MW00423441

Design and Repair of Residential and Light Commercial Foundations

Design and Repair of Residential and Light Commercial Foundations

Robert Wade Brown

McGraw-Hill Publishing Company

New York   St. Louis   San Francisco   Auckland   Bogotá
Caracas   Hamburg   Lisbon   London   Madrid   Mexico
Milan   Montreal   New Delhi   Oklahoma City
Paris   San Juan   São Paulo   Singapore
Sydney   Tokyo   Toronto

Library of Congess Cataloging-in-Publication Data

Brown, Robert Wade.
    Design and repair of residential and light commercial foundations
    Robert Wade Brown.
       p. cm.
    Includes bibliographies and index.
    ISBN 0-07-008192-1
    1. Foundations. 2. House construction. 3. Dwellings—Maintenance
and repair.   4. Industrial buildings—Design and construction.
5. Industrial buildings—Maintenance and repair. I. Title.
TH2101.B729 1990
690'.11—dc20   89-35185
                                                      CIP

Copyright © 1990 by McGraw-Hill, Inc. All rights reserved. Printed in the United
States of America. Except as permitted under the United States Copyright Act of
1976, no part of this publication may be reproduced or distributed in any form or by
any means, or stored in a database or retrieval system, without the prior written
permission of the publisher.

  234567890 DOC/DOC   94321

ISBN 0-07-008192-1

The editors for this book were Joel Stein and Galen H. Fleck, the designer was Naomi
Auerbach, and the production supervisor was Dianne L. Walber. This book was set in
Century Schoolbook. It was composed by the McGraw-Hill Publishing Company
Professional and Reference Division composition unit.

Printed and bound by R. R. Donnelley & Sons Company.

Information contained in this work has been obtained by
McGraw-Hill, Inc., from sources believed to be reliable. However,
neither McGraw-Hill nor its authors guarantees the accuracy or
completeness of any information published herein and neither
McGraw-Hill nor its authors shall be responsible for any errors,
omissions, or damages arising out of use of this information. This
work is published with the understanding that McGraw-Hill and
its authors are supplying information but are not attempting to
render engineering or other professional services. If such services
are required, the assistance of an appropriate professional should
be sought.

For more information about other McGraw-Hill materials,
call 1-800-2-MCGRAW in the United States. In other
countries, call your nearest McGraw-Hill office.

Contents

Preface   v

Introduction   17

Chapter 1. Water Behavior in Soils   5

  1.1   Moisture Regimes   5
  1.2   Soil Moisture versus Water Table   6
  1.3   Soil Moisture versus Aeration Zone   7
  1.4   Gravity and Evaporation   8
  1.5   Permeability versus Infiltration   9
  1.6   Run-off   11
  1.7   Conclusions   12
  1.8   References   13
  1.9   Appendix: Clay Soil   13
  1.10 References   22

Chapter 2. Land Planning and Site Preparation   23

  2.1   Spot Elevation   25
  2.2   Foundations on Filled Slopes   26
  2.3   Site Drainage   27
  2.4   Subsurface Drainage   29
  2.5   Landscaping   31
  2.6   Land Planning   31
  2.7   Foundation Drain Systems   32
  2.8   Storm Drainage and Sediment Basins   34
  2.9   Diversion Terraces and Interceptor Channels   34
  2.10 Steep Slopes   34
  2.11 Energy Dissipators   34
  2.12 Sequence of Construction   35
  2.13 References   35

Chapter 3. Soil Mechanics   37

  3.1   Soil Types   37

3.2   Sand and Gravel   38
3.3   Silts and Clays   38
3.4   Rock   39
3.5   Fill   39
3.6   Foundation on Soil   40
3.7   Shrinkage   40
3.8   Swelling   42
      3.8.1   Atterberg limits   42
3.9   Frost Heaving   43
3.10 Soil Engineering   44
3.11 Soil Classification   44
      3.11.1   Size classification   45
      3.11.2   Sedimentation versus size   46
      3.11.3   Unified classification   47
3.12 Identification   49
      3.12.1   Significance of index properties in residential foundation design   49
      3.12.2   Void ratios and porosity   50
      3.12.3   Relative density   53
      3.12.4   Consistency of soil   54
      3.12.5   Strength of soils   55
3.13 References   56

Chapter 4. General Properties of Concrete   57

4.1   Introduction   57
4.2   Fundamentals   58
      4.2.1   Characteristics of plastic concrete   59
      4.2.2   Characteristics of hardened concrete   60
4.3   Proportioning   63
      4.3.1   Water/cement ratio   65
      4.3.2   Aggregates   65
      4.3.3   Admixtures   66
      4.3.4   Slump test   68
4.4   Placing Concrete   70
4.5   Curing Concrete   70
      4.5.1   Effect of curing on strength   70
      4.5.2   Effect of curing on impermeability   70
      4.5.3   Effect of curing on shrinkage   71
4.6   Mechanical Properties   71
4.7   Reinforcing   72
      4.7.1   Metal reinforcement   72
      4.7.2   Synthetic fiber reinforcement   74
4.8   References   76

Chapter 5. Foundation Design   77

5.1   Introduction   77
5.2   Pier and beam   77
5.3   Slab   79

        5.3.1 Post tension   85
        5.3.2 Design variations   86
        5.3.3 Experimental residential foundation designs   87
    5.4 Basements   92
    5.5 Foundation loads on bearing soils   92
    5.6 References   94

Chapter 6. Soil Stabilization   95

    6.1 Introduction   95
    6.2 Compaction   95
    6.3 Granular Soil   96
    6.4 Foundations on loess   97
    6.5 Foundations on sanitary landfill   97
    6.6 Chemical Stabilization   98
        6.6.1 Stabilizing permeable soils   98
        6.6.2 Pressure grouting   99
    6.7 Stabilizing Impermeable Soils   99
        6.7.1 Clay mineralogy   100
        6.7.2 Laboratory testing of a soil-stabilizing chemical   105
        6.7.3 Field testing of a soil-stabilizing chemical   108
        6.7.4 Pressure injection   114
    6.8 Water Barrier   118
    6.9 Irrigation   119
    6.10 References   119

Chapter 7. Foundation Failures   121

    7.1 Causes of Foundation Failures   121
        7.1.1 Nonexpansive soils   121
        7.1.2 Expansive soils   123
        7.1.3 Summary   127
    7.2 Settlement   127
    7.3 Upheaval   128
    7.4 Occurrence of Settlement versus Upheaval   130
    7.5 Diagnosis of Settlement versus Upheaval   131
    7.6 Sliding   133
    7.7 References   133

Chapter 8. Foundation Repair Procedures   135

    8.1 Introduction   135
    8.2 Pier-and-Beam Foundations   141
        8.2.1 Underpinning   141
        8.2.2 Interior floor shimming—pier-and-beam foundations   144
    8.3 Slab Foundation Mudjacking   146
        8.3.1 Upheaval   146
        8.3.2 Settlement   147
    8.4 Perma-Jack and Variations   151

8.4.1   Deep grouting: introduction   154
8.4.2   Mechanics of grouting applications   155
8.4.3   Placement of injection pipes   155
8.5   Subgrade Waterproofing   157
8.6   Soil Consolidation   158
8.7   Special Problems Which Adversely Affect Leveling   159
8.7.1   Upheaval   159
8.7.2   Warped substructures   159
8.7.3   Construction interferences   159
8.8   Review of Repair Longevity   163
8.9   Conclusions   164
8.10   References   165
8.11   Appendix—Interesting Examples of Repair Techniques   165
8.11.1   Florida   165
8.11.2   London, England   166
8.11.3   Piers—driven steel pipe   168

Chapter 9. Preventive Maintenance   171

9.1   Introduction   171
9.2   Watering   171
9.3   Drainage   173
9.3.1   French drains—subsurface water   174
9.3.2   Water or capillary barriers   175
9.4   Vegetation   176
9.5   References   178

Chapter 10. Foundation Inspection and Evaluation
             for the Residential Buyer   179

10.1   Checklist for Foundation Inspection   180

Appendix A Foundation Engineering   183

A.1   Soil Mechanics and Foundation Engineering   183
A.1.1   Site exploration   183
A.1.2   Compressibility of soil: consolidation and settlement   184
A.1.3   Volume change in noncohesive soil   187
A.2   Stresses in a Soil Mass due to Foundation Pressures   188
A.3   Vertical Surface Loading   190
A.3.1   Boussinesq method for evaluating soil pressure   191
A.3.2   Westergaard's method   193
A.3.3   Application to residential foundation design   194
A.4   Bearing Capacity of Shallow Foundation   196
A.4.1   Shallow foundation bearing capacity equation   196
A.4.2   Hansen equations   199
A.4.3   Bearing capacity of footing on slopes   200
A.4.4   Bearing capacity based on building codes   200
A.4.5   Safety factors in foundation design   202
A.5   Bearing Capacity of Drilled Piers   203
A.5.1   General considerations in analysis   204
A.5.2   Piers in granular soil   206

A.5.3 Piers in cohesive soils   209
A.5.4 Negative skin friction   211
A.5.5 Bearing capacity of rock   212
A.6 References   213

Appendix B—Conversion Factors   215

Appendix C—Abbreviations of Units of Measure   217

Glossary   219
Index   233

Preface

This book is based on 25 years of activity and research devoted to analyzing and correcting foundation failures. It provides a comprehensive source of information about basic foundation construction and behavior. The primary focus is on residential and low-rise commercial structures. The material should prove invaluable to civil and structural engineers, geotechnicians, architects, contractors, developers, and serious engineering students, as well as to realtors, lenders, appraisers, insurers, and homeowners.

Because concrete is one of the major construction materials, the book deals in some detail with the chemistry of cement and the composition of concrete, including special admixtures and reinforcing.

Given that most construction concrete is in contact with the ground, special emphasis is given to soil engineering, site preparation, drainage, and basic foundation design. Each of the foregoing is a factor which influences foundation behavior and, under certain conditions, distress or failure.

The selection of subject matter was influenced by other authors and my associates, to whom I am grateful. The extensive references will enable the serious student to explore the subject in as much detail as he or she wishes.

I am particularly grateful to my friend and colleague, Tom Petry, PhD, PE, Professor of Civil Engineering, University of Texas at Arlington, for his review and comments. I also wish to express appreciation to Brown Foundation Repair and Consulting, Inc., for making the publication possible and to my family for their patience and support in preparing the text, especially my son, Robert Lemoyne Brown, for his editorial assistance, and my daughter, Candy, for the artwork.

Robert Wade Brown

Introduction

A *foundation* is the part of a structure that is in direct contact with the ground and transmits the load of the structure to the ground. Basically there are three different types of foundations: pier and beam, slab, and some combination of the two. The latter, which is often used in commercial constructions, involves a pier-and-beam perimeter with a floating slab floor.

The first type of foundation generally recognized for light commercial and residential construction was the pier and beam. This primitive design involved nothing more than the use of wooden "stumps" placed directly on the soil for structural support. These members, usually cedar or bois d'arc, supported the sole plate as well as the interior girders. Next, the design evolved to the use of a continuous concrete beam to support the perimeter loads with, as a rule, the same wood piers serving to support the interior. This later variation was adopted largely because of the advent of brick or stone veneer, which necessitated a stronger, more stable base.

Further changes in construction requirements, including the awareness of problems brought about by unstable soils, encouraged the addition of concrete piers to support the perimeter beam and concrete piers and pier caps to provide better support for the interior floors (girders). In areas with colder climates or excessively high lot costs, basements are often incorporated into the foundation design. Ultimately, the benefits of costs and pleasing elevations brought about the use of the slab foundation.

Slab construction of one variety or another probably constitutes the majority of new construction in geographic areas exposed to high-clay soils. The particular design of the slab depends upon a multitude of factors. In any event, the structural load is designed to be carried essentially 100 percent by the bearing soil. The steel-reinforced concrete is cast directly into the ground, hence the term slab-on-grade foundation.

Many factors influence the selection and design of the foundation; some are local and some are general. Several of these concerns are discussed.

Special problems arise when the construction is to be in an area in which expansive soils are prevalent. This situation is further aggravated if the particular area also has extreme variations in moisture and temperature. Among all natural disasters, the damage and repair costs resulting from differential foundation movement rank number 1.

Foundations, like all structures, are designed against failure. For purposes herein, "failure" may be defined as either total collapse or a condition exhibiting deflection from the original condition sufficient to require remedial attention. This latter condition, *distress failure*, provides the basis for this book.

Foundation designs against ultimate failure are predicated both on the original nature of the structure (size, loads, type of construction, etc.) and on any later conditions under which the structure must exist. Two principal factors which influence both design and any subsequent failure are the properties of the particular bearing soil, which are compounded by interaction with the climatic conditions. Generally speaking, the stability of the soil is of prime importance. Specifically, that stability is affected by the tendency of the clay constituents for volumetric changes brought about by changes in moisture content.

In simpler terms, foundations constructed on highly active clay soils demonstrate a strong tendency to have distress failures, particularly when located in areas of widely variant climate. Unfortunately, many areas of the United States are susceptible to this coexistence—to one extent or another. The south, midwest, and southwest represent the areas of highest incidence. It is interesting to note that the annual cost to Americans for foundation repairs exceeds $2 billion, according to a study reported by Jones and Holtz.*

In many areas, most foundation failures can be directly attributed to both the clay mineral montmorillonite (or smectite) present in the soil and changes in moisture therein. For example, a relatively pure sodium-substituted montmorillonite clay has the capacity to free-swell up to twentyfold when taken from a dehydrated to a saturated state. Other clays such as illite, attapulgite, and kaolinite also exhibit the swell potential, although to lesser extents. In the course of this swell a confined clay could exert pressures of several tons per square foot. Hence, it becomes quite evident that changes in soil moisture contribute to substantial forces which ultimately cause founda-

---

*D. E. Jones, Jr., and W. G. Holtz, "Expansive Soils—The Hidden Disaster," *Civil Engineering*, vol. 43, August 1973, pp. 49–51.

tion deflections and failure—particularly in the case of residential or light commercial construction.

When a foundation is constructed, it covers or protects an area of bearing soil. The causes for moisture imbalance within this confined area can be those attributable either to variations in natural ambient conditions (rain, heat, wind) and/or to human-created conditions such as domestic water leaks.

Assuming proper drainage at the foundation perimeter, the ambient soil moisture will primarily affect only the outer uncovered soil. The effects of this are generally manifested in failures attributed to settlement or shrinkage of the soil from a loss of water; accordingly, they are referred to as settlement.

Water that collects under the foundation, regardless of origin, is another problem. This water is confined, accumulative, and particularly serious; it accounts for a high percentage of all failures. The source can be from either domestic leaks or nature. Foundation failures resulting from excessive water under the foundation are classically termed *upheaval*.

Both conditions, settlement and upheaval, will be described more fully in following chapters; both are obviously influenced by soil moisture changes—a complex interaction between moisture availability and retention—plus soil character. In order to better understand the overall problem, the topics of hydrology, clay mineralogy, and soil mechanics must be viewed in the perspective of their influences on foundation design.

Other books which address several of the topics in the following chapters are available, but this is the first to deal with the complete spectrum within a single cover.

Water Behavior in Soils

1.1 Moisture Regimes

The regime of subsurface water can be divided into two general classifications: the *aeration zone* and the *saturation zone*. The saturation zone is more commonly termed the *water table* or *ground water*, and it is, of course, the deepest. The aeration zone includes the capillary fringe, intermediate belt (which may include one or more perched water zones), and, at the surface, the *soil water belt*, often referred to as the *root zone* (Fig. 1.1). Simply stated, the soil water belt provides moisture for the vegetable and plant kingdoms; the intermediate belt contains moisture essentially in dead storage—held by molecular forces; the perched ground water, if it occurs, develops essentially from water accumulation either above a relatively impermeable stra-

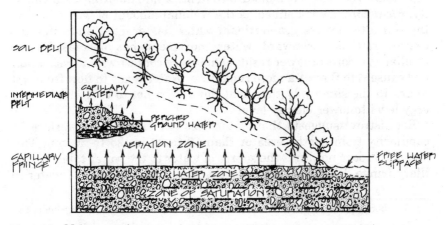

Figure 1.1 Moisture regimes.

tum or within an unusually permeable lens. Perched water occurs generally after a good rain and is relatively temporary; the capillary fringe contains capillary water originating from the water table.

The soil belt can contain capillary water available from rains or watering; however, unless this moisture is continually restored, the soil will eventually desiccate through the effects of gravity, transpiration, and/or evaporation. In doing so, the capillary water is lost. The soil belt is also the zone that most critically influences both foundation design and stability. This will be discussed in the following sections.

As stated, the more shallow zones have the greatest influence on surface structures. Unless the water table is quite shallow, it will have little, if any, material influence on the behavior of foundations of normal residential structures. Further, the surface of the water table, the *phreatic boundary*, will not normally deflect or deform except under certain conditions, such as when it is in the proximity of a producing well. Then the boundary will *draw down* or recede.

In other words, if the water table is deeper than about 10 ft (3 m),* the boundary (as well as the capillary fringe) is not likely to "dome." Should upward deflection or doming occur, it would more likely affect the foundation than would the drawdown mentioned earlier. The relative thickness and depth of the various zones depend upon many factors such as soil composition, climate, and geology. The following paragraphs will provide further detail.

1.2 Soil Moisture versus Water Table

Alway and McDole[1]† conclude that deep subsoil aquifers (e.g., the water table) contribute little, if any, moisture to plants and, hence, foundations. Upward movement of water below a depth of 12 in (30 cm) is reportedly very slow at moisture contents approximating field capacity. *Field capacity* is defined as the residual amount of water held in the soil after excess gravitational water has drained and after the overall rate of downward water movement has decreased (zero capillarity). Soils at lower residual moisture contact will attract water and cause it to flow at a more rapid rate. Water tends to flow from wet to dry in the same way that heat flows from hot to cold—higher energy level to lower energy level.

Rotmistrov[1] suggests that water does not move to the surface by capillarity from depths greater than 10 to 20 in (25 to 50 cm). This statement does not limit the source of water to the water table or capillary fringe. Richards[1] indicates that upward movement of water in

---

*The abbreviations of units of measure used in this book are listed in Appendix C.

†Superscript numbers indicate references at ends of chapters.

silty loam can develop from depths as great as 24 in (60 cm). McGee[1] postulates that 6 in (15 cm) of water can be brought to the surface annually from depths approaching 10 ft (300 cm). Again the source of water is not restricted in origin.

The seeming disparity among the opinions of these hydrologists is likely to be due to variation in experimental conditions. Nonetheless, the obvious consensus is that the water content of the surface soil tends to remain relatively stable below very shallow depths and that the availability of soil water derived from the water table ceases when the boundary lies at a depth exceeding the limit of capillary rise for the soil. In heavy soils (e.g., clays), water loss practically ceases when the water table is deeper than 4 ft (120 cm) even though the theoretical capillary limit might exceed this distance. In silts, the capillary limit may approximate 10 ft (300 cm) as compared to 1 to 2 ft (30 to 60 cm) for sands. The height of capillary rise is expressed by Eq. (1.1).

$$\pi \gamma_T r^2 h_c = T_{st} 2 \pi r \cos \alpha$$

or   (1.1)

$$h_c = \frac{2T_{st}}{r \gamma_T} \cos \alpha$$

where h_c = capillary rise, cm
T_{st} = surface tension of liquid at temperature T, g/cm
γ_T = unit weight of liquid at temperature T, g/cm^3
r = radius of capillary pore, cm
α = meniscus angle at wall or angle of contact

For behavior in soils, the radius r is difficult, if not impossible, to establish. Since the capillary rise varies inversely with effective pore or capillary radius, this value is required for mathematical calculations. However, the value of r for soils is most elusive; it is dependent upon such factors as void ratio, impurities, grain size and distribution, and permeability. Accordingly, capillary rise, particularly in clays, is generally determined by experimentation. In clays, the height and rate of rise are impeded by the swell (loss of permeability) upon invasion of water. Finer noncohesive soils will create a greater height of capillary rise, but the rate of rise will be slower. More information on soil moisture, particularly that dealing with clay soils, will be found in Sec. 6.7.1.

1.3 Soil Moisture versus Aeration Zone

Water in the upper or aeration zone is removed by one or a combination of three processes: transpiration, evaporation, and gravity.

Transpiration refers to the removal of soil moisture by vegetation. A class of plants, referred to as phreatophytes, obtain their moisture, often more than 4 ft (120 cm) of water per year, principally from either the water table or capillary fringe. This group includes such seemingly diverse species as reeds, mesquite, willows, and palms. The remaining two groups, mesophytes and xerophytes, obtain their moisture from the soil water zone. They include most vegetables and shrubs, along with some trees.

In all vegetation, root growth is toward soil with greater available moisture. Roots will not penetrate a dry soil to reach moisture. The absorptive area of the root is the tip, where root hairs occur. The loss of soil moisture due to transpiration follows the root pattern and is generally somewhat circular about the stem or trunk. The root system develops only to the extent necessary to supply the vegetation with required water and nutrition. Roots not accessible to water will wither and die. These factors are important to foundation stability, as will be discussed in following chapters.

In many instances, transpiration accounts for greater loss of soil moisture than does *evaporation*. Another process, *interception*, is the procedure whereby precipitation is caught and held by foliage and evaporated from the exposed surfaces. In densely planted areas, interception represents a major loss of rainfall, perhaps reaching 10 to 25 percent of total precipitation.[1]

1.4   Gravity and Evaporation

Gravity tends to draw all moisture downward from the soil within the aeration zone. Evaporation tends to draw moisture upward from the surface soil zone. Both forces are retarded by molecular, adhesive, and cohesive attraction between water and soil as well as by the soil's ability for capillary recharge. If evaporation is prevented at the surface, water will move downward under the forces of gravity until the soil is drained or equilibrium with an impermeable layer or saturated layer is attained. In either event, given time, the retained moisture within the soil will approximate the "field capacity" for the soil in question.

In other words, if evaporation were prevented at the soil surface, as, for example, by a foundation, an "excessive" accumulation of moisture would initially result. However, given sufficient time, even this protected soil will reach a condition of moisture equilibrium somewhere between that originally noted and that of the surrounding uncovered soil. The natural tendency of uncovered soil is to retain a moisture level above that of the uncovered soil—except, of course, during periods of heavy inundation (rains) wherein the uncovered soil reaches a temporary state at or near saturation. In this latter instance, the moisture content decreases rapidly with the cessation of rain or other sources of water.

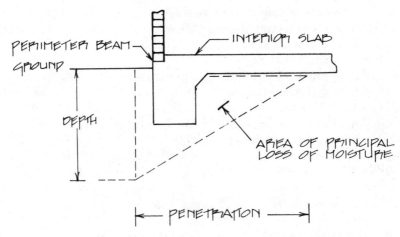

Figure 1.2 Typical loss of soil moisture from beneath a slab foundation during a prolonged drying cycle.

The loss of soil moisture from beneath a foundation caused by evaporation would tend to follow a triangular configuration with one leg vertical and extending downward into the bearing soil and the other leg horizontal and extending under the foundation.[2] The relative lengths of the legs of the triangle depend upon many factors such as the particular soil characteristics, foundation design, weather, and availability of moisture (Fig. 1.2).

In the referenced study, Davis and Tucker reported the depth as about 5 ft (1.5 m) and the penetration as approximately 10 ft (3 m). In any event, the affected distances (legs of the triangle) are relatively limited. As with all cases of evaporation, the greatest effects are noted closer to the surface. In an exposed soil, evaporation forces are ever-present, provided the relative humidity is less than 100 percent. The force of gravity is effective whether the soil is covered or exposed.

1.5 Permeability versus Infiltration

The infiltration feature of soil is more directly related to penetration from rain or water at the surface than to subsurface vertical movement. The exceptions are those relatively rare instances in which the ground surface is within the capillary fringe. Vertical migration or permeation of the soil by water infiltration could be approximately represented by the single-phase steady-state flow equation postulated by Darcy.[3]

$$Q = -\frac{Ak}{\mu}\left(\frac{\Delta P}{L} + g_c\gamma \sin \alpha\right) \qquad (1.2)$$

where Q = rate of flow in direction L
          A = cross-sectional area of flow
          k = permeability
          μ = fluid viscosity
          $\Delta P/L$ = pressure gradient in direction L
          L = direction of flow
          γ = fluid density
          α = angle of dip; $\alpha > 0$ if flow L is up dip
          g_c = gravity constant

If $\alpha = 90°$, $\sin \alpha = 1$ and, simplified,

$$Q = -\frac{Ak}{\mu L}(\Delta P + g_c h\gamma)$$

where $h = L \sin \alpha$ and $g_c h\gamma$ is the hydrostatic head.

If $H = P + g_c h\gamma$, where H is the fluid flow potential,

$$Q = -\left(\frac{Ak}{\mu}\right)\left(\frac{\Delta H}{L}\right)$$

When flow is horizontal, the gravity factor g drops out. Any convenient set of units may be used in Eq. (1.2) so long as they are consistent. Several influencing factors represented in this equation pose a difficult deterrent to mathematical calculations. For example, the coefficient of permeability k can be determined only by experimental processes and is subject to constant variation even within the same soil. The pore sizes, water saturation, particle gradation, transportable fines, and mineral constituents all affect the effective permeability k.

In the instance of expansive clays, the variation is extremely pronounced and is subject to continuous change upon penetration by water. In the case of clean sand, the variation is not nearly as extreme, and reasonable approximations for k are often possible. The hydraulic gradient ΔP and the distance over which it acts ΔL also are elusive values.

In essence, Eq. (1.2) provides a clear understanding of factors controlling water penetration into soils but does not always permit accurate mathematical calculation. The rate of water flow does not singularly define the moisture content or capacity of the soil. The physical properties of the soil and the available and residual water each affect infiltration, as does permeability. A soil section 3 ft (90 cm) thick may have a theoretical capacity for perhaps 1.5 ft of water. This is certainly more water than occurs from a serious storm; hence, the

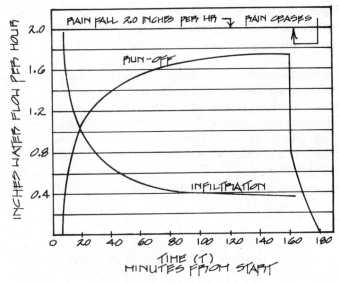

Figure 1.3 Typical case of infiltration versus run-off after a 2 in/hr rainfall.

moisture-holding capacity is seldom, if ever, the limiting criterion for infiltration. That is as it would appear from the foregoing paragraphs.

In addition to the problems of permeability, infiltration has an inverse time lag function (Fig. 1.3). This figure is a typical, graphical representation of the relationship between infiltration and run-off with respect to time. At the onset of rain, more water infiltrates, but over time most of the water runs off and little is added to the infiltration.

Clays will have a greater tendency for run-off, as opposed to infiltration, than will sands. The degree of the slope of the land will have a comparable effect, since steeper terrains deter infiltration. Only the water that penetrates the soil is of particular concern with respect to foundation stability. The water which fails to penetrate the soil is briefly discussed in Sec. 1.6.

1.6 Run-off

The tendency of any soil at a level above the capillary fringe is to lose moisture through the various forces of gravity, transpiration, and evaporation. Given sufficient lack of recharge water, the soil water belt will merge with and become identical in character to the intermediate belt. However, nature provides a method for replenishing the soil water through periodic rainfall. Given exposure to rain, all soils absorb water to some varying degree dependent upon such factors as residual moisture content, soil composition and gradation, and time of exposure. The excess water not retained by the soil is termed *run-off* (Fig. 1.3).

As would be expected, sands have a high absorption rate and clays have a relatively low absorption rate. A rainfall of several inches over a period of a few hours might saturate the soil water belt of sands but penetrate no more than 6 in into a well-graded, high-plasticity soil. A slow, soaking rain would materially increase penetration in either case. The same comparison holds whether the source of water is rain or watering. Later chapters will develop the importance of maintaining soil moisture to aid in preventing or arresting foundation failures.

1.7 Conclusions

What factors have become obvious with respect to soil moisture as it influences foundation stability?

1. Soil moisture definitely affects foundation stability, particularly if the soil contains expansive clays.

2. The soil belt is the zone which affects or influences foundation behavior the most.

3. Constant moisture is beneficial to soil (foundation) stability.

4. The water table, per se, has little, if any, influence on soil moisture or foundation behavior.

5. Vegetation can remove substantial moisture from soil. Roots tend to "find" moisture. In general, transpiration occurs from relatively shallow depths.

6. Introduction of excessive (differential) amounts of water under a covered area are accumulative and threaten stability of some soils. Sources of excessive water could be subsurface aquifers (e.g., temporary perched ground water), surface water (poor drainage), and/or domestic water (leaks or improper watering).

7. Assuming adequate drainage, proper watering (uniformly applied) is absolutely necessary to maintain consistent soil moisture during dry periods—both summer and winter.

The homeowner can do little to affect either the design of an existing foundation or the overall subsurface moisture profile. From a logistical standpoint, about the only control the owner has is to maintain moisture around the foundation perimeter by both watering and drainage control and to preclude the introduction of domestic water under the foundation. Adequate watering will help prevent or arrest settlement of foundations on expansive soils brought about by soil shrinkage resulting from the loss of moisture.

From a careful study of the behavior of water in the aeration zone, it appears that the most significant factor contributing to distress relative to expansive soils is excessive water beneath a protected surface (foundation) which causes the soil to swell (upheaval). From field data collected in a study of more than 2000 repairs, it is an undeniable fact that a wide majority of these instances of soil swell were traceable to domestic water sources as opposed to drainage deficiencies. The numerical comparison of upheaval versus settlement failure is estimated to be in the range of 65:35 or about 2:1. Refer to Chaps. 7 and 8 for more detailed information. Also bear in mind that the data described were accumulated from studies within a C_w rating (climatic rating) of about 20 (Fig. 5.8). This describes an area with annual rainfall in the range of 30 in (75 cm) and mean temperatures of about 65°F (18°C).

1.8 References

1. O. E. Meinzer et al., *Hydrology*, McGraw-Hill, New York, 1942.
2. R. C. Davis and Richard Tucker, "Soil Moisture and Temperature Variation Beneath a Slab Barrier on Expansive Clay." *Report No. TR-3-73*. Construction Research Center, UTA, May, 1973.
3. S. J. Pirson, *Soil Reservoir Engineering*, McGraw-Hill, New York, 1958.
4. David B. McWhorter and Daniel K. Sunada, *Ground-Water Hydrology and Hydraulics*, Water Resources, Ft. Collins, Colo., 1977.

1.9 Appendix: Clay Soil

Preceding sections have insinuated the influence of hydrology on foundation stability. This is most certainly true when the foundation bearing soil contains an expansive clay. One complex and misunderstood aspect is the effect roots have on soil moisture. Without question, transpiration removes moisture from the soil. Exactly how much, what type, and from where represent the basic questions. If the roots take only pore (or capillary) water and/or remove the moisture from depths deeper than about 3 to 7 ft (1 to 2 m), the moisture loss is not likely to result in shrinkage of the soils to the extent that foundation stability will be threatened.

Logically, in semiarid climates (Fig. 5.8), the root pattern would tend to develop toward deeper depths. In wetter areas, the root systems would be closer to the surface. In that instance, the availability of moisture would be such that the roots' needs could be supplied without

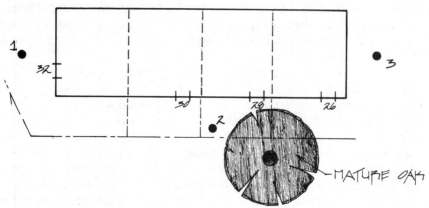

Figure 1.4   Location plan.

desiccation of the soil; see Figs. 1.4 and 1.5 and Table 1.1. [An explanation of the Atterberg limits (LL, PL, and PI) is given in Chaps. 3 and 5.]

The soil is identified as London clay with physical and chemical characteristics similar to those of many of the typical fat clays found in the United States. The London climate has a C_w factor in the range of 35 to 40, which is similar to that for Mississippi and Washington (Fig. 5.8). Note that the soil moisture content remains constant from 2 to 5 m (6.6 to 16.4 ft) despite the close proximity of the mature oak tree. While this observation might be surprising, it was by no means an isolated instance. The test borings provided data on the loss of soil moisture, but there was nothing to indicate the root pattern, which is not critical but would have been interesting. It should be noted, however, that all tests commenced below the 2-ft (0.6-m) level, which seems to be the maximum depth from which roots remove moisture in this environment. (Refer to Sec. 6.7.1, "Clay Mineralogy," for additional information concerning the water behavior in clay soils.)

In areas with more extreme climates and the same general soil, the root development pattern would more closely resemble that in Fig. 1.6. It is worthy of mention that during earlier growth stages, particularly if the tree was being conscientiously watered, the root system might be quite shallow—within the top 1 ft (30 cm) or so. Dry weather (lack of "surface" moisture) forces the roots to seek deeper soils for adequate water. The surface roots can remain dormant in a low-moisture environment for extended periods of time and become active again when soil moisture is restored.

Although the so-called fat clays are generally impermeable, thus limiting true capillary transfer of water, intrinsic fractures and fissures allow the tree or plant root systems to pull water from soil a ra-

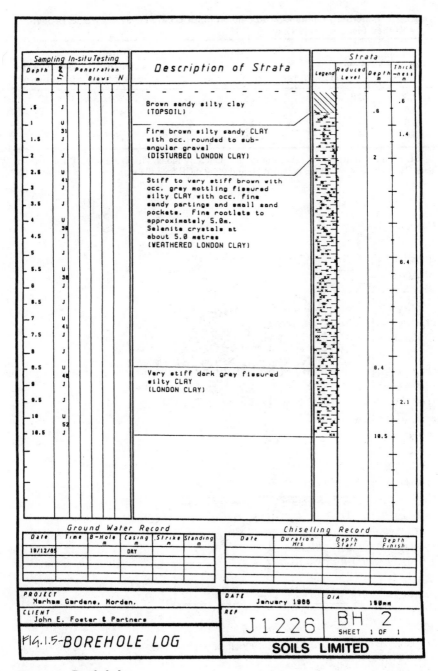

Figure 1.5   Borehole log.

TABLE 1.1   Atterberg Limits and Soil Moisture for London Clay BH No. 2: Brown-Gray Mottled Fissured Silty Clay

Depth		LL, %*	PL, %*	PI*	Natural moisture content, %	Soil classification
m	ft					
2.00	6.6	93	27	66	30	CE
3.5	11.5	86	27	59	30	CV
4.5	14.8	89	28	61	30	CV
5.00	16.4	85	26	59	29	CV

*LL = liquid limit; PL = plastic limit; PI = plasticity index. The British Soil Classification uses CV for soils with an LL between 70 and 90 and CE for soils with an LL in excess of 90.

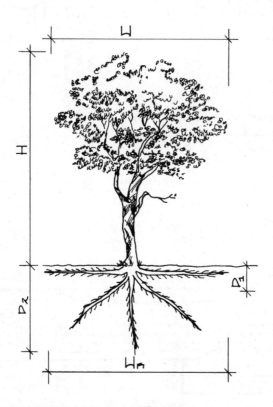

W – DIAMETER OF CANOPY (UNPRUNED) DRIP LINE
H – HEIGHT
D₁ – DEPTH OF LATERAL ROOTS
D₂ – DEPTH OF DEEP ROOTS (TAP ROOTS.)
W_R – DIAMETER OF LATERAL ROOTS

Figure 1.6   Root system.

dial distance away in excess of the normal foliage radius. A side point worthy of mention is that when transpiration is active, evaporation diminishes. (The shaded areas lose less moisture.) The net result is often a conservation of soil moisture.

With respect to Fig. 1.6, Dr. Don Smith, Botanist at North Texas State University, Denton, Texas, suggests certain generalities:

1. D_1 is in the range of 2 ft (0.6 m), maximum.

2. W_R is in the range of 1.25 × W, where W is the natural canopy diameter (unpruned).

3. When moisture is not readily available at D_1, the deeper roots D_2 increase activity to keep the trees' needs satisfied. If this is not possible, the tree wilts.

4. H has no direct correlation to W_R, D_1, or D_2 except the indirect relation that H is relative to the age of the tree.

T.T. Koslowski,[1] and the National House-Building Council,[2] suggest values for D_2 and the effective D_1 shown in Table 1.2. Another important point is that soil moisture losses from either transpiration or evaporation normally occur from relatively shallow depths. Tucker and Poor[3] report test results which indicate that 84 percent of total soil moisture loss occurs within the top 3 to 4 ft (1 to 1.25 m) (Fig. 1.9). The soil involved was the Eagleford (Arlington, Tex.) with a PI in the range of 42. Other scientists, such as Holland and Lawrence[4] report similar findings. The latter report soil moisture equilibrium below about 4 ft (1.25 m) from test data involving several different clay soils in Australia with PIs ranging from about 30 to 60.

Drs. Tom Petry and Clyde Armstrong presented a paper in 1981 which included a figure illustrating the differential movement in a slab foundation versus the proximity of trees.[5] Figure 1.7 is a modified reproduction of their figure. Generally, the data seem too random to interpret; however, following the surmise of Petry and Armstrong, it

TABLE 1.2a   Depth of Tree Roots, Plains Area, United States*

Name	Age, years	D_2, ft (m)
Plantanus occidentalis (American sycamore)	6	7 (2.1)
Juglans nigra (black walnut)	6	5 (1.5)
Quercus rubra (red oak)	6	5 (1.5)
Carya ovata (shag bark hickory)	6	5 (1.5)
Fraxinus americana (ash)	6	5 (1.5)
Populus deltoides (poplar or cottonwood)	6	6 (1.8)
Robinia pseudoacacia (black locust)	Unknown	24–27 (7.3–8.2)

*After Ted Koslowski.[1]

TABLE 1.2b   Depth of Tree Roots, London, England, (PI above 40)*

Name	Age	D_1† m (ft)		H (height), m (ft)	
High water demand					
Elm	Mature	3.25	(10.6)	18–24	(59–79)
Oak	Mature	3.25	(10.6)	16–24	(52–79)
Willow	Mature	3.25	(10.6)	16–24	(52–79)
Moderate water demand					
Ash	Mature	2.2	(7.2)	23	(75)
Cedar	Mature	2.0	(6.6)	20	(65.6)
Pine	Mature	2.0	(6.6)	20	(65.6)
Plum	Mature	2.0	(6.6)	10	(32.8)
Sycamore	Mature	2.2	(7.2)	22	(72)
Low water demand					
Holly	Mature	1.55	(4.9)	12	(39.4)
Mulberry	Mature	1.45	(4.7)	9	(29.5)

*After National House-Building Council, UK.[2]
†Interpolation of *maximum* depth of root influence on foundation design at $D = 2$ m, per Ref. 2. Refer also to Fig. 1.7 for D and Fig. 1.6 for D_1.

would appear that the transpiration loss which influences foundation stability generally occur at D/H distances between about 0.35 and 1.0.

The modified curve indicates that the ΔM occurring at D/H greater than 1.0 is due to causes other than transpiration. At $D/H = 0.35$, the ΔH caused by transpiration is 0.125 ft (0.34 to 0.125 ft) at which point approximately 63 percent of ΔM would seem to be relative to transpiration. At $D/H = 0.75$, only 4 percent of the ΔM would seem to be attributable to transpiration. Except for the use of H as a significant factor, these data do not differ materially from the statements made by Dr. Smith. If H were replaced by W, the canopy width, there would seem to be general agreement. The data given in Fig. 1.7 make no statement regarding the encroachment of roots beneath the slab.

Consider the following restatement of the data expressed by Fig. 1.7. Neglect the house (since foundation subsidence, under the prevailing conditions, is correlated to moisture loss) and concentrate on transpiration loss versus distance from the tree trunk (Fig. 1.8). At distances greater than H, the tree appears to make no contribution to moisture loss. Approximately 85 percent of the transpiration loss occurs between $0.35H$ and $0.5H$. Only 4 percent of total moisture loss would be anticipated for the interval between $0.5H$ and $0.75H$.

If H were equatable to W, these data would appear to mirror the statements of Dr. Smith: The $0.5H$ would roughly equate to the canopy width W, and $0.75H$ would roughly equate to $1.5W$. One important factor is that the data in Fig. 1.7 were accumulated under strict ambient conditions; the trees were not domestically watered during the entire study. Also, the data were quite random, as mentioned earlier, and should not be considered to be definitive or exact.

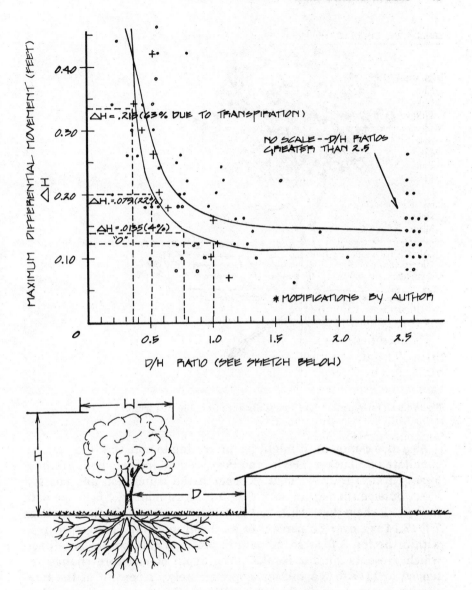

Figure 1.7   Maximum differential movement versus *D/H* ratio.

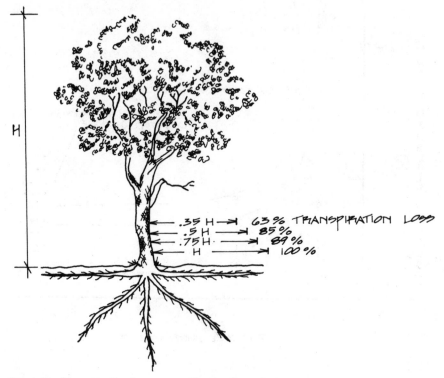

Figure 1.8   Transpiration loss versus distance from the tree trunk.

As a side comment, it might be interesting to note that the data accumulated by Tucker, Davis, and Poor seem to indicate both minimal losses (if any) in soil moisture beneath the foundation and shallow losses outside the perimeter[3,6] (Fig. 1.9). As a matter of fact, the data in Fig. 1.9 show that, while soil moisture varies to a depth of perhaps 7 ft (2.14 m), over 85 percent of total soil moisture change occurred within the top 3 ft or so. Komornik presents data on an Israeli soil which presents similar results.[7] The depth of moisture change extended to 11½ ft (3.5 m), but approximately 71 percent of the total change occurred within the top 3.2 ft (1 m). These observations, again, would seem to support the foregoing conclusions and opinions.

Another source of similar information is *Building Near Trees*.[2] This periodical presents data compatible with those previously cited. Again the only question involves the issue of whether the tree height H is the important dimension describing root behavior or the canopy width W is the true concern, as apparently believed by most botanists.

Other authorities who agree with the statements concerning shallow feeder roots are John Haller[8] and Neil Sperry.[9] Haller states that

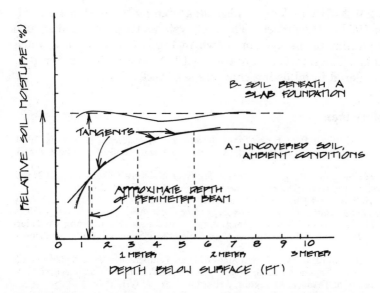

Figure 1.9 Typical loss of soil moisture versus depth during a prolonged drying cycle. The tangent lines indicate the dramatic change in comparative soil moisture versus depth. (*From Tucker and Davis.*)

the majority of feeder roots are found within 1 to 1½ ft (30 to 45 cm) of the surface. He explains that "it is here that the soil is the richest and aeration the simplest." Both air and nutrition (water) are required by the healthy tree. Deeper root systems are present, but their primary function is to provide stability to the tree. In fact, the tap roots have the principal relationship to tree height. This correlation is exploited by the Japanese to dwarf trees by shortening the tap roots.

Many geotechnical engineers do not seem to share the views expressed by the botanists. Dr. Poor seems to feel that the radial extent of a tree's root pattern is greater ($1H$ to $1.5H$) and the depth of moisture loss to transpiration is deeper.[3] Part of the apparent basis for his beliefs are presented in Fig. 1.7. Two-thirds of the trees involved in this study were fruitless mulberry, elm, cottonwood, and willow. Each of these trees represents a variety with typically extensive root systems. One interesting question would be whether the root systems he describes were nutrient roots and were present before the slab foundations were placed. Publication sponsored by FHA/HUD have also suggested a potential radial root pattern extending to $1.5H$.

No one referenced in this study stated or implied that there were no exceptions; the positions taken were intended to be general. However, the data as interpreted by the author do seem to provide a limit on root radius of $0.5W$ (canopy width) and on transpiration effective depth of less than 2.0 ft (61 cm). This is also suggested by the author's experience from 1963 to the present. The root systems for plants and shrubs would be similar to the system shown in Fig. 1.6, except on a much smaller scale. The interaction of tree root behavior to foundation failure is considered in following chapters, especially 7 and 9.

1.10 References

1. T.T. Kozlowski, *Water Deficits and Plant Growth*, vol. 1, Academic, New York, 1968.
2. "Building Near Trees," *Practice Note 3 (1985)*, National House-Building Council, London.
3. Richard Tucker and Arthur Poor, "Field Study of Moisture Effects on Slab Movement," *Journal of Geotechnical Engineering*, vol. 104 N GT, April 1978.
4. John E. Holland and Charles E. Lawrence, "Seasonal Heave of Australian Clay Soils," *4th International Conference on Expansive Soils*, ASCE, June 16–18, 1980.
5. Thomas M. Petry and Clyde J. Armstrong, "Geotechnical Engineering Considerations for Design of Slabs on Active Clay Soils," ACI Seminar, Dallas, February 1981.
6. Richard Tucker and R.C. Davis, "Soil Moisture and Temperature Variations Beneath a Slab Barrier on Expansive Soils," *Report No. TR-3-73*, Construction Research Center, University of Texas at Arlington, Arlington, Tex., May 1, 1973.
7. D. Komornik et al., *Effect of Swelling Clays on Piles*, Israel Institute of Technology, Haifa, Israel.
8. John Haller, *Tree Care*, Macmillan, New York and Collier-Macmillan, London, 1986, p. 206.
9. Neil Sperry, *Complete Guide to Texas Gardening*, Taylor Publishing Co., Dallas, Tex., 1982.

Land Planning and Site Preparation*

A concept of grading design is essential in developing the physical form of the construction site. This grading concept must strengthen the overall project rather than detract from it, as often happens. Appearance, utilization, cost, future maintenance, and safety are a few of the concerns.

Positive drainage, an important concept in grading, allows storm water run-off to flow away from the structure. When water flows away from structures toward drainage facilities, flooding is prevented, and in areas with expansive soils, expensive foundation problems can often be avoided. Studying existing topography will aid in designing a proper drainage system around the structure which consequently minimizes both problems. The following terms are used in grading (see also Fig. 2.1).

Grade	Percent of rise or fall per 100 ft (30 m). A fair rule of thumb is ¼ in/ft (6 mm/30 cm).
Crown	Provides for run-off of water on roads or walks.
Cross slope or pitch	Provides for run-off on paved areas and is given as inches per foot (millimeters per centimeter) or a whole number.
Wash	Provides for run-off on steps and is given in inches per foot, usually ⅛ to ¼ in/ft, (3–6 mm/30 cm).
Batter	Amount of deviation from vertical such as 2 in/ft (5 cm/30 cm) for a vertical surface such as a wall.

*Special appreciation is extended to Dr. Abdulkarim Nikmanesh, Visiting Professor, Civil Engineering Department, Southern Methodist University, Dallas, Tex., for contributing to and providing editorial assistance with this chapter.

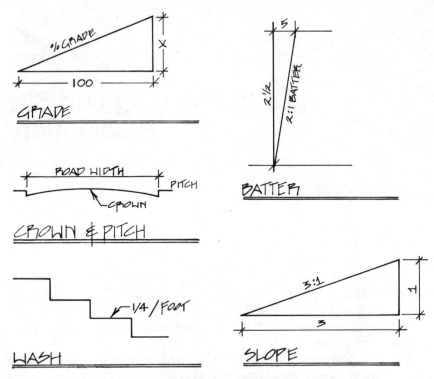

Figure 2.1 Different terms used in grading. (*From Rubenstein, Ref. 6.*)

Slopes	The ratio of horizontal to vertical maximum slopes.
Cut and fill	Cut is indicated when a proposed contour is moved back into an existing slope; fill is indicated when a proposed contour is moved away from an existing slope. It is the purpose of earthwork calculation to determine if a balance exists between cut and fill or whether material will have to be added to or carried away from the site.

The following are some slopes of interest:

Solid rock	¼:1
Loose rock	½:1
Loose gravel	1½:1
Firm earth	1½:1
Soft earth	2:1
Mowing grass	3:1

2.1 Spot Elevation

The grading plan is significant in the technical development of the
site plan. The major consideration in a grading plan is to set trial or
preliminary spot elevations in order to achieve a positive drainage
pattern. The following factors should be considered in setting preliminary spot elevations:

1. Setting the first-floor elevations of buildings, generally a minimum
   of 6 in (1.3 cm) above the intended final grade
2. Meeting existing building elevations and relating grading to adjacent properties so as not to disturb existing grade or disposal run-
   off
3. Relating elevation of roads, walks, parking, and other activities to
   building elevations to achieve positive drainage
4. Saving the cost of unnecessary retaining walls where other types of
   grading can be used
5. Generally balancing cut-and-fill areas to avoid the transport of material to or from the site

Table 2.1 lists commonly accepted gradients for various situations.

After preliminary spot elevations are studied in relation to each
other, preliminary contour lines are drawn on the grading plan at a
chosen contour interval such as 1, 2, or 5 ft (30, 60, or 150 cm). When
the proper balance of cut and fill has been obtained, final spot elevations and contour lines are set. Finished spot elevations are placed at
the following locations.

1. First-floor elevations of buildings
2. All corners of buildings and door stoops or landings
3. Corners of parking areas, terraces, or other paved areas

TABLE 2.1 Gradients

Desirable grades	Maximum, %	Minimum, %
Streets (concrete)	8	0.50
Parking (concrete)	5	0.50
Service areas (concrete)	5	0.50
Main approach walls to buildings	4	1
Stoops or entries to buildings	2	1
Collector walks	8	1
Terraces and sitting areas	2	1
Grass recreational areas	3	2
Mowed banks of grass	3:1 slope	—
Unmowed banks	2:1 slope	—

4. Corners at the tops of landings and bottoms of steps

5. Top and bottom of walls, curls, and gutters

Existing topsoil. Two types of grading that reshape existing contours are *rough grading* (before construction) and *finished grading* (after construction). Before rough grading is begun, existing topsoil should be stripped from the area to be graded and stockpiled away from the construction area. Topsoil of good quality can be reused in the finished grading process. Consider the kind of soil, how it reacts in cut-and-fill situations, its bearing capacity, and its expansive tendencies.

Erosion control plans. Many states require erosion and sedimentation control plans during site construction. Factors to consider in developing these plans are the type of soil on the site, topographic features of the site, type of development, amount of run-off, staging of construction, temporary and permanent control facilities, and maintenance of control facilities during construction.

During construction, minimizing the area and time of exposure of disturbed soil is important. If earth-moving activities are not to be completed within at least 20 days, interim stabilization measures, such as temporary seeding and mulching, should be carried out.

2.2 Foundations on Filled Slopes

Another special problem that may be encountered after site grading is that of a foundation located on or adjacent to a filled slope (Fig. 2.2). From the figure it can be seen that the lack of soil on the slope side of the footing will tend to reduce the stability of the footing and favor sliding. In this case, the overall stability of the slope should be

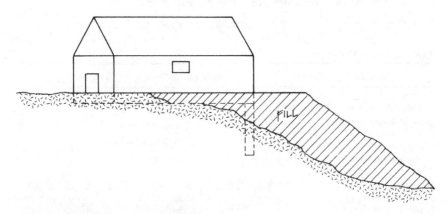

Figure 2.2 Construction on a filled slope.

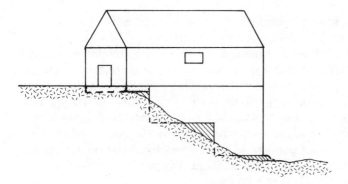

Figure 2.3 Step beam construction on a slope.

checked for the effect of the footing load. This can be done by using slope stability charts (Figs. A.14 and A.15) on computer programs.

If slope stability is questionable, retaining walls are often required. To prevent the future movement or sliding of fill and consequently potential foundation failure, retaining walls which have been designed to withstand the downhill stress are sometimes used. Figure 2.2 shows construction on a filled slope. Piers can be drilled through the fill into undisturbed soil and used to support the foundation, or a step beam which conforms to the contour of the land as illustrated in Fig. 2.3 can be designed. Either approach will reduce or neutralize the downhill stress.

2.3 Site Drainage

In residential areas, natural drainage should be used as much as possible in the design and layout of housing. It is useful to keep the cost of the storm water system down, since water control can be one of the higher-cost items in site development. Natural methods often allow water to percolate into the soil and recharge the groundwater system.

Controlling storm water run-off is a major factor in preparing a grading plan. To prevent problems caused by flooding, the principle of positive drainage is required: Storm water is diverted from the foundation and transported from the site in a storm drainage system. Spot elevations are set at critical points adjacent to a building to provide drainage. Advantageous points must be chosen for placement of catch basins and their connection to existing drainage channels in the area.

Surface drain systems, which are referred to as storm sewers, are constructed with tight or closed joints. Surface drainage can be provided by adjusting around slopes to allow for run-off of storm water and interception at various intervals in catch basins. This is the common conception of the accommodation of surface water (rainfall) in area development.

The design of a drainage system is based on the amount of rainfall to be carried away at a given time. Run-off is the portion of precipitation that finds its way into natural or artificial channels either as surface flow during the storm period or as subsurface flow after the storm has subsided. Run-off is determined by calculating the volume of water discharged from a given watershed area and is measured in cubic feet of discharge water per second or in acre-inches per hour, depending upon the mathematical units utilized. To calculate run-off, the rational formula of Eq. (2.1) can be used.

$$Q = CiA \qquad (2.1)$$

where Q = storm water run-off from an area, acre-in/hr
  C = coefficient of run-off (percent of rainfall that runs off depending on the characteristics of the drainage area)
  i = average intensity of rainfall (in/hr) during the time of concentration for a selected location and rainfall frequency
  A = area, acres

Note: Q can be expressed in acre-centimeters per hour if i is expressed as centimeters per hour.

The rational method can be used for drainage areas less than 5 mi^2 (13 km^2) and is most frequently used on areas up to ½ mi^2 (1.3 km^2).

In urban areas, the frequency of rainfall generally considered for design purposes is the greatest rainfall during the 10-year period. In residential areas, this may be reduced to a 2- to 5-year period. For the design of storm drains and inlet systems to accommodate this precipitation, inlet times of 5 to 15 min are generally used. Beyond this criterion, specific drain design varies by community. Rainfall intensity duration curves, in inches per hour, are available from the local weather bureau or city engineering office. These data can be used to specify the inlet placement and size.

Catch basins and drop inlets. Catch basins intercept storm water and separate the sediment before the water enters the outlet line. The catch basins must be cleaned periodically to prevent clogging. Drop inlets do not have sediment traps below the outlet line and must be designed with self-cleaning water velocities in order to function properly. Drop inlets are often used in low-maintenance areas where sediment would clog improperly maintained catch basins. Both structures generally use cast-iron grates to allow water to enter the basin. Catch basins or drop inlets are generally placed 100 to 200 ft (30 to 60 m) apart on roads but closer as necessary where swales around buildings in developed areas increase the localized volume of water to be handled.

Manholes are used as a means of inspecting and cleaning sewer lines. They are placed at these points:

1. Changes of direction of pipelines

2. Changes in pipe sizes

3. Changes in pipe slope

4. Intersection of two or more pipelines

5. Intervals not greater than 300 to 500 ft (90 to 150 m)

Pipes. Pipes used in closed systems are generally concrete, vitrified clay, cast iron, galvanized corrugated metal, or, on occasion, plastic (PVC or ADS). In some cases where corrugated-metal pipe is used, it has a paved invert for flow where the slope of the pipe is small, such as 0.5 percent (or 0.005 ft/ft). Comfortable pipe slope is generally desirable at 1 percent (or 0.01 ft/ft). Pipe inverts are, by design, set below frost level so that flow will not stop in winter.

2.4 Subsurface Drainage

Subsurface drainage involves the control and removal of soil moisture such as underground streams, perched water, or percolated water. It is concerned with the following:

1. Carrying water away from impervious soils, clay, and rock

2. Preventing seepage of water through the foundation walls

3. Lowering water tables in low flatland

4. Preventing unstable subgrade or frost heaving

5. Removing surface run-off in combination with underground drainage

Subsurface drainage may be accomplished by providing a horizontal passage in the subsoil that collects gravitational water and carries it to outlets. Subsurface drain lines either have open joints or use perforated pipe. Flow into subsurface drains is affected by soil permeability, depth of drain below soil surface, size and number of openings in the drain, drain spacing, and diameter. Drainage can be accomplished by one or more of the following types of systems (see also Fig. 2.4):

1. *Gridiron.* Used where laterals enter the main from one side. Mains and laterals may intersect at angles of less than 90°.

2. *Interceptor.* Used near the upper edge of a wet area to drain

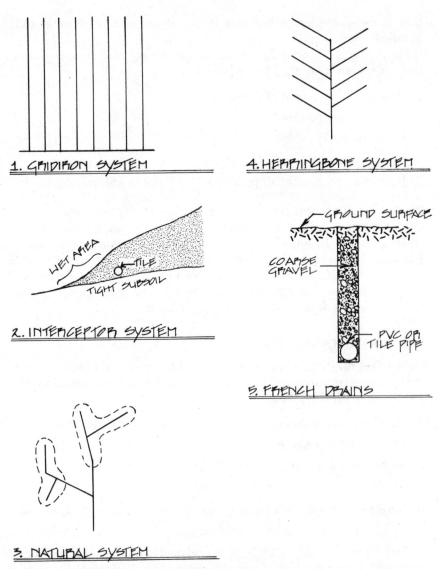

Figure 2.4   Different forms of site drainage.

such an area. Outlets should discharge flow without erosion and prevent flooding when they are submerged. Tile or pipe lines should be placed 2½ to 5 ft (75 to 150 cm) below the soil surface or as necessary to intercept and divert the subsurface flow. In moderately permeable soils, a space approximately 24 ft (7.2 m) wide should be used for each 1 ft (30 cm) of depth below soil surface. In general, depth varies with soil permeability and water table fluctuation.

3. *Natural.*   Used for areas that do not require complete drainage or where existing topography provides adequate drainage.

4. *Herringbone.*   Used in areas of land with a concave surface with land sloping in either direction. This system should not have angles over 45°.

5. *French drains.*   This procedure is used to intercept and divert subsurface water. More on this subject will be presented in Chap. 9. The slope of tile or pipe may vary from a maximum of 2 to 3 percent for a main to a desirable minimum of 0.2 percent for laterals. A minimum fluid flow velocity of 1.5 ft/sec (46 cm/sec) is sometimes used. Drainage tile, ADS or PVC pipe, varying in size from 4 in (10 cm) as a minimum to 6 to 8 in (15 to 20 cm) is used most frequently. The PVC pipe is perforated or slit to permit the water to enter. Generally, ADS is wrapped in a geotextile material which serves as a filter. Drainage tiles may be perforated or laid with loose joints for the same purpose. The trench is often lined with screen or geotextile prior to installing the pipe and gravel, to help prevent fouling of the system.

2.5   Landscaping

Landscaping, for purposes of discussion, involves a combination of factors such as drainage control, planting, and watering. Chapter 9 will provide a more extensive discussion of these subjects.

2.6   Land Planning

The land use depends on the architectural arrangement of a plan in terms of type of activities, linkages, and densities. Activities must be grouped so they will function in relation to each other. When land uses have been established, the linkages between them must be evaluated. Linkage may be the movement of people, goods, waste, communication networks, or a collection of amenities such as views. Land use also involves the concept of density, or number of families per acre. In community development plans, density standards must be adhered to.

The type of construction also will influence the land use plan. If a plan is not economically feasible because of excessive site work, an alternative may be necessary. A particular land use may require a specific type of site—flat, rolling, or hilly. In general, the following subjects should be considered in a land planning study:

1. Visitor and other parking
2. Vehicular circulation patterns

3. Pedestrian circulation

4. Steps and ramps

5. Handicap ramps

6. Bikeways

7. Pavements

8. Walls and retaining walls

9. Sculpture

10. Fountains and pools

11. Night lighting

12. Pedestrian lighting

13. Benches

14. Seating in conjunction with raised tree planters

15. Tree planters and pots

16. Telephone booths

17. Plant material—recreational plans

18. Noise

19. Erosion control

20. View control

21. Parks and trees, shrubs, and flowers

In designing residential projects, careful consideration must be given to configuration and placement of housing on the land and the relationship of the units to each other, access to public facilities, and amenities.

2.7 Foundation Drain Systems

Foundation drain connections.   Until about 25 years ago, most foundation drains were connected to the sanitary sewers where such were available; otherwise, they were served by sump pumps. With the growing demands for increased sewage treatment capacities, it became logical to eliminate as much extraneous inflow as possible. Some municipalities have already begun to prohibit foundation drain connections into sanitary sewers, preferring connection to the storm sewer.

It is not economically feasible to size storm sewers to accommodate every possible run-off. Occasionally, rainfall is such that the storm sewer backs up to levels above the basement or lower-floor grade. Con-

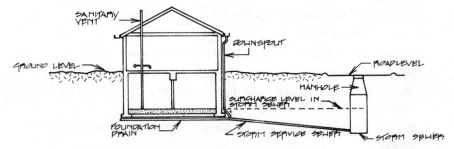

Figure 2.5 Foundation gravity drains and downspouts connected to a storm sewer. (*From Ref. 6.*)

sequently, storm water backs into the foundation drains and causes flooding, the very condition it was originally designed to prevent (Fig. 2.5).

The condition becomes considerably more severe when roof water leaders are also connected to the foundation drain outlet pipe. This drastically increases the volume of water which the drain must accommodate. In addition, this practice can result in flooded basements due to the hydrostatic pressure buildup in the external soil as a result of the drainage breakdown.

If foundation drains are connected by gravity to a storm sewer of insufficient capacity and the hydraulic grade line exceeds the basement elevation, protection against flooding of basements will not be obtained. An alternative solution is a separate foundation drain collector, which is a third pipe installed in the same trench as the sanitary sewer but with connection only to the foundation drain (Fig. 2.6). This method has several advantages, and for many new areas, it may be the best and least-expensive solution. A foundation drain collector will:

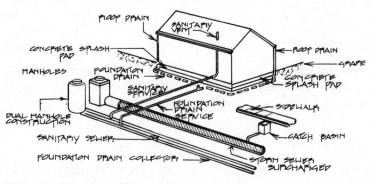

Figure 2.6 Foundation gravity drain connected to a foundation drain collector. (*From Ref. 6.*)

1. Eliminate the probability of hydrostatic pressure on basements due to surcharged sewers.

2. Eliminate infiltration into sanitary sewers from foundation drains.

3. Permit shallow storm sewers designed for lower rainfall intensity, which could reduce the length of storm sewers and result in cost savings for the system.

4. Permit positive design of both the minor and major storm drainage systems.

2.8   Storm Drainage and Sediment Basins

The storm drainage system can be effective in controlling sediment by using straw bale barriers that are cleaned after each storm or, alternatively, a sediment basin designed to collect run-off. The basins can be a temporary control during construction, or they can be cleaned out and turned into an improvement, such as a fountain, upon completion of construction. Ponds often are created for schools as nature study areas, supplemental water sources for fire protection, or recreation.

The spillway of a pond should be designed for the highest rainfall over the past 50 years, whenever flooding would threaten buildings or roads. A drop inlet trickle tube with holes drilled in the rise pipe can be used in sediment ponds during construction.

2.9   Diversion Terraces and Interceptor Channels

Diversion terraces may be constructed upgrade of a project site to convey run-off around the disturbed area. Interceptor channels may also be used within a project area to reduce the velocity of flow and thereby limit erosion.

2.10   Steep Slopes

Whenever possible, steep slopes should be avoided. A desirable maximum is 3:1 slope. This may be planted with grass and can be mowed with a tractor.

2.11   Energy Dissipators

Where water run-off from an outlet pipe is discharged, energy dissipators may be required to control the velocity of run-off. End walls with outlets into streams may need a paved bottom and rubble riprap around them for protection from undercutting during periods of high water.

2.12 Sequence of Construction

Phasing of construction helps limit erosion, as does stockpiling topsoil in the construction area and using temporary seeding. Another way is to construct the storm water system as early as possible. Base courses can be placed for roads and parking so that, if needed, construction workers can park in these areas until surfacing is finished. This limits disturbance of other areas and thereby limits erosion.

2.13 References

1. *Building Code Requirements for Reinforced Concrete* (ACI 318-71). American Concrete Institute, 1975.
2. *Design and Control of Concrete Mixtures.* Portland Cement Association, 1968.
3. Harvy M. Rubenstein, *A Guide to Site and Environmental Planning*, Wiley, New York, 1980.
4. J. T. Adams, *The Complete Concrete Masonry and Brick Handbook*, ARCP Publishing, New York, 1979.
5. Joseph E. Bowles, *Foundation Analysis and Design*, McGraw-Hill, New York, 1977.
6. *Modern Sewer Design.* American Iron and Steel Institute, Washington, D.C., 1980.
7. Whitney Clark Huntington and Robert E. Mickadeit, *Building Construction Materials and Types of Construction*, Wiley, New York, 1975.

Soil Mechanics*

The term *soil* generally describes all the loose material constituting the earth's crust, in varying proportions, and includes three basic materials: air, water, and solid particles. The solid particles have been formed by the disintegration of different rocks. The nature of this origin helps determine the soil behavior. The content of water and/or air, represented as the porosity, further influences soil behavior.

Generally, the higher the porosity, the lower the compressive or bearing strength and the higher the permeability. For purposes herein, porosity is defined as the ratio of combined volume of water and air to the total volume of the soil sample. Another property often used along with (or rather than) porosity is the void ratio. *Void ratio* is defined as the ratio of total voids to solids volume.

3.1 Soil Types

As far as construction practices are concerned, the major classification divisions of soil are by particle size: fine-grained or coarse-grained. The *coarse-grained* soils are the gravels and sands; the *fine-grained* soils consist of silts and clays. The Unified Soil Classification System identifies the groups with the symbols G for gravels, S for sands, M for silts, C for inorganic clays, O for organic silts and clays, and Pt for peat. In many cases, two symbols are used in combination to more precisely describe the soil; examples are GC, a clayey gravel, and SM, a silty sand.

The gravels and sands are further identified as well graded or

---

*Particular appreciation is extended to Tom Petry, Ph.D., P.E., Associate Professor, Civil Engineering, University of Texas at Arlington, for his editorial assistance with this chapter.

poorly graded by combining the letters W for well graded and P for poorly graded (e.g., GW is a well-graded gravel and SP is a poorly graded sand.) "Well graded" signifies a wide distribution in grain size, and "poorly graded" signifies predominately one grain size.

The silts and clays are cross-classified as highly compressible or plastic H or of medium to low compressibility or plasticity L. A highly plastic, inorganic clay would be designated as CH. An organic clay with low to medium compressibility would be labeled OL. For a more in-depth discussion of the Unified Soil Classification System, see Ref. 1.

3.2 Sand and Gravel

The sands and gravels are the easiest soil types to distinguish. They consist of coarse particles which range in size from 3 in (7.6 cm) in diameter down to small grains which can be barely distinguished by the unaided eye as separate grains. Another principal parameter is whether the mixture of particles is well graded. If there is a fairly even distribution of grain sizes, the soil is termed well graded. If a majority of particles are of one particular size, the soil is said to be poorly graded.

The bearing, or shear strength, of a sand or gravel depends solely upon the internal friction between grains. Generally speaking, bearing strengths are high and foundation failures are relatively infrequent in these materials, provided they are sufficiently dense. Any settlement which might occur takes place almost immediately upon application of load and does not materially affect the stability of the foundation. Often, the shear strength increases as the grain size increases, and a well-graded soil is most preferred. The sands and gravels are noncohesive, indicating that there is no attraction or adhesion between individual soil particles.

3.3 Silts and Clays

Silts are finer than sands but coarser than clays. They represent soil particles of ground rock which have not yet changed in mineral character. Generally, silts are more stable than clays with respect to construction problems; clays represent the basic "culprits" in foundation instability. They are the finest possible particles, usually smaller than $1/10,000$ in (0.0025 mm) in diameter. As will be mentioned in Chaps. 6 and 7, the clays exhibit peculiar properties which are also deterrent to foundation stability. The silts and clays are cohesive in nature and tend to compress, deform, and creep under constant load. Clays are particularly vulnerable to volumetric changes induced by moisture variation. Silts also tend to compress, deform, and creep under load and may derive their strength from friction, cohesion, or some combination of the two.

A simple empirical method for determining the type of soil is to disperse a quantity of soil into a container of water and note the rate of sedimentation. Sand and gravel will settle quickly—within about 30 sec. Silts will settle within 15 to 60 min. Clay particles will remain suspended for periods of several hours.

3.4 Rock

Rock may not always be a superior foundation bed. The bearing qualities of rock are dependent upon such factors as the presence of bedding planes, faults, joints, weathering, and cementation of constituents. In many cases the presence of "rock" as a foundation bearing results in faulty assumptions of foundation stability. So-called solid rock, if the implication were correct, would produce a proper foundation bearing. However, in some cases, the "solid" rock is not, in fact, solid and unexpected foundation failures result.

3.5 Fill

The preceding discussion has been limited to native or virgin soils. What happens if the construction site is not level and requires filling? The back-filled soil should be placed at approximately the same dry unit weight and nature as it possessed before removal. Generally, the nature of the replaced soil is not difficult to reproduce, but the "original" dry unit weight may be more elusive. Dry unit weight is an intricate balance of compaction and moisture content.

Compaction of gravel is primarily affected by the load applied during the vibration-densification process; proper compaction of sands is normally done when they are saturated and loaded with vibratory machinery. Achieving satisfactory results in clays and plastic silts requires proper control of moisture content and type of compaction.

As shown in Fig. 3.1, there is an optimum amount of water that is needed to provide maximum dry unit weight. When dry of optimum, the soils are not "lubricated" sufficiently to assist in the compaction. On the other hand, when soils are wet of optimum, the available water interferes with air trying to escape as the voids are reduced. It is, therefore, most advantageous to compact these materials near optimum water content. Clays are best compacted in relatively thin layers (6 to 12 in or 15 to 30 cm) by using sheepsfoot rollers. Plastic silts respond best to compaction in thin layers and to pneumatic rollers.

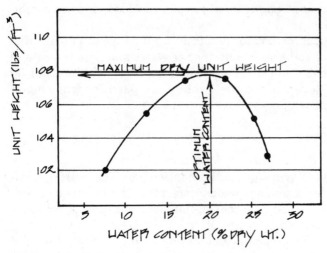

Figure 3.1   Optimum dry unit versus water content.

3.6 Foundation on Soil

The foundation load imposed on the supporting soil depends, to a large extent, upon the design of the foundation and the character of the particular bearing soil. Figure 3.2 shows the distribution of foundation pressure versus depth in bearing soils. For simplicity, the illustration relates to spread footings of a limited area. An approximate relationship would hold for strip footings, e.g., foundation beams. The width of the footing shown in Fig. 3.2 is represented by W and the bearing load by Q or pressure q ($q = Q/A$).

The effects of the load are generally diminished at a depth of about $2W$. Immediately under the footing the pressure is, of course, q. At a depth of approximately $\frac{1}{2}W$ the load is $0.8q$. At a depth of W, the pressure is approximately $0.5q$. Obviously, the effects of a bearing load on the underlying soil diminish rapidly with depth. This relationship will be further discussed in Chap. 5; see also Figs. 3.2 and A.7. This representation deals with the effects of mechanical loading, but another problem can exist with soils containing expansive clays wherein changes in soil volume can be caused by variations in water content.

3.7 Shrinkage

Shrinkage of compressible clays caused by reduced water content or subsequent swelling from rehydration can produce serious damage in residential buildings. Rarely, if ever, will the natural soil exist at the

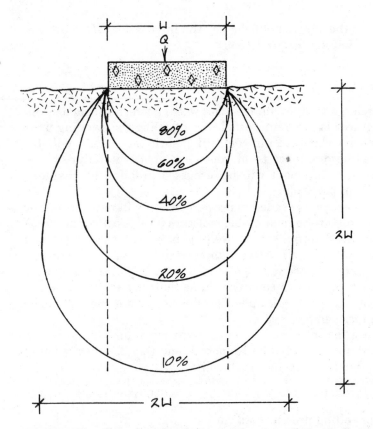

Figure 3.2 Foundation load distribution into bearing soils (vertical).

optimum or stable soil moisture condition. Therefore, some knowledge of the relative ambient moisture content of the native soil is desirable.

The *shrinkage limit* is the water content at which there is no further indication of volume decrease with further decrease in water content. It is usually designated SL or W_{SL}. The shrinkage limit also represents the water content at which the soil changes from a solid to a semisolid state.

Filling of shrinkage cracks with water during wet periods consequently swells the clay and can close the cracks. Repeated cycles of shrinking and swelling can cause increased fissuring of the soil and enormous damage to residential and other light buildings. As soils swell, they increase (moisture content) W and decrease γ_d, resulting in loss of strength. As they shrink, this is reversed, but volume, and hence support, is lost. The type of damage and reducing the damage will be discussed in subsequent chapters (particularly Chap. 7). For more information, readers can refer to the papers published by the International Conferences on Expansive Soil in 1959 and 1980.[2]

3.8 Swelling

Clay soils undergo volume change upon wetting which is called swelling. The engineer is more interested in controlling the swelling pressure in expansive clays than in controlling shrinkage, principally because of the inordinate costs of repairing upheaval failures. The rationale for this statement will be discussed in following chapters, again Chap. 7 in particular.

The pressure which is needed to prevent swelling in natural soils as they take on moisture to their stable moisture level is called the *swelling pressure*. To determine the swelling pressure, an undisturbed specimen of natural clay is fitted into a consolidation apparatus and subjected to water. A strain gauge affixed to the top of the apparatus (the only moving surface) measures volume change, and swell stress is determined by load/area. A graph of swell versus water content can be plotted; see, for example, Fig. 6.2.

The pressure to control soil swelling (expansion) may be evaluated from an equation, suggested by Komornik and David, which is based on statistical analysis for an Israeli soil[3]:

$$\log P_s = 0.0208 LL + 0.000665\gamma_d - 0.0269W - 1.868 \qquad (3.1)$$

where P_s = swelling pressure, kg/cm^2
   LL = liquid limit, percent
   γ_d = natural dry density of soil, kg/cm^2
   W = natural moisture content, percent

Any loading in excess of P_s can control the heave and thus prevent serious foundation movement (1 kg/cm^2 = 14.6 lb/in^2; 1 kg/m^3 = 0.06 lb/ft^3).

3.8.1 Atterberg limits

The Atterberg limits are often used to describe a soil's expansive tendencies. The key descriptions include the liquid limit LL, plastic limit PL, plasticity index PI, shrinkage limit SL, and in situ moisture content, W. Simply stated, LL represents the moisture content at which the soil changes from a liquid into a plastic state; PL represents the moisture content at which the soil changes from a plastic state into a semisolid; and PI is the difference between the two.

The greater the range between LL and PL, the more potentially expansive the soil can be. SL represents the moisture content below

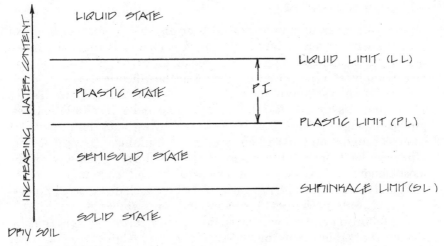

Figure 3.3 Atterberg limits and related indices.

which the soil no longer decreases in volume. (The soil is changing from a semisolid state to a solid; Fig. 3.3.) More information concerning the Atterberg limits can be found in Chaps. 1 (Table 1.1), 5, and 6.

3.9 Frost Heaving

Frost heaving occurs when a mixture of soil and water freezes. When the soil freezes, the total volume may increase by as much as 25 percent, dependent upon the formation of ice lenses at the boundary between the frozen and unfrozen soil. This swell can create distress in foundations. As an example, the Structural Research Department of the Hydro Electric Power Commission, Toronto, Canada, produced tests which indicated that a bond between concrete and frozen soil could approach 400 lb/in^2. Based on this, the uplift (heave) on a 10-in- (25-cm-) diameter pier in a frost zone reaching 4 ft (1.2 m) might approximate 600,000 lb (272.2 t). This obviously exceeds normal foundation loads and would easily result in structural failure.

Generally, the finer the soil, the greater the capillary effects and, consequently, the greater the moisture content. However, relatively pure clays are not prone to frost heave because water movement is restricted, particularly near the surface where temperatures are most extreme. Silts, on the other hand, are most susceptible to frost heave. They are fine-grained and permeable, and they do not possess the swell propensity characteristic of clays (when subjected to available water). Obviously, frost heave is not a problem in mild climates.

3.10 Soil Engineering

There are numerous publications concerning the performance of soil as a support for heavy buildings, but few for residential structures. Surface slab foundation pressures are sufficiently light that they can be carried by the surface soils with minor modification.

Foundation problems in the midwest, particularly in Texas, Louisiana, Mississippi, Oklahoma, Colorado, and several other states, provide enough reasons to understand and investigate the behavior of soils as foundation support for residential buildings. Several factors affect the behavior of soil as a foundation material; among them the most important may be expansiveness of the soil, particularly in the design of residential slab foundations. Others include physical properties of the soil, mechanical behavior, and soil stabilization.

The following section will cover the most important factors that influence the soil behavior and, accordingly, the design of residential or light commercial foundations, particularly slab on grade. They include soil classification, soil compressibility indices, strength parameters, bearing capacity, earth pressure, settlement, soil improvement and compaction, and fill treatment, with special emphasis on the soil mechanics principles most applicable to residential and low-rise commercial foundation analysis and design.

For a representative application of engineering judgment as it concerns a foundation problem, supplemental information will be provided. It is based on the author's experience with expansive soils in such areas as Texas, Louisiana, Arkansas, Oklahoma, New Mexico, Mississippi, Colorado, Florida, and England.

Generally, the properties of soil cannot be determined with the same degree of accuracy as those of other construction materials. That is largely because the properties of soils vary over a wide range in a small geographical area. However, physical properties of soils such as grain size distribution, plasticity, permeability, compressibility and consolidation, shrinkage, swelling, and shear resistance can provide valuable information for the engineer to use in the design of a residential foundation. It is also reasonable and economical to have a geotechnical engineer sample and test the soil profiles, particularly when the proposed building site is in an area where expansive soils are prevalant.

3.11 Soil Classification

In general, soils are classified as cohesive and noncohesive. Cohesive soils, such as clay, possess shearing resistance that is largely independent of normal stress. Noncohesive soils, such as sand, have no shearing resistance, except as developed by friction caused by normal internal pressure between the grains. Most natural and undisturbed soils are a mixture of cohesive and noncohesive materials. Other useful classifications in foundation engineering are size classification and the Unified Soil Classification System.

3.11.1 Size classification

Size classification requires determination of the percent of particles by weight in each of the sizes between minimum and maximum. Mechanical analysis (sieving or screening) is generally used for coarse-grained soil, and sedimentation tests are used for analyzing fine-grained soils. In sieve analysis, the weight of material retained on each sieve is converted to a percent of the total soil sample taken from the site. Then the data are shown as a particle/size distribution curve plotted on semilog coordinates with the sieve size on the horizontal logarithmic scale and the percent by weight smaller than a particular sieve opening on the vertical arithmetic scale.

Based on this sieve analysis, soil can be categorized as well-graded, uniform, or gap-graded. A coarse-grained soil is described as well-graded if there is no excess of particles in any one size range and if no intermediate sizes are lacking. A coarse-grained soil is described as poorly graded if (1) a high proportion of the particles have sizes within narrow limits (a uniform soil) or (2) particles of both large and small sizes are present but show a relatively low proportion of particles of intermediate size (gap graded).

Among these, the well-graded soil could be a good material for foundation support, especially if the particle size distribution involves diameters retained on the No. 200 sieve. Based on the sieve analysis, soils categorized as poorly graded often require the addition of materials to create a stable foundation base.

The grain size plot can provide some other information such as "effective size" and the "uniformity coefficient." The effective size of a sand is the particle size corresponding to 10 percent by weight passing that sieve; it is indicated by D_{10}. By knowing the effective size, permeability and capillarity can be estimated. The ratio D_{60}/D_{10} is defined as the *uniformity coefficient*, where D_{60} represents the grain diameter (or sieve size) which passes 60 percent by weight and D_{10} is the grain diameter or sieve size which passes 10 percent by weight. The ratio, indicated by C_u, provides more information about the range of particle sizes in the soil. For example, a sand with a C_u greater than 10 is a well-graded soil and one with a C_u less than 5 is considered a

TABLE 3.1   Different Classifications Based on Grain Size

U.S. Bureau of Soils Classification, mm						
2.0	1.0	0.5	0.25	0.1	0.05	0.005
Fine gravel	Coarse sand	Sand	Fine sand	Very fine sand	Silt	Clay

M.I.T. Classification, mm									
2.0	0.6	0.2	0.06	0.02	0.006	0.002	0.0006		0.0002
Coarse	Medium	Fine	Coarse	Medium	Fine	Coarse	Medium		Fine (colloidal)
	Sand			Silt			Clay		

TABLE 3.2   Comparison of Grain Size and Sieve Size, American Standard and British Standard

British Standard sieves		American Standard sieves	
Sieve number or size, in	Sieve opening, μm*	Sieve opening, μm*	Sieve number
¼ in	6350	6350	3 (¼ in)
³⁄₁₆ in	4760	4760	4
⅛ in	3180	3360	6
No. 7	2411	2380	8
No. 14	1204	1190	16
No. 25	599	590	30
No. 36	422	420	40
No. 52	295	297	50
No. 72	211	210	70
No. 100	152	149	100
No. 200	76	74	200

*1 μm (micrometer) = 0.001 mm = 0.00004 in. British Standard sieve openings are as given in B.S. 410.
SOURCE: Donald W. Taylor, *Soil Mechanics*, Wiley, New York, 1948.

uniform soil. Tables 3.1 and 3.2 illustrate the different soil classifications based on sieve opening or grain size.

3.11.2   Sedimentation versus size

The particle size and distribution information of silts and clays is obtained by a sedimentation method. This is necessitated by the extremely fine particle size. The method is based on Stoke's equations and is not an exact method for clay because most clay particles are flat or plate-shaped (as opposed to spherical) and some clays develop electrostatic forces or hydrogen bonding which inhibits gravity-induced settlement (sedimentation). Generally, the settling velocity can be expressed, from Stoke's law, as Eq. (3.2).

$$V_s = g_c D_p^2 \left(\frac{\gamma_p - \gamma_f}{18\mu} \right) \quad \text{ft/sec}$$

or   (3.2)

$$D_p = \sqrt{\frac{18\mu V_s}{g_c(\gamma_p - \gamma_f)}} \quad \text{ft}$$

where V_s = settling velocity
g_c = gravitational constant, ft/sec^2
D_p = diameter particle, ft^3
γ_p = particle density lb/ft^3
γ_f = fluid density, lb/ft^3
μ = fluid viscosity, lb/(ft·sec)

More information and details are described by ASTM Test D 422.

3.11.3 Unified classification

The Unified Soil Classification System, developed by Casagrande,[4] is based upon both grain size and plasticity properties of the soil and is recommended for soil analysis in residential design (Fig. 3.4).

The liquid limit LL is determined by the use of a Casagrande liquid limit device. The liquid limit is the water content at which soil "flows." ASTM Test D 4318 explains the laboratory procedure using the Casagrande device to determine LL.

The plastic limit PL is the water content at which the soil can be rolled into a thread ⅛ in (0.3 cm) in diameter before breaking. The plasticity index PI is defined as

$$PI = LL - PL \quad (3.3)$$

and indicates the range of the water content over which the soil remains plastic.

The liquidity index LI is defined as

$$LI = \frac{W - PL}{LL - PL} = \frac{W - PL}{PI} \quad (3.4)$$

where W is the natural water content of the soil. If the value of LI is less than 1, the water content W is less than the liquid limit, and LI near zero indicates that W approaches PL.

Even a small amount of clay mineral in a soil can have an important effect on the index properties of the soil. The basic clays of con-

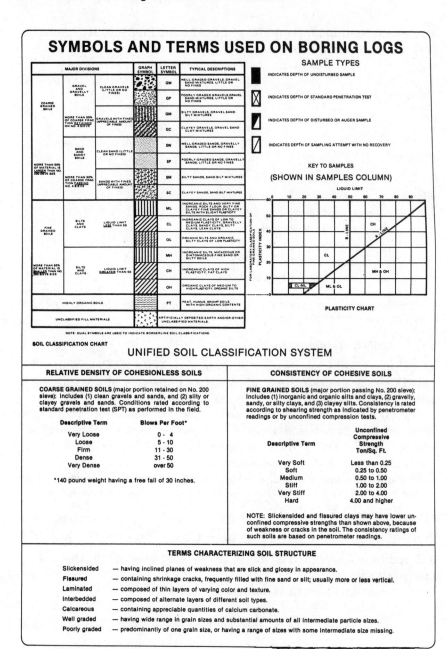

Figure 3.4   Unified Classification.

cern to soil engineers are montmorillonite, attapulgite, illite, chlorite, and kaolinite. Among these clay minerals, kaolinite has minimal and montmorillonite maximal effect on the activity of the soil.

Activity is defined as the ratio of the plasticity index to the percent of clay sizes, as in Eq. (3.5).

$$\text{Activity} = \frac{\text{PI}}{\text{\% of clay sizes in soil samples finer than 2 }\mu\text{m by weight}} \quad (3.5)$$

Note: $1 \,\mu\text{m} = 1 \times 10^{-3} \,\text{mm} = 0.001 \,\text{mm} = 3.9 \times 10^{-5} \,\text{in} = 0.000039 \,\text{in}.$
The values given in Table 3.3 are a range for an active clay. For residential foundations, activity should be less than 1; otherwise, the soil should be treated or altered.

TABLE 3.3   Relative Activity of Clays

Clay	Activity
Inactive clay	Less than 0.75
Normal clay	0.75–1.25
Active clay	Greater than 1.25

3.12 Identification

Casagrande's plasticity chart, which classifies soils based on LL and PI, is useful for soil study in foundation design. The A line divides the plasticity chart in Fig. 3.4 into areas representing different soil types. The areas above the A line represent inorganic and those below organic or silty soils.

Several organizations and individuals, among them A. A. Wagner, have also devised charts and tables for the classification of soils. None of these alternatives have had the acceptance of Casagrande's charts.

3.12.1 Significance of index properties in residential foundation design

In general, clay has a strong surface charge, thin particles, obviously greater attached viscous water, and, consequently, plasticity. Dependent on particle shape and structure, the liquid limit could be an indication of compressibility and, finally, settlement. A high plasticity index is indicative of a soil that will shrink a great deal when moisture is removed (dehydration) and swell when moisture is added (hydrated).

Highly plastic soil can create a high pressure (many tons per square foot) from expansion caused by increasing moisture content. Therefore, extreme care must be taken in the design of foundations to con-

TABLE 3.4   Potential Soil Volume Change as Related to Plasticity Index (PI), Liquid Limit (LL), and Shrinkage Limit (SL)

Potential for volume change	Plasticity index PI	Liquid limit LL, %	Shrinkage limit SL, %
Low	< 18	20–35	> 15
Medium	15–28	35–50	10–15
High	25–41	50–70	7–12
Very high	> 45	> 70	< 11

SOURCE: W. G. Holtz and H. J. Gibbs, *Transactions ASCE*, vol. 121, 1956.

trol or resist moisture variations if the structure is to withstand the stress. A claylike soil with PI greater than 15 can create serious problems for the foundation by absorbing water and subsequently expanding. As will be seen later, the load associated with the residential or light commercial foundation is not generally sufficient to control expansion. As a result, soil modification and/or special foundation designs become important. See in particular Chaps. 5 to 8.

Generally, the lower the shrinkage limit and the wider the range of plasticity index, the greater the potential for change of volume. Swelling pressure, and consequently upheaval, will occur unless the building provides enough weight to restrain the swelling pressure. Interior areas of the building pose the greater concern (vertical movement) due to characteristically lighter loads. [In residential and light commercial construction, the perimeter carries something like 75 to 80 percent of the total weight (load).] Interior areas of the building cause the greatest concern because the structural loads there are characteristically less than at the perimeter. Residential buildings cannot restrain pressures required for controlling swelling pressure. Table 3.4 is a guide in evaluating the soil volume change based on indices.

3.12.2 Void ratios and porosity

Soils seldom, if ever, exist in "pure" form; instead they are conglomerations of several constituents. Further, a quantity of soil does not contain solid material(s) only. Three basic conditions are necessary to describe a soil mass:

1. A two-phase soil is one which consists of solids and air
2. A saturated two-phase soil consists of solids and water
3. A three-phase soil consists of solids, air, and water

In the real world of foundation design, condition 3 is most common. Schematically, condition 3 can be represented as in Fig. 3.5. For condition 2, $V_a = 0$ and $V_v = V_w$. Conversely, for condition 1, $V_w = 0$ and

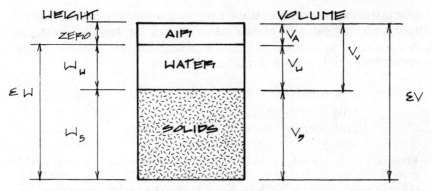

Figure 3.5   Schematic of a three-phase soil.

$V_a = V_v$. From these relationships it can be shown that:

$$\text{Void ratio } e_o = \frac{V_v}{V_s}$$

$$\text{Porosity } n = \frac{V_v}{\Sigma V}$$

$$\% \text{ saturation } S\% = \frac{V_w}{V_v}$$

$$\% \text{ Water } W\% = \frac{W_w}{W_s}$$

Also, G_s = specific gravity of solids

γ_s = unit weight of solids

γ_w = unit weight of water (62.4 lb/ft^3 or 9.8 kN/m^3)

ρ = bulk (mass) density

Then
$$V_w = \frac{W_w}{\gamma_w} = W\% \times V_s \times G_s$$

$$V_s = \frac{W_s}{\gamma_s} \quad (\gamma_s = G_s \times \gamma_w)$$

$$W_w = W\% \times \gamma_s = W\% \times V_s \times G_s$$

$$W_s = V_s \times \gamma_s$$

$$V_w = S\% \times V_v = S\% \times e_o \times V_s$$

$$= W\% \times V_s \times G_s$$

Hence
$$W\% \times V_s \times G_s = S\% \times e_o \times V_s$$

or
$$W\% \times G_s = S\% \times e_o$$

The latter expression is useful for plotting water content versus void ratio at various percents of saturation. (Often the specific gravity of soil is assumed to be about 2.7, unless actual data are available.) The relation between G_s and ρ can be expressed as:

$$G_s = (\rho_s \div \rho_w)(1 + e_o) - (e_o \times S)$$

where ρ_s = bulk density of soil
ρ_w = bulk density of water

Example 3.1   A soil weighs 115 lb/ft^3 (1842 kg/m^3) at a moisture content of 30 percent. The specific gravity G_s of the soil solids is 2.68 [γ_s = 2.68 × 62.4 lb/ft^3 (1000 kg/m^3) = 167 lb/ft^3 (2675 kg/m^3)]. Assume for simplicity a sample of 1 ft^3 (0.028 m^3). Determine V_w, V_s, V_{air}, V_{voids}, e_o, n, and S percent.

Solution

$$\Sigma V = 1.0 \text{ ft}^3 \ (0.028 \text{ m}^3)$$

$$W = 115 \text{ lb/ft}^3 \ (1842 \text{ kg/m}^3) = W_w + W_s$$

$$W\% = \frac{W_w}{W_s} = 0.3 \ (\text{or } 30\%)$$

$$\frac{115 - W_s}{W_s} = 0.3 \qquad 115 - W_s = 0.3 W_s \qquad 1.3 W_s = 115$$

$$W_s = \frac{115}{1.3} = 88.5 \text{ lb } (40.1 \text{ kg})$$

$$W_w = 115 - 88.5 = 26.5 \text{ lb } (12 \text{ kg})$$

$$V_w = \frac{W_w}{\gamma_w} = \frac{26.5 \text{ lb}}{62.4 \text{ lb/ft}^3} = 0.42 \text{ ft}^3 \ (0.012 \text{ m}^3)$$

$$V_s = \frac{W_s}{\gamma_s} = \frac{88.5 \text{ lb}}{167 \text{ lb/ft}^3} = 0.53 \text{ ft}^3 \ (0.015 \text{ m}^3)$$

Then
$$V_{air} = \Sigma V - V_w - V_s = 1 \text{ ft}^3 - 0.42 \text{ ft}^3 - 0.53 \text{ ft}^3$$

$$= 0.05 \text{ ft}^3 \ (1.4 \times 10^{-3} \text{ m}^3)$$

$$V_{voids} = V_a + V_w = 0.05 \text{ ft}^3 + 0.42 \text{ ft}^3$$

$$= 0.47 \text{ ft}^3 \ (0.0133 \text{ m}^3)$$

$$e_o = \frac{V_v}{V_s} = \frac{(0.47 \text{ ft}^3) \ (0.0133 \text{ m}^3)}{(0.53 \text{ ft}^3)(0.015 \text{ m}^3)} = 0.89$$

$$\text{Porosity } n = \frac{V_v}{\Sigma V} = \frac{0.41}{1} = 0.41 = 41\%$$

Saturation
$$S\% = \frac{V_w}{V_v} = \frac{0.42 \text{ ft}^3}{0.47 \text{ ft}^3} = 0.89 = 89\%$$

3.12.3 Relative density

In general, coarse-grained soils with high unit weights have better shear strength and less tendency for settlement. High density is an indication of compaction, and the void ratio is low. A comparison of dense and loose conditions is presented by determining the relative density D_r and expressing the value as a percent. High values of D_r indicate a dense soil and can be expressed by the relationship

$$D_r = \frac{e_{max} - e_o}{e_{max} - e_{min}} \times 100\% = \frac{\gamma_{dmax}}{\gamma_d} \times \frac{\gamma_d - \gamma_{dmin}}{\gamma_{dmax} - \gamma_{dmin}} \times 100\% \quad (3.6)$$

where $e_o = \dfrac{\text{total volume of voids}}{\text{total volume of solids}} = \dfrac{V_v}{V_s}$

$\gamma = \dfrac{\text{mass of soil}}{\text{volume of soil}} \times \text{gravity acceleration} = \rho_s g_c$

$ = \dfrac{\text{weight of soil}}{\text{volume of soil}} \times \text{unit weight of water} = G_s \times \gamma_w$

e_{max} = void ratio of the granular soil in its loosest condition

e_{min} = void ratio of the granular soil in its densest condition

e_o = void ratio of the soil in natural conditions

γ_d = dry unit weight, (weight of soil)/(volume of soil)

γ_{dmax} = maximum dry unit weight

γ_{dmin} = minimum dry unit weight

g_c = gravity acceleration

The maximum dry unit weight can be determined in the laboratory by compacting the soil. The minimum density is determined by letting the soil flow into the test container through a funnel. The relative density above 65 percent could be an appropriate value for residential foundations. The typical relative densities are shown in Table 3.5. Relative densities pertain to variations in the soil's bulk density and are not to be confused with specific gravity (or specific weight).

Clays normally have specific gravities higher than those of sand, gravel, silt, or peat; they range from about 2.63 for kaolinite and 2.76

TABLE 3.5   Values of Relative Density

Condition	D_r, %	γ, lb/ft^3	γ, kg/m^{3*}
Loose	< 35	< 90	< 1442
Medium dense	35–65	90–110	1442–1762
Dense	65–85	110–130	1762–2063
Very dense	> 85	> 130	> 2063

*1 kg/m^3 × 0.00981 = 1 kN/m^3.
SOURCE: David F. McCarthy, 1977.

for montmorillonite to 2.84 for illite. The specific gravity of sand, on the other hand, ranges from about 2.6 to 2.65. Soils, which consist of a combination of materials, will most often have specific gravities ranging between about 2.6 and 2.75. Soil bulk densities vary substantially from these ranges as illustrated in Table 3.5. For example, the bulk density of a dry soil weighing 110 lb/ft^3 would be 1.76 g/cm^3.

3.12.4 Consistency of soil

It is important to study the consistency of the undisturbed soil, particularly clays. Consistency is referred to by texture and strength of the soil and is categorized as soft, medium, stiff, very stiff, and hard. Unconfined compressive strength or shear strength (cohesion) of clays represents the consistency of the soil. Shear strength of clay can be taken as half of the unconfined compressive strength. The cohesion can be determined by triaxial or uniaxial compressive tests. A vane-shear device or pocket penetrometer and rule-of-thumb test can be used for quick approximation of the shear strength of the soil, and sometimes they are sufficient for residential foundation design. Table 3.6 shows an approximation of the relation between soil consistency and soil strength.

TABLE 3.6 Consistency and Strength of Undisturbed Clay Soils

Consistency	Shear strength τ_f, tons/ft^2 (t/m^2)	Unconfined compression strength q_u, tons/ft^2 (t/m^2)	Rule-of-thumb test, or feel to touch
Soft	0.25–0.5 (2.44–4.88)	Less than 0.5 (< 4.88)	¼-in- (0.6-cm-) diam. pencil makes 1-in (2.5-cm) penetration with moderate effort
Medium		0.5–1.0 (4.88–9.76)	
Stiff	0.5–1.0 (4.88–9.76)	1.0–2.0 (9.76–19.52)	¼-in- (0.6-cm-) diam. pencil makes ½-in- (1.2-cm-) penetration with moderate effort
Very stiff	1.0–3.0 (4.76–29.28)	2.0–4.0 (19.520–39.040)	¼-in- (0.6-cm-) diam. steel rod makes ¼-in- (0.6-cm-) penetration with considerable effort
Hard	Greater than 3.0 (> 29.28)	Greater than 4.0 (> 39.04)	¼-in steel rod can penetrate less than ⅛ in (0.3 cm). Fingernail marks hardly possible

Sensitivity (a ratio of unconfined compressive strength of undisturbed clay to unconfined compressive strength of the remolded clay) and relative density can be chosen as references for consistency determinations of cohesive and granular soils. In clays, low sensitivity ranges between 2 and 4. Between 5 and 8, clay is considered to be sensitive and above 8, extrasensitive.

3.12.5 Strength of soils

The principal strength factor of concern with soils is the *shear strength*, which can be calculated from Coulomb's equation:

$$\tau_f = C + \sigma \tan \phi \quad \text{(cohesion plus friction)}$$

Or in some texts

$$S = c + \sigma \tan \phi \tag{3.7}$$

where S or τ_f = shearing resistance of soil at failure, shear strength
  C = apparent cohesion of soil (zero for cohesionless soils)
  σ = normal stress on shear plane
  ϕ = angle of shearing stress of soil, often assumed to be zero for very soft soils

Coulomb's equation is often shortened to:

$$S \text{ or } \tau_f = C = q_u/2 \quad \text{for plastic, fine-grained soils}$$

or S or $\tau f = \sigma \tan \phi$ for ideal sand and coarse-grained soils of no plasticity

Laboratory tests are normally used to provide the data necessary to solve Coulomb's equation. Triaxial shear tests can provide the shearing stress versus effective normal stress data required to plot the Coulomb failure envelope. From this line, the intercept (y axis) is C, the apparent cohesion, and the slope (with x axis) is $\tan \phi$. A simplified test can be used to estimate the apparent cohesion of saturated clay soils. This is the vane test, in which

$$C = \frac{\tau}{\pi\left(\dfrac{d^2 h}{2} + \dfrac{d^3}{6}\right)}$$

where τ = torque required to rotate vane
  d = vane width
  h = vane height

The units must be consistent: lb/ft^2 or kg/cm^2 for $\tau_f(S)$, C, σ, and q_u; ft-lb or kg-cm for τ; cm or ft for d and h.

Additional information on foundation engineering will be found in the Appendix following Chap. 10. This topic is more technical and mathematical by nature but is necessary to provide both an insight to the design capacity of soils and a procedure for evaluating various underpinning options.

3.13 References

1. T. W. Lambe and R. V. Whitman, *Soil Mechanics*, Wiley, New York, 1969.
2. Donald Snethen (ed.), *Expansive Soils*, Vols. 1 and 2, ASCE International Conference, Denver, Colo., June 1980.
3. A. Komornik and D. David, "Prediction of Swelling Pressures of Clays," *Proc. ASCE, J. of SMFE*, vol. 95, pp. 209–225, 1969.
4. A. Casagrande, "Classification and Identification of Soils," *Trans. ASCE*, vol. 113, p. 901, 1948.

4

General Properties of Concrete*

4.1 Introduction

Virtually all modern structural foundations are constructed of rein-forced Portland cement concrete, a material with high inherent com-pressive strength, durability (when properly proportioned and placed), and versatility in the shapes and forms into which it can be molded. Internal steel and/or fiber reinforcement imparts the necessary tensile and shear strengths to concrete structures.

Ordinary concrete is obtained from a specific mix consisting of ce-ment, water, aggregates, and, as necessary, special admixtures. The concrete is then placed in forms, normally containing steel reinforc-ing. Most often the mix is batched at a concrete plant and supplied to the user ready for use, thus the term "ready-mix" concrete.

All constituents are measured in definite quantities for the given concrete composition. A preliminary laboratory test procedure selects the concrete proportions in order to provide a desired performance such as frost resistance, impermeability to water, strength, and ap-pearance.

Production of Portland cement takes place by mining the raw ma-terials in great quantities and then firing them in huge kilns. The pro-cess is intended to ensure the homogeneity of the product. The basic raw materials are calcium carbonate ($CaCO_3$), sand, shale or clay, cal-cium sulfate ($CaSO_4$), and various special-performance ingredients as the specific purpose might dictate.

According to the purpose for which the concrete is required, the mix

---

*Special appreciation is extended to James D. Irwin, President, ECI Services, Inc., for his contribution to and editorial assistance with this chapter.

may contain cement from one of the following groups: *ordinary Portland* cement, *finely ground Portland* (high early), *coarse-ground Portland* (slow set), *nonshrinking* cement, *super-sulfate* cement (sulfate resistant), and *heat-resistant* cement. See Sec. 4.2 for more details of various cement types. Other than grind size, changes in performance of cement are also altered by changes in chemical composition. For example, the set time (and strength development) can be retarded by the addition of calcium lignosulfonate or accelerated by using calcium chloride. Along these same lines, sulfonated naphthalenes can be used to reduce the water-to-cement ratio and substantially increase ultimate compressive strength of the concrete. In specialty applications, the homopolymer of polyvinyl acetate is used to increase bond strengths between concrete and steel, or concrete to concrete, as in the case of overpours.

4.2 Fundamentals

Portland cement concrete consists of two phases: (1) a chemically active paste which gives the plastic mixture workability, cohesiveness, and gradual hardening and gives the hardened concrete strength, durability, and impermeability and (2) chemically inert fillers known as aggregates.

The desired properties of both the freshly mixed and the hardened concrete can be selected from a broad spectrum of values by first choosing one of several available types of Portland cement and then proportioning the ingredients in accordance with established guidelines to be discussed later. The normal types of Portland cement are designated as Type I through Type V, each of which is manufactured to conform to ASTM specifications C-150.

Type I. Normal Portland cement, used for construction, pavements, beams, columns, floor slabs, bridges, sewers, culverts, soil-cement mixtures, and other general construction purposes that are not subject to sulfate hazard.

Type II. Modified Portland cement, similar to Type I except with a lower content of tricalcium aluminate, and in some instances, a coarser grind. Type II is used where light sulfate resistance is required. This cement generates heat at a slower rate and, accordingly, is used in structures of large dimensions and massive pours where moderate heat of hydration is desirable. These include applications such as dams, heavy retaining walls, and nuclear reactors and even less massive pours where the concrete is placed in conditions of elevated temperatures.

Type III. High early strength cement, used where high strength is desired at a very early period, such as precast concrete. Increasing the tricalcium silicate content accelerates the heat of hydration and strength development. Also, Type III is a finer grind that promotes a more rapid rate of hydration due to the increased surface area exposed to water. This cement is more suitable for cold-weather construction, but even under these conditions, it should not be used for massive pours because the high heat of hydration tends to cause expansion and cracking.

Type IV. Low-heat cement, used in massive pours, such as large gravity dams, to diminish heat cracking as described for Type II. The amount of tricalcium silicate is also reduced and the dicalcium silicate is increased.

Type V. Sulfate-resistant, used in structures exposed to severe sulfate action such as wastewater treatment plants and drainage structures that carry wastewater with high sulfate content. In composition, this cement is similar to Type II except that the tricalcium aluminate content would be further decreased and the calculated free lime increased.

Air-entrained cement. Air-entrained cement, indicated by the letter A following the type, contains an additive which promotes the stabilization of microscopic air bubbles which increase the resistance to scaling and spalling often caused by contraction and expansion in freezing and thawing cycles. Air-entrained concrete has been successfully used in pavements in the northern states since the 1940s.

4.2.1 Characteristics of plastic concrete

The attributes of freshly mixed plastic concrete necessary for successful placement are workability, paste content, and rate of hardening.

4.2.1.1 Workability. The ease with which concrete is placed depends on its fluidity, cohesiveness, the amount of paste in excess of that required to fill the voids between the aggregate particles and coat the individual particles, and pumpability in certain instances. A rough measure of workability is determined by testing the *slump*, which represents the subsidence of a conical specimen 12 in (30.5 cm) high with top and bottom diameters of 4 in (10.2 cm) and 8 in (20.3 cm), respectively, when the mold is lifted away. See Sec. 4.3.4 or ASTM C-143 for details of this test. More fluid mixes have higher slumps which are often needed for narrow form dimensions, closer reinforcement spacing, or other factors which inhibit thorough consolidation by internal or external vibration.

Control of the slump can be achieved by varying the paste content of the mix and/or introducing various types and amounts of chemical admixtures, which are discussed in Sec. 4.3.3. Other factors affecting the slump are the temperature of the mix, time elapsed after combining the cement and water, and changes in aggregate gradation.

4.2.1.2 Paste content. A concrete mixture must contain enough paste to coat the aggregate particles, fill the voids between the particles, and coat the formed and finished surfaces of the monolith. Paste in excess of these requirements separates the aggregate particles, thereby facilitating their flowing past each other, giving the mixture fluidity, and increasing the slump. Increasing the slump by adding only water to the plastic mix, rather than both water and cement in their original proportions, reduces potential strength, durability, and other desired properties. Excess paste increases plastic and drying shrinkage of the concrete.

4.2.1.3 Rate of hardening. As with all chemical reactions, the rate of hardening of cement paste is temperature-dependent. Other factors that influence the rate of hardening are the type and amount of cement, the type and amount of chemical admixtures, and the amount of water relative to the amount of cement (the water/cement ratio). Concrete must harden at a rate slow enough that it can be transported, placed, and finished while still plastic but fast enough to prevent costly delays in finishing and unwanted deformation in slip-form and extrusion operations.

4.2.2 Characteristics of hardened concrete

The desired characteristics of hardened concrete include durability, strength, resistance to abrasion and impact, impermeability, and, in some instances, unit weight.

4.2.2.1 Freeze-thaw durability. The ability of mature concrete to resist deterioration due to repeated cycles of freezing and thawing is primarily a function of density and entrained air content. Greater density resulting from lower water/cement ratios reduces the amount of free water within the concrete subject to freezing, and the near-microscopic bubbles of entrained air provide reservoirs into which freezing water can expand, thereby relieving the internal pressures that otherwise result in spalling of exposed surfaces. Properly proportioned air-entrained concrete should be protected from freezing until its compressive strength has reached at least 500 lb/in².

Entrained air content approximating 9 percent by volume of the $-\frac{1}{4}$-in fraction of the concrete mix (total paste and fine aggregate) has been found to be optimum for durability. Higher air content provides little additional durability and is detrimental to ultimate strength. Entrained air should not be used in high-strength concrete (5000 lb/in² and above) because of the strength reduction, even though the concrete may otherwise be used in freeze-thaw environments. The greater density of these concretes provides adequate durability.

4.2.2.2 Strength. The ultimate strength of concrete is determined by the water/cement ratio and is influenced by the mechanical and chemical characteristics of the Portland cement, pozzolans, aggregates, and chemical admixtures and the curing conditions. Flexure, shear, and bond strengths are important in structural design, but they are generally proportional to compressive strength, which is more conveniently and reliably measured by standardized tests. Therefore, the term "strength" usually is understood to mean compressive strength unless otherwise indicated.

In addition to the ultimate strength, the rate of strength increase is, in many instances, an important consideration. Ordinary concrete containing Type I Portland cement and no admixtures at 70°F (21°C) can be expected to attain approximately 50 percent of its 28-day strength in 3 days, 70 percent in 7 days, and 85 percent in 14 days. This rate of strength increase can be accelerated by changing to Type III cement, using certain chemical admixtures, and/or elevating the initial concrete temperatures by heating mixing water and/or steam curing. Higher strengths at all ages can, of course, be obtained by increasing cement or producing the concrete with lower slump (reducing water).

4.2.2.3 Resistance to abrasion and impact. Although tests to quantify abrasion and impact resistance have not been developed, these properties are of extreme importance, especially for such applications as hydraulic structures exposed to running water, pavement or structures subjected to heavy foot and/or vehicular traffic, and highway median barriers. Impact resistance (ductility) can be improved by incorporating certain synthetic fibers in the plastic mix. Abrasion resistance is increased by lower water/cement ratios, abrasion-resistant aggregates (such as crushed granite), or applying abrasion-resistant coatings such as those containing epoxy resin with quartz, granite, or steel filings as aggregate.

4.2.2.4 Impermeability. The accumulation of moisture on concrete floor slabs on grade is the result of either (1) the condensation of moisture from the air in contact with a surface having a temperature lower than the dew point of the air or (2) the migration of moisture through the slab at a rate faster than it evaporates from the surface. The former condition is not related to the quality of the concrete and can be eliminated by raising the temperature of the slab or lowering the dew point of the air. The latter condition can be avoided by placing impermeable ("waterproof") concrete, installing an effective vapor barrier on the subbase before the slab is poured, or using a coarse-grained fill material for the subgrade to minimize capillary vapor pressure. It can be alleviated on existing slabs by drying the concrete with forced warm air and applying a sealer such as methyl methacrylate to the dried surface.

To determine if the moisture resulted from condensation or migration, thoroughly dry a test area the size of a small pane of glass. Run a continuous bead of calking compound around the perimeter of the glass and place the glass, calking side down, on the dried area. If, after several hours, moisture beads form on the underside of the glass, the problem is migration through the concrete. Moisture on top of the glass is from condensation.

Good-quality concrete is, for all practical purposes, impermeable. Therefore, the best assurance of getting impermeable concrete is to properly place, compact, vibrate, and cure a dense, high-quality mix. The so-called waterproofing admixtures are often solutions of chlorides and stearates which are of marginal value and can have detrimental side effects such as corrosion of imbedded metals, increased drying shrinkage, and reduced resistance to freeze-thaw deterioration. No admixture can make poor-quality concrete impermeable. Only by improving the quality of the concrete can admixtures contribute to reducing permeability. Entrained air bubbles tend to block the capillary paths through the concrete and thereby reduce permeability.

Tests have shown that, when properly placed and compacted and with 7 days effective curing, impermeable concrete can be made with a water-cement ratio of 5.6 gal/sack of cement. This corresponds to a 28-day compressive strength of about 4400 lb/in^2 (308 kg/cm^2). With *14* days effective curing, impermeable concrete can result from a water-cement ratio of 7.2 gal/sack [27.3 l/sack with a 28-day strength of about 3000 lb/in (210 kg/cm^2)]. Adequate curing is as important as mix proportions in achieving waterproof concrete. See Sec. 4.5 for more information on curing.

4.2.2.5 Unit weight (density). The unit weight of concrete is seldom a consideration except in multistory structures to minimize the dead load on the supporting structural elements. The use of heavyweight (high-density) concrete is limited to such structures as nuclear containment vessels, in which heavy aggregates such as granite or lead shot are used.

The weight of concrete can be reduced significantly by using special lightweight aggregates and entrained air. Structural lightweight concrete can be produced to weigh 100 lb/ft³ (1602 kg/m³). Nonstructural floor fill and insulating concretes weighing as little as 60 to 90 lb/ft³ (961 to 1442 kg/m³) can be produced by using plastic foams to replace conventional coarse aggregates.

4.2.2.6 Drying shrinkage. The reduction in dimensions of a concrete structural member resulting from drying shrinkage is an important consideration in such structures as bridges and multistory buildings. The cracks in residential construction and paving are largely cosmetic problems except where moisture penetration or insect infestation through the cracks can lead to more serious consequences.

Drying shrinkage is primarily a function of the amount of mixing water in the plastic mix and subsequent curing and to a lesser extent certain characteristics of the aggregates and cement. Reducing the amount of mixing water (lower slumps) or the use of water-reducing admixtures tends to reduce drying shrinkage, as does moist curing. The latter is most often achieved in the field through the use of curing compounds (chemical films) or plastic sheets (polyethylene) applied directly on the finished surface.

The development of shrinkage cracks is dependent not only on the amount of shrinkage but also on the time at which this shrinkage occurs relative to the rate of hardening and strength gain of the concrete. Therefore, the rate of bleeding of the fresh concrete, temperature, and other evaporative conditions influence the development of shrinkage cracks.

4.2.2.7 Other characteristics of hardened concrete. In unusual instances, such qualities as creep, conductivity (sound, thermal, electrical), and color may be a consideration. These require special selection of cements, aggregates, and/or admixtures as well as trial batch tests to determine beforehand if the requirements will be met.

4.3 Proportioning

The quantity of each ingredient of a concrete batch required to produce both a plastic mix and a finished product having predetermined characteristics can be estimated by using guidelines that have been developed by various concrete engineers over the years. These guide-

TABLE 4.1   Water/Cement Ratios

Water/cement ratio, lb/lb or kg/kg	Approximate 28-day compressive strength, lb/in^2 (kg/cm^2), when entrained air is		
	0%	4%	8%
0.7	2500 (175)	2000 (140)	
0.6	3500 (245)	2500 (175)	1500 (105)
0.5	4500 (315)	3500 (245)	2500 (175)
0.4	5500 (385)	4500 (315)	3500 (245)

lines require preliminary test data on pertinent characteristics of each of the ingredients. The type of the cement generally gives sufficient information about a particular ingredient, since limitations on its properties are established by ASTM C-150. Water, for example, is required to be potable.

Limitations on the characteristics of the aggregates are established by ASTM C-33, but variations within those limitations are critical. The sieve analysis (gradations) and specific gravities of the particular aggregates to be used must be determined. The properties of the particular chemical and mineral admixtures to be used are usually determined by trial batches.

The quantity of each of the ingredients required for a batch of concrete is usually computed on the basis of absolute volume, which is then converted to weight by using the specific gravity of each of the materials. Data such as those presented in Tables 4.1 and 4.2 are helpful in estimating these quantities. Other tables based on various approaches to estimating the quantities of aggregates needed to fill the remaining volumes have been devised by the Portland Cement Asso-

TABLE 4.2   Total Mixing Water versus Slump

Maximum aggregate size, in	Total water per cubic yard*					
	1- to 2-in slump		3- to 4-in slump		5- to 6-in slump	
	lb	kg	lb	kg	lb	kg
3/8	340	155	370	168	400	182
1/2	330	150	350	159	380	173
3/4	310	141	340	155	360	164
1	296	135	320	145	340	155
1½	280	127	300	136	320	145
2	260	118	280	127	310	141
3	240	109	260	118	290	132

*1 yd^3 = 0.76 m^3.

ciation, the National Ready Mix Concrete Association, the American Concrete Institute, and others and are available in their publications.

4.3.1 Water/cement ratio

The ultimate compressive strength, as well as most of the other critical characteristics of concrete, is determined by the relative proportions of water and Portland cement in the paste. Depending on the other factors such as chemical characteristics of the cement, fly ash, and admixtures and curing conditions, the water/cement ratios given in Table 4.1 should yield the approximate compressive strengths in 28 days.

Since the amount of mixing water required is determined by the slump, aggregate gradation, temperature, the characteristics and amounts of any admixtures, and the amount of entrained air, these factors must be determined to arrive at the approximate amount of cement required for a given water/cement ratio.

Table 4.2 gives the approximate total mixing water (including free water in aggregates) requirements for various slumps, and maximum aggregate sizes at 70°F (21°C) without water-reducing admixtures or entrained air.

4.3.2 Aggregates

Aggregates for Portland cement concrete are generally chemically inert granular materials such as sand, gravel, and various kinds of crushed stone. On occasion, such materials as crushed blast furnace slag, kiln-burned clay or shale, vermiculite, lead balls or slugs, sea shells, wood chips, and fibers of steel or plastics may be substituted or used to supplement the normal aggregates. Entrained air and preformed plastic foam, being inert, are treated as parts of the aggregate system.

4.3.2.1 Gradation. Since the sole function of the aggregates is to occupy space (thereby minimizing the amount of the more expensive cement required to produce a given quantity of concrete with given properties), the aggregates must (1) minimize the interparticle void space and (2) minimize the total surface area of the particles that must be coated with paste. This is where the *gradation* of the aggregates becomes important.

Aggregates containing roughly equal amounts of each intermediate particle size from the largest (several inches) to the smallest (No. 100 sieve) have been found to meet both these criteria. Limitations on the percents of the intermediate sizes are given in ASTM C-33 for both fine aggregate (smaller than the No. 4 standard sieve) and coarse aggregate (larger than the No. 4 sieve). The sum of the percents of the aggregates larger than each of the standard sieves from the No. 100 up to the largest particle (expressed as a decimal fraction) is known as the fineness modulus. This is a useful index number indicating the relative fineness or coarseness of the aggregates, and it is used to estimate relative proportions of fine and coarse aggregates.

4.3.2.2 Other aggregate characteristics. In addition to being inert and well-graded, aggregates should be (1) free of deleterious materials such as silt, clay, coal, and trash, (2) strong to resist crushing, splitting, and abrasion, and (3) sound to resist exposure to water, weather, and chemical attack.

4.3.3 Admixtures

Defined as any ingredient in Portland cement concrete other than cement, water, or aggregate, the most commonly used admixtures are chemical ones (ASTM C-494 describes the seven basic types in terms of performance) and pozzolans or pozzolan substitutes such as fly ash, volcanic ash, pumice, or silica fume.

4.3.3.1 Chemical admixtures. The proprietary chemical admixtures (Table 4.3) are formulated to meet the performance requirements of ASTM C-494 in the following categories:

Type A   Water-Reducing Admixtures
Type B   Retarding Admixtures
Type C   Accelerating Admixtures
Type D   Water-Reducing Retarders
Type E   Water-Reducing Accelerators
Type F   High-Range Water Reducers
Type G   High-Range Water-Reducing Retarders

Other requirements such as maximum shrinkage, relative durability, and flexural and compressive strengths at various ages are given in ASTM C-494. Most of the chemical admixtures presently available are in the form of concentrated liquids.

4.3.3.2 Pozzolans. Pozzolanic admixtures are materials, liquid or granular, that contain free silica which can react, in the presence of water, with the free lime liberated by the chemical reaction between Portland cement and water. This lime-silica reaction results in the formation of additional cementing compounds, which increases the potential strength of the cement-water paste. Pozzolans and chemical

TABLE 4.3   ASTM C-494 Chemical Admixture Requirements

	A	B	C*	D	E	F*	G*
Minimum reduction in water requirement for given mix and slump	5%	—	—	5%	5%	12%	12%
Acceleration of initial set, hr	1.0 max	—	1.0– 3.5	—	1.0– 3.5	1.0 max	—
Acceleration of final set, hr	1.0 max	—	1.0 min	—	1.0 min	1.0 max	—
Retardation of initial set, hr	1.5 max	1.0– 3.5	—	1.0– 3.5	—	1.5 max	1.0– 3.5
Retardation of final set, hr	1.5 max	3.5 max	—	3.5 max	—	1.5 max	3.5 max
Minimum 28-day compressive strength*	110%	90%	100%	110%	110%	110%	110%

*C, 125% at 3 days; F, 140% at 1 day; G, 125% at 1 day

admixtures can be used independently of each other or together. In the latter instance, they are introduced into the mixer separately.

The most commonly used pozzolan is fly ash, a by-product of coal-fired power plant furnaces. Its advantages include economy (it is less expensive than cement, which it partially replaces to produce concrete of given qualities), availability, and the reduction in the heat of hydration liberated by the reduced cement content. The same statement applies to volcanic ash in areas where it is available. Both materials are subject to significant variations in quality due to variations in their silica, free lime, and detrimental carbon content from source to source as well as from a given source.

A new pozzolan beginning to be used is silica fume. Because of its ultra-fine grain size, very high free silica content, and absence of carbon, it has produced greater concrete strengths than were heretofore considered possible.

4.3.3.3 Entrained air. The intentional entrainment of air in concrete usually involves no chemical reaction. Dissolving a soapy substance in the mixing water to form a film encapsulating each air bubble folded into the mix by the action of the mixer prevents the bubbles from coalescing and floating out of the mix. That is, the nearly microscopic air bubbles are stabilized in the mix. They are considered to be a part of the aggregate system, since they merely occupy space and are not involved in any chemical activity. However, since the bubbles are like tiny balloons, they are easily deformed, and they flow past rigid aggregate grains much easier than the aggregate particles pass each other. The result is increased flowability or slump, or equal slump with less mixing water. The resulting decrease in the water/cement ratio partially offsets the loss in strength because of the reduction in effective cross-sectional area of the concrete due to the bubbles.

A rough estimate of the effect of entrained air on compressive strength is computed by reducing the strength 4 percent for each percent (by volume of the total mix) of entrained air after positive adjustment for the lower water/cement ratio. Since the reduction in water requirement due to entrained air is greater for leaner than for richer mixes, entrained air usually results in a net gain in strength in lean mixes, little change in average mixes, and net losses in rich mixes. For that reason, entrained air should not be incorporated in 5000 lb/in^2 (350 kg/cm^2) or stronger designs.

The benefits of entrained air include a manyfold increase in durability, increased workability and cohesiveness and reduced permeability, segregation, and bleeding. The reduction in bleeding can reduce drying shrinkage and the development of shrinkage cracks, but it can present finishing difficulties by causing the slab surface to dry prematurely and crust and harden from the top down. This can lead to uneven troweled surfaces, blistering, or scaling, with the extent being further influenced by ambient conditions, finishing techniques, and other circumstances.

4.3.4 Slump test

The slump test (ASTM C-143) can be used as a rough measure of the consistency and mobility of the concrete. Slump is then used as a relative measure of the degree of wetness or flow of the concrete, such as stiff, medium, or wet. It should not be considered an exact measure of workability and should not be used to compare mixes of entirely different proportions or with different kinds of aggregates.

Changes in slump reflect variations in grading or proportion of the aggregates, changes in the water content of the sand, or changes in the mix water. Variations should be addressed immediately to maintain proper consistency by adjusting amounts and proportions of sand and coarse aggregate or by changing water, with caution given to maintain the specified water/cement ratio.

The dimensions of a slump cone are shown in Fig. 4.1. To perform the slump test, the cone is set on a flat surface and filled with concrete in three layers of equal volume. Each layer is tamped 25 blows with a 5/8-in (1.59-cm) diameter rod. The cone is then removed and set beside the slumping concrete on the flat surface. A straightedge is extended from the top of the cone over the concrete. The slump is the vertical distance, in inches, between the bottom of the straightedge to the top of the concrete (Fig. 4.2).

Figure 4.1 The dimensions of a slump cone.

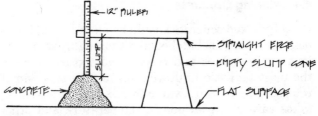

Figure 4.2 Slump test.

TABLE 4.4   Recommended Slumps for Concrete

| | Slump, in (cm) | |
Types of structures	Minimum	Maximum
Massive sections, pavements, and floor laid on ground	1 (2.54)	4 (10.16)
Heavy slabs, beams or walls, tank walls, posts	3 (7.62)	6 (15.24)
Thin walls and columns, ordinary slabs or beams, vases and garden furniture	4 (10.16)	8 (20.32)

SOURCE: J. T. Adams, 1979.

To avoid mixes that are too stiff or too wet, slump falling within the limits given in Table 4.4 are recommended. The table lists a few kinds of structures as typical examples of each range of slump. In all cases, slump should not exceed the point at which segregation begins to occur with the placement method being used.

It should be borne in mind that, by whatever method or means the batch design was conceived, it is only an estimate. Only by committing this combination of materials to a concrete mixer can the resulting slump, air content, yield, unit weight, strength and other properties be confirmed. A typical batch design for 3000 lb/in^2 (2.06 kN/cm^2) concrete is given in Table 4.5. These proportions are based upon the assumption that inert ingredients are in a saturated surface dry condition, meaning that they contain all the water they are capable of adsorbing. If the aggregate contains excess free water, correction should be made in the amount of added water. The resultant composition would have a slump of approximately 4 to 5 in (10.2 to 12.7 cm).

TABLE 4.5   Mixture for 1 yd^3 (0.76 m^3) of 3000 lb/in^2 (210 kg/cm^2) Concrete

Material	Amount per 94-lb (42.5-kg) sack of cement	Total amount per yard
Cement (5 sacks)	— —	470 lb (212 kg)
Sand	314 lb (142.5 kg)	1570 lb (712 kg)
Coarse aggregate	345 lb (157 kg)	1725 lb (784 kg)
Water, max	7 gal (26.5 l)	35 gal (132.5 l)

4.4 Placing Concrete

Freshly mixed concrete should be placed in its final position as soon as possible after it is batched and thoroughly mixed. Time limits for various temperatures and types of admixtures have been proposed, but the most realistic limitation on mixing time simply allows only one retempering (adding water to mixed concrete) of any one batch. This takes care of variations in temperature and other conditions detrimental to the concrete. The quantity of water added should not be more than that resulting (even temporarily) in the maximum allowable slump.

Concrete placement methods should be such that segregation of the mix is minimized. Pumping is preferable to flowing the mix down long flat chutes or dragging piles of concrete horizontally. Tremies should be required when concrete is to be dropped over 3 ft (0.9 m). The beginning of segregation with the placement method used should be the factor limiting maximum allowable slump.

4.5 Curing Concrete

Although it is desirable to produce concrete with the lowest water content compatible with job conditions and other considerations, once the concrete is in place every effort should be made to prevent the escape of water.

4.5.1 Effect of curing on strength

Since only the surface of each grain of cement is initially in contact with the water, and water penetrates the grains gradually, the formation of the gel which gives the paste its strength takes place over an indefinite period of time terminated only by the lack of additional free water with which the cement can react.

Concrete will continue to gain strength almost indefinitely, at least for several years, as long as free water is available in the mix. When this free water is lost to evaporation in a few days or a month, the ultimate potential strength of the concrete can never be realized. From a practical standpoint, concrete should be cured (prevented from drying, even on the surface) for 14 days after placement. Seven days should be the absolute minimum.

4.5.2 Effect of curing on impermeability

Adequate curing is equal in importance to a low water/cement ratio in the achievement of impermeable concrete. Refer to Sec. 4.2.2.4 for more detailed discussion.

4.5.3 Effect of curing on shrinkage

Shrinkage occurs only when water leaves the concrete. The longer adequate curing is maintained, the more tensile strength the concrete develops to withstand shrinkage-induced stresses. Refer to Sec. 4.2.2.6 for additional discussion.

4.6 Mechanical Properties

Compressive strength. The compressive strength is dependent upon the mix (the water/cement ratio) and the quality of curing; it can be obtained in excess of 10,000 lb/in² (700 kg/cm²). Commercial production of concrete with ordinary aggregate is usually in the 3000 to 7000 lb/in² (210 to 490 kg/cm²) range with the design $f'_c = 3000$ to 4000 lb/in² (210 to 280 kg/cm²) being most common.

Tensile strength V. The tensile strength of concrete is relatively low, about 10 to 15 percent of the compressive strength. The modulus of rupture as measured from 6-in- (15.24-cm-) square beams somewhat exceeds the real tensile strength. The value of $7.5V = f'_c$ or $(V = f'_c/7.5)$ is often used for the modulus of rupture, depending on the type of flexure test used.

Shear strength. The shear strength of concrete varies from 35 to 80 percent of the compressive strength.

Strain. Maximum strain, that is, 0.0025 in/in, measures the useful limit for most concretes except those of low strength or those made with lightweight aggregate. Observations show that unit strains of 0.0035 to 0.0045 were obtained for concretes with f'_c over 6000 lb/ft² (420 kg/cm²).

Modulus of elasticity. When E_c or the term "modulus of elasticity" is used, it is usually the secant modulus based on ACI code and taken (for W_c values between 90 and 150 lb/ft³) as

$$E_c = W_c^{1.5} \, 33 \sqrt{f'_c} \qquad lb/in^2 \qquad (4.1)$$

where W_c is the weight of concrete in pounds per cubic foot. For normal-weight concrete, W_c may be taken as 145 lb/ft³ (2323 kg/m³). Thus, $E_c = 57,000 \sqrt{f'_c}$.

Shrinkage. As concrete loses moisture, it tends to shrink. Accordingly, the differential moisture changes cause differential shrinkage tendencies which produce internal stresses. Stresses due to differential shrinkage can be large, and they are the reason for insisting on moist curing conditions. Shrinkage is usually expressed in terms of the shrinkage coefficient S, which is the shortening or shrink per unit length. This coefficient varies, with values commonly 0.0002 to 0.0006 and sometimes as much as 0.0010.

4.7   Reinforcing

Inherently, concrete is strong in compression but weak in tension. For this reason, reinforcing is used within the concrete to provide the desired tensile strength. As a rule, steel bar or welded wire is used for this purpose.

4.7.1   Metal reinforcement

Metal reinforcement, at the time concrete is placed, should be free from rust scale or other coatings which could destroy or reduce the concrete-to-steel bond. The steel reinforcement and thickness of concrete over the reinforcement should be roughly as follows:

1. Where concrete is cast against and permanently exposed to the ground, the thickness of concrete between the reinforcement and the earth should be at least 3 in. Concrete exposed to weather should have at least 1½-in cover over reinforcement. Other concrete should have ¾-in minimum cover.

2. In slab on grade with desirable soils (nonexpansive and competent bearing) and minimal load, very little reinforcing is required. In most installations, electric-welded wire fabric (WWF) is specified; the most common type is a fabric with 10-gauge rods in both directions forming a 6-in-square hole, designated 6 × 6–10/10 WWF. The wire mat is generally situated at or near the middle of the concrete.

3. For prestressed concrete or heavily reinforced residential foundations, ACI specifications should be followed as discussed in subsequent chapters. In any event, for heavier construction or at unfavorable sites, steel reinforcement is suggested, if not demanded. The side distance of rebar from forms or earth faces should be at least 3 in (7.62 cm) or the diameter of the bar, whichever is greatest. The thickness of concrete above and below the reinforcing steel will vary with design requirements. Generally, the minimum distance between bars is the diameter of the largest-diameter bar, or ¼ in (0.6 cm) greater than the diameter of the largest aggregate. As a rule, greater distances are preferred. Splices in rebar should be staggered and overlapped, at least 30 bar diameters for steel in tension and 24 bar diameters for steel in compression. In most beam designs, two sets of reinforcement are specified. The top set will be as near the top of the

TABLE 4.6   Reinforcement: Grades and Strength

	Minimum yield strength f_y, lb/in^2 (kg/cm^2)	Ultimate yield strength f_u, lb/in^2 (kg/cm^2)
Billet steel		
Grade 40	40,000 (2800)	70,000 (4900)
60	60,000 (4200)	90,000 (6300)
75	75,000 (5250)	100,000 (7000)
Rail Steel		
Grade 50	50,000 (3500)	80,000 (5600)
60	60,000 (4200)	90,000 (6300)
Deformed wire		
Reinforced	75,000 (5250)	85,000 (5950)
Fabric	70,000 (4900)	80,000 (5600)
Cold-drawn wire		
Reinforced	70,000 (4900)	80,000 (5600)
Fabric	65,000 (4550)	75,000 (5250)

beam and the lower set as near the bottom of the beam as possible to maintain minimum coverage.

Reinforcing bars are made from billet steel in many grades. Rail steel bars rerolled from old rails also are available. The modulus of elasticity E_c is usually taken as 29×10^6 lb/in^2, and the yield points and ultimate strength are as given in Table 4.6.

All standard bars are round, medium-grade, deformed steel suitable for working stress of 20,000 lb/in^2 (1400 kg/cm^2), designated by size as No. 2 to No. 18. The bar weights and nominal areas, diameters, and perimeters are tabulated in Table 4.7.

TABLE 4.7   Nominal Dimensions of Round Bars

Bar dimen. no.	Unit wgt./ft		Diameter d		Cross-sectional area (CSA)		Circumference	
	lb	(kg)	in	(cm)	in^2	(cm^2)	in	(cm)
2	0.167	(0.076)	0.250	(0.635)	0.05	(0.32)	0.786	(2.0)
3	0.376	(0.17)	0.375	(0.95)	0.11	(0.71)	1.178	(2.99)
4	0.668	(0.3)	0.500	(1.27)	0.20	(1.29)	1.571	(3.99)
5	1.043	(0.47)	0.625	(1.59)	0.31	(2.0)	1.963	(4.99)
6	1.502	(0.68)	0.750	(1.9)	0.44	(2.84)	2.356	(5.98)
7	2.044	(0.93)	0.875	(2.22)	0.60	(3.87)	2.749	(6.98)
8	2.670	(1.21)	1.000	(2.54)	0.79	(5.1)	3.142	(7.98)
9	3.400	(1.54)	1.125	(2.86)	1.00	(6.45)	3.544	(9.0)
10	4.303	(1.95)	1.250	(3.175)	1.27	(8.19)	3.990	(10.13)
11	5.313	(2.41)	1.375	(3.49)	1.56	(10.06)	4.430	(11.25)
14	7.65	(3.47)	1.750	(4.45)	2.25	(14.52)	5.32	(13.51)
18	13.60	(6.17)	2.250	(5.715)	4.00	(25.8)	7.09	(18.0)

The data presented in Tables 4.6 and 4.7 are used in mathematical formulas to determine the steel reinforcement requirements for the foundation. The specific equations utilized are dependent upon such factors as soil conditions, structural design and loading of the foundation, yield stress of steel f_y, and minimum compressive strength of concrete f_c. The formulas may be relatively simple or somewhat complicated. The empirical version suggested by the BRAB bulletin [Eq. (4.2)] is applicable for simple, lightly loaded slab foundations (Type II).[4]

$$A_s = \frac{FLW_d}{2f_y} \quad \text{in}^2/\text{ft of width} \tag{4.2}$$

where A_s = cross-sectional area of steel per foot of width, in^2
    F = coefficient of friction, 1.25
    L = longest dimension of slab, ft
    W_d = dead load weight of slab, lb/ft^2 or estimated as 12.5 lb/ft^2 per inch of thickness
    f_y = minimum steel yield strength, lb/in^2, often assumed to be 45,000 for Type II slabs.

Once the foundation designs exceed these very basic requirements, the calculations become more involved. In the latter case the reader is directed to texts specific on the subject.[4-6] In any event, once the value of A_s (or A'_s in the case of steel at the top of a beam) is established, Table 4.7 will facilitate the rebar selection. For example, should A_s turn out to be 0.6 in^2 (3.87 cm^2), reference to Table 4.7 would suggest the use of two No. 5's (0.31 in^2 × 2 = 0.62 in^2) or possibly one No. 7 (0.60 in^2). In practice, the most common choice would be two No. 5's.

4.7.2 Synthetic fiber reinforcement

In recent years, a new commercial alternative to secondary reinforcement has been introduced. The product is a synthetic fiber cut into ½- to 2-in lengths which is mixed into the concrete at the rate of 1½ lb/yd^3 of concrete. The use of ½- or ¾-in does not affect the water/cement ratio required to maintain a constant slump. The 2-in fiber sometimes can require the addition of water to provide constant slump because of the vertical support provided by the longer fibers. Polyester and polypropylene are the two most common materials currently being used.

The impetus behind the advent of synthetic fibers lies in the inherent tendency of concrete to crack. There is one basic reason why cracks occur in concrete: The stresses that exist exceed the strength of the concrete at a specific time. Stresses from external forces can be offset by providing design changes to concrete structures, pavements, and slabs. However, the intrinsic stresses caused by shrinkage within the concrete itself have historically been a problem to control because of their unpredictable variety and occurrence.

Synthetic fibers automatically provide dimensional stability to concrete by reducing or relieving the intrinsic stresses until the concrete has gained sufficient strength to sustain the stresses without cracking. The elimination or reduction of early crack formation substantially reduces the number of weak planes and potential future crack formation due to drying shrinkage.

The suggested benefits of synthetic fibers are dual: (1) Shrinkage cracking caused by intrinsic stresses that occur naturally in new concrete is inhibited; (2) synthetic fibers are a proven, safe, practical alternative to welded wire fabric for crack control. They provide identical physical properties in every direction throughout the mass. Welded wire fabric is located in only a single plane and does not reduce the tendency of concrete to crack. It can only help hold cracks together after they occur.

Synthetic fibers have a high energy absorbent capacity. In the hardened concrete, the presence of millions of fibers increases the ductility of the concrete, improves its resistance to impact and abrasion. This reduces shattering and fragmentation under shock loading—a real asset for precast products and industrial applications. It dramatically reduces concrete permeability. It cannot rust or stain surfaces; it is noncorrosive and alkali-resistant. The action of the fibers is purely mechanical, not chemical, and it requires no changes in mix proportions. It eliminates the need for hoists, cranes, or labor placement time, contrary to wire mesh, and thereby reduces construction costs.

Fibers intercept shrinkage cracks in their microscopic state and thereby stop propagation. The cracks are unable to develop into macrocracks and potential trouble. Being totally inert, the fibers do not affect the setting characteristics of concrete. They enhance all surface treatments and textures, including pressed form, hard troweled, broomed, and exposed aggregate. The flexural capacity of slabs containing fibers is equal to or higher than that of slabs containing welded-wire fabric or just plain concrete slabs.

Conversely, synthetic fibers are not intended for:

1. The control of cracking as a result of external stresses (structural)

2. Increasing the elastic modulus of PC concrete in pavement or slabs on grade

3. Higher structural strength development

4. The elimination or reduction in curling and/or creep

5. The justification for a reduction in the size of the support columns

6. The replacement of any structural steel reinforcement

7. The unlimited elimination of control joints

8. The thinning out of bonded or unbonded overlay sections.

The proof of a process is confirmed by successful field performance. Synthetic fibers have been widely used with apparent success. Some interesting applications for fibers include precast products, water- and sewage-treatment plants, office buildings, streets, malls and concourses, and industrial plants.

4.8 References

1. F. M. Lea and C. H. Desch, *The Chemistry of Cement and Concrete*. Edward Arnold, London, 1956.
2. G. E. Troxell and H. E. Davis, *Concrete*. McGraw-Hill, New York, 1956.
3. *Building Code Requirements for Reinforced Concrete, ACI 318–83*. American Concrete Institute, Detroit, Mich., 1983.
4. Federal Housing Administration; *Criteria for Selection and Design of Residential Slabs-on-Grade*, National Academy of Science, Report No. 33, 1968.
5. Philip Ferguson, *Reinforced Concrete Fundamentals*, Wylie, New York, 1973
6. John Faber and Frank Mead, *Foundation Design Simply Explained*, Oxford University Press, London, 1961.

5

Foundation Design

5.1 Introduction

A *foundation* is the part of a structure that is in direct contact with the ground and transmits the load of the structure to the ground. The load W_T is the sum of live loads W_L and dead loads W_D. The *dead load* is the weight of the empty structure; the *live load* is the weight of the building contents plus wind, snow, and earthquake forces where applicable. The magnitude of W_T is often assumed to be in the range of 200 to 400 lb/ft^2 (976 to 1952 kg/m^2) for residential construction of no more than two stories. This load must be supported by the soil. The characteristic of the soil which measures its capacity to carry the load is the unconfined compressive strength q_u. Compressible soils will normally have a q_u of less than 2000 lb/ft^2 (9760 kg/m^2). The actual value of q_u is determined by laboratory tests. As discussed in earlier chapters, other factors, such as climatic condition and bearing soil characteristics, also influence foundation design. Basically there are two different types of residential foundations: pier and beam and slab. (In some areas a third type is recognized; it utilizes piles for the basic support.)

5.2 Pier and Beam

The first type of foundation generally recognized for residential construction was the pier and beam. This primitive design involved nothing more than the use of wood "stumps" placed directly on the soil for structural support. These members, usually cedar or bois d'arc, supported the sole plate as well as the interior girders. Next the design evolved to the use of a continuous concrete beam to support the perimeter loads with, as a rule, the same wood piers serving to support the interior. This variation was precipitated largely by the advent of the brick or stone veneer. Further changes in construction requirements, including the awareness of problems brought about by unstable soils, encouraged the addition of concrete piers to support the perimeter beam and concrete piers and pier caps to provide better support for the interior floors (girders).

For purposes of the following discussion, pier-and-beam construction is the design whereby the perimeter loads are carried on a continuous beam supported by piers drilled into the ground, presumedly to a competent bearing soil or stratum. The interior floors are supported by piers and pier caps which sustain the girder and joist system of a wood substructure. All foundation components are assumed to be steel-reinforced concrete. For practical purposes, there are two principal variations of the pier-and-beam design: the normal design whereby the crawl space is on a grade equivalent to the exterior landscape and the relatively new low profile, whereby the crawl space is substantially lower than the exterior grade (Figs. 5.1 and 5.2).

The stability of the pier-and-beam design depends, to a large extent, upon the bearing capacity of the soil at the base of the piers. Assuming ideal conditions, this principle will produce a stable foundation. Difficulties with this design can occur if a stable bearing material is not accessible as a pier base. In some instances, piers are belled to spread the structure load and allow the use of less-competent soils to support the weight. Belled piers might also provide an adequate resistance to upheaval in plastic-clay soils. The belled area tends to anchor the pier and the attached beam. However, should the upward force (upheaval) be transmitted to the beam, a cracked foundation could result. The use of void boxes under the beams has provided some limited protection against upheaval stress. However, proper moisture control still has the most successful stabilizing effect. Effective exterior grade,

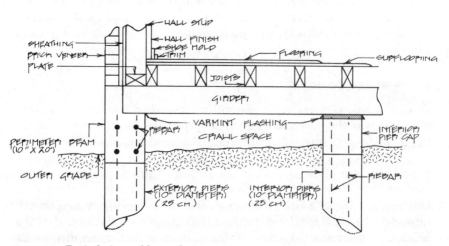

Figure 5.1 Typical pier-and-beam design.

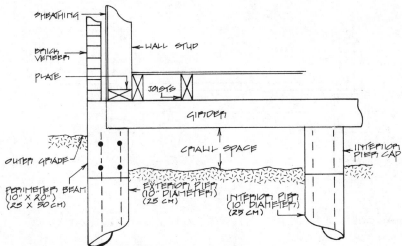

Figure 5.2   Typical low-profile pier-and-beam design.

adequate watering, and sufficient ventilation are all forms of proper moisture control.

The low-profile design presents inherent problems relative more to excessive moisture than to actual foundation distress. The low-profile design encourages the accumulation of water under the floors, which tends to result in mold, mildew, rot, termites, and, if neglected, differential foundation movement. In this instance, proper ventilation and proper exterior grade will normally arrest the serious structural distress. In persistent problems of moisture accumulation, forced-air blowers to provide added ventilation and/or chemical treatment to kill the mildew can be beneficial. The practice of covering the crawl space with polyethylene sheets should be avoided. Although the film reduces the humidity in the crawl space, it also develops a "terrarium" beneath it with subsequent threat to the foundation. In no event should the air vents be below the exterior grade. This oversight would channel surface water directly into the crawl space.

In certain areas with soil problems more serious than those experienced in the United States, more intricate foundation design is suggested. For example, in Adelaide, Australia, where PIs often fall in the range of 60 or more, a "pier and beam" design illustrated by Fig. 5.3 is used. Note that both examples lack the conventional piers associated with the pier and beam depicted in Figs. 5.1 and 5.2. (Actually, this design is not typical to the U.S. pier and beam; it is referred to as such because the interior floors do not rest on bearing soil.)

5.3   Slab

Slab construction of one variety or another probably constitutes the majority of new construction in geographic areas exposed to high-clay

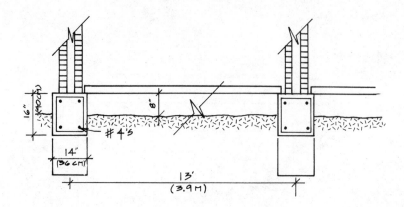

A. SOILS WITH PLASTICITY INDEX (PI) LESS THAN 10.

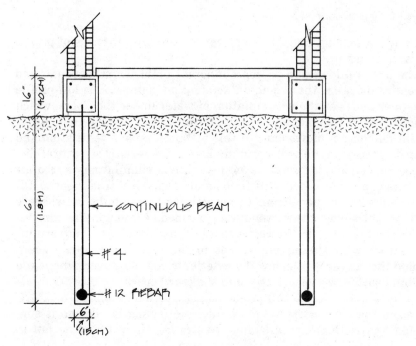

B. SOIL WITH PI GREATER THAN 60 BUT LESS THAN 100.

Figure 5.3   Australian "pier and beam." (A) Soil with a plasticity index (PI) less than 10. (B) Soil with PI greater than 60 but less than 100.

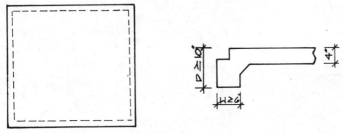

Figure 5.4 Typical FHA Type I slab.

soils. The particular design of the slab depends upon a multitude of factors. As stated earlier, the purpose of this book is not to delve into structural design but to present a study of foundation failures. Accordingly, the handling of slab design will be cursory.

In any event, the structural load is designed to be transmitted essentially 100 percent to the bearing soil. For want of a place to start, the FHA (or HUD) designs pose a handy reference. Most of the FHA material was apparently obtained from independent research; fortunately, many of the data are available to the industry. One example is the much referenced publication *Criteria for Selection and Design of Residential Slab on Ground*, BRAB publication No. 33.[1] Many other publications have been sponsored by the government, but as far as analysis can determine, none have substantially changed the principal design criteria postulated by the BRAB publication.

Slab foundations come in various configurations as determined by such factors as soil conditions, load considerations, and the variable nature of weather (Figs. 5.4 to 5.7). As a rough rule of thumb, soil expansion greater than about 3 percent is considered potentially dangerous and requires special design considerations.

Another factor which suggests special concern would be any anticipated condition wherein the foundation could be expected to act as a bridging member. The BRAB book addresses this as a support factor C, which accommodates minimal cantilever conditions. Ideally, C

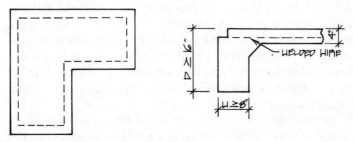

Figure 5.5 Typical FHA Type II slab.

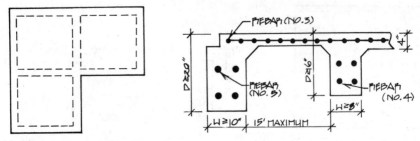

Figure 5.6   Typical FHA Type III slab.

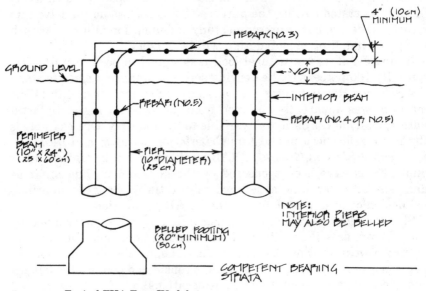

Figure 5.7   Typical FHA Type IV slab.

would be 1.0, indicating 100 percent support by the soil. As the support factor deviates below 1.0, special design considerations are demanded.

Figures 5.4 to 5.7 depict typical representations of various slab designs—based to a large extent on FHA design. Since structural design is basically beyond the scope of this book, the primary concern will be major differences in design. Bear in mind that the resistance of a beam to differential deflection is influenced more by depth than by width. In fact, other things being equal, a twofold increase in depth will improve the resistance to deflection by a factor of 8.

Table 5.1 presents some of the major differences in soil (based on classification) and climatic conditions which combine to influence the

TABLE 5.1   Soil Differences and Climatic Conditions That Influence Foundation Design

Soil type	Minimum densities q_u	Climatic rating C_w	Slab type	Reinforcement
Gravel	All densities	All	I[a]	None except wire mesh at openings, step-downs, etc.
Gravel sands, low-PI silts, and clays	Dense	All	I	Same
Same	Loose (noncom-pacted)	All	II[b]	Lightly reinforced wire mesh, rebar in perimeter beam
Organic or inorganic clay and silts	PI < 15 and $q_u/W_T \geq 7.5$	All	II	Same
Same	PI > 15	$C_W > 45$	II	Same
Same	PI > 15, $q_u/W_T \geq 7.5$	$C_W < 45$	III	Rebar plus interior beams
Same	q_u/W_T between 2.5 and 7.5	All	III	Same
Same	$q_u/W_T < 2.5$	All	IV	Structural slab (not supported directly on soil)

[a]Maximum partition load 500 lb/ft (757 kg/m).
[b]Maximum partition load 500 lb/ft (757 kg/m) unless loads are transmitted to independent footings.
SOURCE: Simplified from BRAB Report 33.

acceptable foundation design. The symbol W_T designates the total unit foundation load, dead load plus live load ($W_D + W_L$), and q_u represents the unconfined compressive strength of the soil.

Note in particular the dependence of the design upon the plasticity index PI and climatic conditions C_w. The PI is a dimensionless constant which has a direct relation to the affinity of the bearing soil for volumetric changes with respect to moisture variations. The higher the value of the PI, the greater the volatility of the soil. Generally, the volumetric changes are directly related to clay content of the soil as well as differential moisture. [For example, Poor and Tucker[2] reported in their study that a slab foundation (typical FHA II) constructed on a soil with a PI of 42 experienced a vertical deflection of about 1¼ in (3.175 cm) upon a change in soil moisture content of 4 percent]. The PI is determined as the difference between the liquid limit LL and the plastic limit PL. (As noted in earlier chapters, these terms represent part of the classical Atterberg limit determinations.)

The liquid limit is determined by measuring the water and the number of blows required to close a specific-width groove of specified length in a standard liquid limit device. The plastic limit is determined by measuring the water content of the soil when threads of the soil ⅛ in (0.3175 cm) in diameter begin to crumble.[3] Finally, q_u is the unconfined compressive strength of the proposed bearing soil.

Again referring to the BRAB report, only the top 15 ft of bearing soil influences foundation stability. The top 5 ft carries about 50 percent of the imposed load, the second 5 ft 33 percent, and the final 5 ft about 17 percent.

Figure 5.8 shows the climatic ratings C_w for the United States (U.S. Department of Commerce). As a matter of interest, the British Standards Institute *Code for Foundations*, CP2004:1972,[4] states that seasonal variations in their heavy clay soils occur to a depth of 1.5 to 2.0 m (5 to 6 ft) under areas not watered. They further suggest that foundations for traditional masonry structures be founded at a depth of at least 1 m (3 ft) to reduce relative movement to acceptable limits. Their heavy clays are quite similar to those of the United States. In essence, as the design and environmental conditions become more severe, the

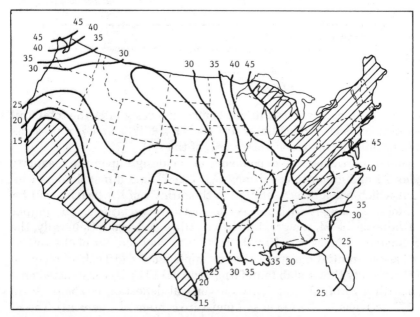

Figure 5.8 Climatic ratings for continental United States.

slab must be strengthened. This is accomplished by increasing the size and the frequency of both the beams and reinforcing steel.

5.3.1 Post tension

A relatively recent innovation is the use of post-tension stress to the slab. Concrete has limited tensile strength but is adequate in compression. The stress cables are intended to enhance the tensile strength of the slab through the compressive effects of the cable tension. So it is in theory; in practice, the results do not always meet expectations. Perhaps the problem lies with the fact that, in field performance, the compressive loads are not always perpendicular to the stress and the vectors that are created destroy the benefits of the principle. The author's experiences indicate that failures with post-tension residential slabs are more likely, on a percentage basis, than with conventional deformed-bar slabs. This same observation has been documented by others.[5] As indicated above, many of these problems may be caused by field practices and, as such, may not reflect a design defect.[5] Figure 5.9 illustrates a typical post-tension slab.

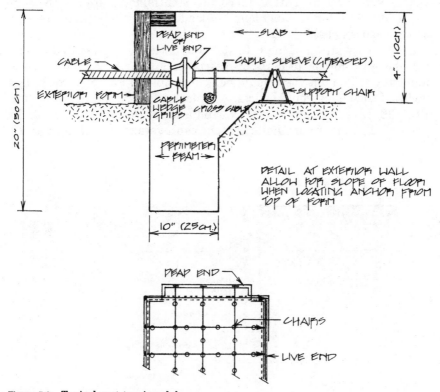

Figure 5.9 Typical post-tension slab.

5.3.2 Design variations

Special construction, and/or site conditions, suggest various changes or considerations for foundation design. For example, in areas with low or moderately expansive soil, often of a low- or noncohesive nature, a typical design might be similar to that shown in Fig. 5.10. Areas representing this criterion include parts of Florida, Oklahoma, and other states.

A somewhat similar design is used in the United Kingdom, where the soil is both expansive and cohesive (Fig. 5.11). The montmorillonite content averages 20 to 40 percent, which is roughly equivalent to that exhibited by the more volatile U.S. soils. The climate in the United Kingdom is such that soil moisture remains both high and relatively constant year round. Typically, a London clay might have a PL = 26, LL = 69, and PI = 43 and a moisture content of 30 percent. With an initial, reasonably consistent moisture content of this magnitude, little swell potential remains; however, a loss of soil moisture could create substantial subsidence. Tomlinson suggests that a minimum foundation depth to guard against seasonal moisture variations would be 3 ft (0.9 m). This assumes a residential foundation with bearing loads of 1.0 ton/ft (3030 kg/m) of load bearing wall (perimeter) on a stiff fissured clay.[6]

Another variation of the U.S. slab foundation is represented by the raft design common to parts of Australia. Figure 5.12 shows such a foundation. The top view would be comparable to Fig. 5.6, except the width of the beam would be less. A typical Adelaide soil might have a PL = 30, LL = 90, and PI = 60 + and a moisture content of 15 to 35 percent. The montmorillonite content can average something like 70

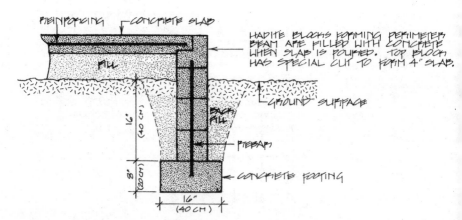

Figure 5.10 Variation: slab foundation.

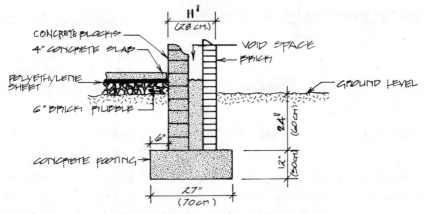

Figure 5.11 Variation: slab foundation, United Kingdom (typical).

percent. In areas with PI of 10 or less, the foundation design is almost identical to that for the monolithic U.S. slabs.

Foundation designs are as numerous as societies. However, the foregoing will give the reader a brief glimpse at some of the more interesting accepted practices.

5.3.3 Experimental residential foundation designs

The foundation study presented in the BRAB booklet was continued to some extent in 1976–1979.[7] During this period, 11 houses with slab foundations were constructed by utilizing various approaches in-

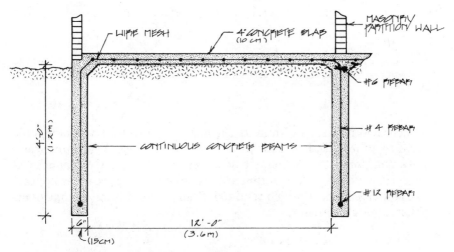

Figure 5.12 Variation: slab foundation, Australia.

TABLE 5.2 **Experimental Foundation Designs**

| Foundation type | Perimeter beam | | | Movement | |
	Width, in (cm)	Depth, in (cm)	Protective measure	Deflection, in (cm)	Differential, in (cm)
1. Monolithic	12 (30)	18.5 (47)	Impermeable barrier to 5 ft (1.5 m)*	+0.7 (1.8)	+0.4 (1)
2. Monolithic*	12 (30)	18.5 (47)	Granular barrier to 5 ft (1.5 m)*	+0.3 (0.76)	+0.25 (0.6)
3. Monolithic	12 (30)	18.5 (47)	Irrigation	+0.55 (1.4)	+0.3 (0.76)
4. Monolithic	8 (20)	14 (36)	Irrigation	+0.9 (2.3)	+0.3 (0.76)
5. Monolithic	8 (20)	14 (36)	Granular barrier to 5 ft (1.5 m)*	+0.4 (1)	+0.25 (0.6)
6. Monolithic	8 (20)	14 (36)	Impermeable barrier to 5 ft (1.5 m)*	+0.6 (1.5)	+0.4 (1)
7. Monolithic BRAB	10 (25)	35 (89)		+0.55 (1.4)	+0.25 (0.6)
8. Monolithic*	4 (10)	8 (20)	Extended beam depth by 5 ft, not monolithic	+1.2 (3.0)	+0.8 (2)
9. Post-tension	10 (25)	14 (36)		+0.9 (2.3)	+0.4 (1)
10. Post-tension	8 (20)	20 (50)		+1.0 (2.5)	+0.6 (1.5)
11. Post-tension beam only	10 (25)	23 (58)		+0.8 (2)	+0.5 (1.3)

*Bearing soil was prewetted to a moisture content of PL+2 to 3 percent to a depth of 5 ft (1.5 m).

tended to minimize or eliminate the foundation stability problems relative to differential soil movement. Once in place, the foundations were monitored for movement behavior over the next 41 months. A synopsis of the type foundation and experimental approaches appears in Table 5.2. Factors which tend to influence the volume change of expansive soils include:

1. Thickness of soil stratum

2. Weather extremes (moisture and temperature)

3. Characteristics of particular soil (clay content, type of clay, particle size, and exchange cations)

4. Stress conditions inherent to the soil

5. Stress conditions (load) created by structure

6. Apparent permeability of the soil

7. In situ density and moisture content and variations of the soil

8. Presence of organic material

9. Landscaping and vegetation

These factors influenced the design approaches considered in this study. The soil at the test site can be characterized as follows:

1. *Clay content:* Montmorillonite content varied from a low of 11 percent at 7 to 8 ft (2.1 to 2.4 m) to a high of 37.5 percent at 3 to 4 ft (0.9 to 1.2 m). Illite content varied from a high of 50.6 percent at 7 to 8 ft (2.1 to 2.4 m) to a low of 25 percent at 3 to 4 ft (0.9 to 1.2 m).

2. *Atterberg limits:* The Atterberg limits indicated LL generally in the high 60s with variations from 65 to 73 and PL in the high 20s with a low at 26 and a high at 31. (Data were recorded at 1-ft intervals to a 10-ft depth.) The PIs then varied between 39 and 43 with the average of about 40. In situ moisture content was a high of 36.3 percent at the surface and a low of 25.4 percent at 8 to 9 ft. In most cases, the W percent was within 1 to 2 percent of the PL, below in 80 percent of the tests and above in the remaining 20 percent. Linear shrinkage (LS) varied between 24 percent (8 to 10 ft) and 20 percent (4 to 5 ft). Free swell varied from about 14 percent (18 tons/ft^2 swell pressure) at a soil moisture of 12 percent to less than 1 percent at moisture contents above 24.5 percent.

3. *Weather conditions:* Weather typical to the area would be windy, 33-in (83.8-cm) annual rainfall (80 percent of which is often recorded in 15 days) with temperature ranges frequently between lows of 10°F (−12°C) and highs in excess of 110°F (43°C), subject to change.

4. *Site Elevation and Vegetation:* The lots are basically flat with only scattered trees. The trees are generally pin oak, mulberry, cottonwood, and weeping willow. Most of the trees were probably planted after 1976.

In Table 5.2, "deflection" refers to general displacement of the perimeter beam during the term of the study. This movement is not necessarily a problem, since the design of the slab is intended to allow the foundation to "float" as a unit. The differential movement between various locations along the perimeter beam represents the area of most concern because this, in effect, reflects the stress subjected to the foundation. As an arbitrary rule of thumb, differential movement less than ⅜ in (0.95 cm) is not considered as threatening to the safety of the structure. As noted, the measurements were taken on the perimeter beams and do not reflect interior movement in the slab. The latter would have been both interesting and important. The conclusions to be derived at the termination of this 41-month study would seem to indicate (Table 5.2):

1. The post-tension slabs seemed least impressive. [Tests 9, 10, and 11 each with differential movements in excess of 0.4 in (1 cm).]

2. The BRAB design was most effective with the 35-in- (88.9-cm-) deep perimeter beam. [Test 7 with 0.25-in (0.6-cm) differential movement.]

3. The extended beam depth was not effective under the circumstances. [Test 8 with 0.8-in (2-cm) differential movement.]

4. The irrigation system seemed marginally effective. [Tests 3 and 4 with 0.3-in (0.76-cm) differential movement.]

5. The impermeable barrier did not seem to be effective. [Tests 1 and 6 with differential movement in excess of ⅜ in (0.95 cm).] Refer to Fig. 9.5 for the barrier design.

6. The granular barrier seemed to inhibit deflection, particularly *differential* movement. (Tests 2 and 5.)

7. Prewetting the bearing soil to 5 ft (1.5 m) did not prove to be conclusive. Considering the site and weather conditions, the prewetting may have resulted in adverse performance of barriers. [Tests 1, 2, 5, and 6 with only 2 and 5 showing differential movements less than ⅜ in (0.95 cm).]

8. Glass fiber (rather than rebar) was used as the principal reinforcing material in tests 2 and 8. In test 2, rebar was used in beams and step-downs. In test 8, rebars were used in the beam at 4-ft (1.2-m) centers vertically and 18-in (0.5-m) centers horizontally. What influence, if any, this change in reinforcement alone had on the results is subject to question. However, with benefit of hindsight, it would seem that both test 2 and test 8 were failures.

Subsequent attention should be given to two factors: (1) What was the precise weather cycle during the 41 months over which the study was conducted? (2) What has happened since? The evidence is that, by October 1987, the slab described as test 2 had failed. This would tend to suggest that only test 7 showed real merit with some question of credence being given to 5 and perhaps 3. A suggestion was made to HUD for a complete reevaluation and update of all foundation behavior. This would provide a 10-year history and possibly develop more definitive information. Through 1988, no decision had been rendered on the suggestion.

A request to the National Climatic Data Center produced data which provides a fair analysis of the DFW weather for the years 1976 through 1979. [The site was in Grand Prairie, Texas, about 13.8 miles (22.2 km) from the Dallas–Fort Worth airport.] Table 5.3 depicts a generalized synopsis of the weather conditions prevailing during the study period.

The overall weather variations between 1976 and 1979 were quite extreme. The extremely hot, dry years of 1977 and 1978, following the abnormally wet 1976, would suggest that preponderant soil (and foundation) movement would be settlement (negative movement). In 1979, the rain returned and would perhaps be expected to reverse the trend established in 1977 and 1978. In essence, neither of these expectations seemed to materialize. The data presented in the study generally reflect upward movement of the slabs throughout the entire period. (The individual data plots did vacillate, but the overall curve trend was consistently away from zero elevation to the positive direction.)

TABLE 5.3   Weather Analysis

Year	Mean temp., °F	Months with 100°F +	Annual water, in		Wind, mph	Months with over 10-mph wind
			Rain	Snow and sleet		
1979	63.9	3	32.42	2.5	9.7	5
1978	64.4	4	24.37	18.4	9.3	4
1977	66.2	4	27.19	5.4	9.3	6
1976	64.3	1	35.63	5.0	8.7	3
Normal	65.5	5	32.3	NA	10.9	8

Summary

1976 Unusually wet, moderate temperatures, low winds
1977 Unusually dry, hot, moderate wind
1978 Unusually dry, moderate wind, and hot
1979 Moderately wet, windy with broader temperature variations

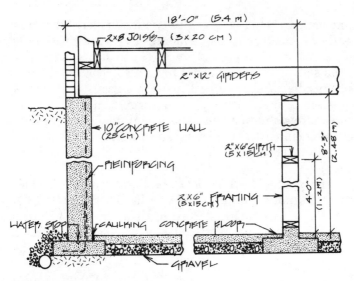

Figure 5.13 Basement construction.

5.4 Basements

Generally, in present times, the use of basements as part of the foundation design is limited to areas where either real estate costs are
quite high or a deep frost line exists. The reason for this trend is simple. It is much less expensive to spread out than to excavate. Figure
5.13 presents a typical basement-foundation design. In the past, when
coal furnaces were prevalent, at least partial basements were common
in areas not inclusive in the land cost–frost line criterion. In that
event, the furnaces and coal storage were situated below the floors
and necessitated some basement.

5.5 Foundation Loads on Bearing Soils

Generally speaking, the in-depth study of structural engineering, en-
compassing such factors as foundation design and load distribution to
the bearing soils, is considered beyond the scope of this book. However, since load distribution to the soil affects foundation stability,
restoration of failures, and prevention, a cursory examination of foundation types has been provided. Again, the comments are limited to
residential and light commercial construction. The load distribution
transmitted to the soil is the next consideration.

First, consider the case of the conventional spread footing. The
spread footing can be part of the original construction, e.g., Type II
foundations where partition loads exceed 500 lb/ft (757 kg/m), or incorporated into repair procedures for correcting foundation problems.

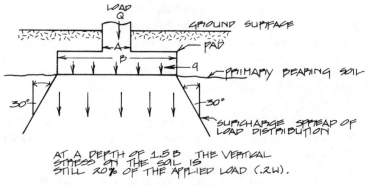

AT A DEPTH OF 1.5 B THE VERTICAL
STRESS ON THE SOL IS
STILL 20% OF THE APPLIED LOAD (.2H).

Figure 5.14 Foundation loads on bearing soils.

One point of interest is the spread distribution of the load over the soils beneath the footing (see Fig. 5.14).

Assume the base of the footing at zero. The applied load is spread laterally and downward at an angle of approximately 30°. As the load is spread 1.73 ft (0.5 m) vertically (down), the lateral component (out) is 1 ft (0.3 m). As mentioned earlier, the BRAB report indicates that loads are carried 50 percent by soils within the top 5 ft (1.5 m) under the foundation and 83.3 percent by soils within the top 10 ft (3 m). Other authorities have indicated even shallower depths (Figs. 3.2 and 3.11). Hence, for all practical purposes, any stress effects below about 10 ft (3 m) would be, at most, minimal. The lateral distance within which the soil behavior materially affects the spread footing would then be a *maximum* of 10 ft/1.73 or 5.78 ft (1.77 m).

As a practical point, it becomes obvious that any attempt to maintain soil moisture by watering must certainly be performed within the 5.8-ft (1.77-m) distance. Watering beyond this distance away from the foundation would have little, if any, effect on the foundation or the foundation-bearing soils, assuming, of course, that the exterior grade is away from the foundation, as would be proper. In practice, watering to maintain moisture should be as near the foundation as practical. This is further substantiated by several authorities referred to in Chap. 1, such as Alway, McDole, Rotmistrov, and Richards (as well as the above-mentioned BSI report[4]), who generally agree that upward movement (evaporation) of water in silty loam does not develop from depths greater than 24 in (0.6 m). Restoring soil moisture at this depth under the foundation would favor watering within about 12 in (0.3 m).

Slab foundations distribute the loads directly to the surface (or shallow) soils. The perimeter beam carries several times that load borne by the interior slab. The surcharge load distribution from the perim-

eter beam is approximately the same as that indicated for spread footings in Fig. 5.14. These points are important to remember, because
they influence repair techniques for correcting foundation failures.

Pier-and-beam load distribution is somewhat more complex. The
foundation loads are carried by intermittent, relatively shallow piers
which, in turn, transmit the stresses to the soil via end bearing and
skin friction (except in clay soil where little, if any, design consideration is given to skin friction). Accordingly, the load distributions
would deviate more from the examples cited. Nonetheless, the identical theory would apply.

As suggested in foregoing paragraphs, the foundation design has
some influence over the extent of, or resistance to, movement. The perimeter beam has the greatest structural strength and carries the
greatest structural load. The only force tending to cause downward
movement (settlement) is the structural load itself—with, say, 100 to
200 lb/ft^2 (488 to 976 kg/m^2) for a normal single-story residence or,
since about 75 percent of the total structural load is carried by the perimeter beam, something like 600 to 900 lb/ft (909 to 1364 kg/m) on
the beam. Accordingly, settlement normally progresses from the perimeter to within, and the greatest deflection is most probable at a
corner. In contrast, upheaval generally attacks the foundation's weakest point (the interior slab), and the potential disruptive force is substantially greater. The soil described by Tucker and Poor[2] can have a
confined expansive force of 9000 lb/ft^2 (43,920 kg/m^2) at 23 percent
moisture content. Largely because of the gross imbalance in the applied forces and the magnitude of moisture change, upheaval normally occurs more rapidly and to a greater extent than settlement
does.

5.6 References

1. Federal Housing Administration. "Criteria for Selection and Design of Residential
Slab-on-Ground," *Report No. 33*, National Academy of Sciences, 1968.
2. R. L. Tucker and A. Poor, "Field Study of Moisture Effects on Slab Movements,"
Journal of the Geotechnical Engineering Division, ASCE, April 1978.
3. T. W. Lambe and R. V. Whitman, *Soil Mechanics*, Wiley, New York, 1969.
4. British Standards Institute, "Code of Practise for Foundations," *Report
CP2004:1972*, p. 31.
5. P. M. Allen and W. D. Flanigan, "Geology of Dallas, Texas, United States of
America," Association of Engineering Geologists, 1986.
6. M. J. Tomlinson, *Foundation Design and Construction*, 2d ed., Wiley Interscience,
New York, 1969.
7. A. Poor, "Experimental Residential Foundations on Expansive Clays," *HUD Contract No. H-2240R*, four reports, 1976–1979.
8. J. Ambrose, *Simplified Design of Building Foundations*, Wiley Interscience, New
York, 1981.

Chapter

6

Soil Stabilization

6.1 Introduction

"Soil stabilization" refers to a procedure for improving the natural soil properties in order to provide more adequate resistance to erosion, loading, landsliding, water seepage, or other environmental forces. In foundation or geotechnical engineering, soil stabilization is divided into two sections: (1) mechanical stabilization, which improves the structure of the soil (and consequently the bearing capacity), usually by compaction, and (2) chemical stabilization, which improves the mechanical properties of the soil by adding or injecting a chemical agent such as lime, fly ash, or bituminous emulsions. Generally, the chemical either reacts with the soil or provides an improved matrix which binds the soil.

In residential foundations, soil stabilization refers not only to improvement of the compressive strength or shear strength but also to increasing the resistance of the soil to dynamic changes. The latter tend to destroy both the soil's integrity and its structure. Generally, the first condition relates to stress applied to the soil by the foundation and the latter to the conditions imposed by the environment.

Among the different mechanical stabilization techniques such as preloading (to reduce future settlement), drainage (to speed up settlement), compaction or densification (using a vibrofloat), compaction is generally the least expensive alternative for residential and commercial buildings.

6.2 Compaction

Compaction may be accomplished by excavating the surface soil to a depth for residential up to 4 ft (1.3 m) and for commercial up to 6 ft (1.8 m) and then backfilling with controlled layers and compacting the fill to 95 percent compaction. Often the fill material is a replacement type such as some nonplastic (low-plasticity-index) soil. In the case of uniform soil (sand), the addition of a fine soil to improve the grain size distribution is advised. The standard compaction tests utilized to evaluate these processes include one of the following:

1. *ASTM D698-70*, consisting of 5.5-lb hammer, 12-in drop, $\frac{1}{30}$-ft^3 mold. Three layers of soil at 25 blows/layer may be used.

2. *ASTM D-1557-70*, consisting of 10-lb hammer, 18-in drop, $\frac{1}{30}$-ft^3 mold, five layers at 25 blows/layer.

Specific details of compaction tests, equipment, and quality control are beyond the scope of this book. The interested reader should consult publications in the references for this chapter.

The undrained shear strength of a soil acceptable for a housing site should not be less than 800 lb/ft^2 (3904 kg/m^2). In a nonexpansive fill with up to 600 lb/ft^2 (2928 kg/m^2), undrained shear strength, compaction, preloading, and grout injection are beneficial for improving the soil for light residential construction. For heavier foundation loads, piers or other forms of structural enhancement might be required. This might encompass a more sophisticated foundation design, soil improvement, or both. A discussion of specific soils amenable to mechanical improvement follows.

6.3   Granular Soil

Granular soils are those comprised of particles larger than 0.0075 mm (No. 200 sieve). After proper compaction, most soils are modified to possess volume stability and improved frictional resistance, but they often retain high permeability. In order to offset that property, bonding or cementation is implemented to provide cohesion under both moist and dry conditions. Silty clay constituents (or other cementitious materials) can decrease the danger of instability under dry or, particularly, wet conditions. Laboratory tests are performed to determine the optimum conditions of compaction or soil modification.

In general, a sandy soil, particularly after stabilization, has a high bearing capacity, but footings should be placed at a sufficient depth so the soil beneath the footing is confined. Foundations in stabilized sand may consist of spread footings, mats, piles, or piers, dependent principally upon the soil density, thickness, cost of soil modification, and building loads.

In sand deposits (without compaction) spread footings are used if the deposit is sufficiently dense to support the loads without excessive settlement. Piers in loose sand deposits should be drilled to firm underlying strata. Skin friction can be considered in the design (or load) criteria for sand or granular soil. The foundation should not be located on sand deposits such that the relative density is less than 60 percent or a density of 90 percent of the maximum cannot be attained in the soil laboratory. An exception would be where the loose material is completely penetrated, usually by driven piles.

6.4   Foundations on Loess

Loess is a fine-grained soil formed by the deposit of wind-borne particles. This soil covers 17 percent of the United States. Depths of loess deposits range from 3.3 to 164 ft (1 to 50 m), and depths of 6.6 to 9.9 ft (2 to 3 m) are common. Loess has a specific gravity from about 2.6 to 2.8 and in situ dry density from about 66 to 104 lb/ft^3 (1057 to 1666 kg/m^3) with 90 percent particle size passing a No. 200 sieve. The plastic limits range from 10 to 30 percent. Standard compaction tests produce dry densities of 100 to 110 lb/ft^3 (1602 to 1762 kg/m^3) at optimum moisture content of 12 to 20 percent.

As a foundation soil, a loess soil with a bulk density greater than 90 lb/ft^3 (1442 kg/m^3) will often exhibit quite limited settlement. The problem with loess is the changing of bearing capacity with saturation. Soil bearing capacity can drop to 90 percent or less of that of the dry loess upon saturation. This soil is silt-cemented by calcareous materials, and consequently the addition of water destroys the cement bonds. Eroded loess is commonly referred to as a silt deposit. Loess below the permanent water table is, however, relatively stable because the water content is constant. Compacted loess can be a satisfactory foundation material for mats and spread footings if the specific gravity is more than 1.6 g/cm^3 or the bulk density is about 100 lb/ft^3 (1602 kg/m^3).

Loess can be stabilized by using lime, lime fly ash, or cement, each followed by compaction. In general, compaction is required above the permanent water table or the full depth of the loess deposits, whichever is first accessible. Piers are commonly suggested if in-place specific gravity of the loess is under 1.44 g/cm^3 (90 lb/ft^3 or 1442 kg/m^3). Piles should be driven or piers drilled through the loess into the underlying soil layer unless the loess terminates below the water table. Again, loess is often stable within or below the water table.

6.5   Foundations on Sanitary Landfill Sites

"Sanitary landfill" is a euphemism for "garbage dump." Within urban areas, it often becomes necessary to develop a former sanitary landfill for construction. In most instances, the opportunity for soil improvement by normal compaction techniques is denied. Landfill usage for one- or two-story residential buildings, apartments, office buildings, etc., [where the required bearing capacity is within the range of 0.5 to 1 ton/ft^2 (4.88 to 9.766 t/m^2)] can be acceptable if the site is stabilized by grout injections or modified by the addition of lime or cement or, perhaps, by adequate compaction. In this way, the use of continuous foundations may provide adequate bridging capacity over local soft spots or cavities. Otherwise, piers should be driven to a firm layer underlying the landfill.

Compaction of expansive clays. When the subject soil is basically an expansive clay, compaction alone is most often inadequate to prepare the site for foundation support. Herein, it is desirable to alter the soil's behavior through either the use of chemicals or pressure grouting or, occasionally, some combination of both. Overconsolidation of shallow or surface soils should be avoided (see Sec. A.1.1).

6.6 Chemical Stabilization

The soil upon which a foundation is supported influences or dictates the structural design and ultimate stability of the constructed facility. Earlier chapters have dealt with the pertinent physical properties inherent to and desirable within a bearing soil. Some discussion has been devoted to problem soil components such as the expansive clays. Criteria for overcoming the clay problems through design and maintenance of the foundation have been discussed. This section will address other options: (1) impart beneficial properties to the otherwise problem soil or (2) alter the offending clay constituent to reduce or eliminate the volatile potential. Chemical stabilization represents a classic approach to this problem and will be separated into two categories: (1) permeable soils which generally include noncohesive materials such as sand, gravel, organics, and occasionally silts and (2) the nonpermeable soils which generally are cohesive in nature and contain the clays (e.g., montmorillonite, attapulgite, chlorite, illite, and kaolinite).

6.6.1 Stabilizing permeable soils

Generally, the concerns with noncohesive, permeable soils involve measures to control or prevent sloughing, improve bearing strengths, reduce creep or lateral shifting, control water flow, etc. To best provide this function, stabilizing chemicals which develop a cementitious matrix are used. These additives include such materials as cement slurry, fly ash or pozzolanic earth in lime or cement slurries, sodium silicates (water glass) mixed with a strong acid, and methyl methacrylate polymerized by a peroxide catalyst. The basic nature of the individual soil particle is unchanged; the particles are merely cemented together by the cementitious material filling the void (or pore) space.

As a rule, the stabilizing materials are introduced into the soil, through some variation of pressure injection, often to depths of 10 to 20 ft (3 to 6 m). Injection pipes are mechanically driven or washed down by water to total depth. Once grout injection commences, the pipe is slowly withdrawn. In other words, injection proceeds from the bottom toward the surface and generally continues at each level until either refusal or some predetermined maximum injection pressure is reached. Varying from one type of material to another usually involves little more than changing the mixer and/or pump. For more information on this subject, see Secs. 6.6.2 and 8.4.

6.6.2 Pressure grouting

Pressure grouting can often be used to improve the bearing capacity of soils with little or no permeability. The key is to compress the soil material to a factor above the anticipated load. For example, if a compressible organic/inorganic fill could be grouted to a pressure of 100 lb/in^2 (7 kg/cm^2) (actual), the soil theoretically could support a load of up to 14,400 lb/ft^2 (70,272 kg/m^2), not taking into account any safety factors. (Actual pressure implies the true compressive pressure on the soil matrix, and not gauge pressure at the surface.)

6.7 Stabilizing Impermeable Soils

For purposes of our discussion, the impermeable soils are generally cohesive with appreciable clay content. As a rule, the clay constituent will be one of expansive nature. The problems generated by a clay are influenced directly by variations in available moisture, the result of which is either shrinking or swelling. This volatile nature causes serious concern regarding the design, construction, and stability of foundations.

For example, a typical Eagle Ford soil (Dallas, Tex.) with a PI of about 42 will exhibit a confined swell pressure of about 9000 lb/ft^2 (43,928 kg/m^2) when the moisture content is increased from 23 to 26 percent. In this example, the problem clay constituent is montmorillonite, which is present at up to 50 percent of the total solids volume. Considering that the preponderant weight of a residential or light commercial structure is carried by the perimeter beam and that load is less than 1000 lb/ft^2 (4880 kg/m^2) (single-story construction), it becomes obvious that structural instability is imminent. What must eventually happen if the soils' upward thrust is 9000 lb/ft^2 (43,928 kg/m^2) and the maximum structural resistance is less than 1000 lb/ft^2 (4880 kg/m^2)? The building will rise. [The interior floor area often represents loads as low as 50 to 100 lb/ft^2 (244 to 488 kg/m^2).] Because of the difference in structural resistance as well as the heterogeneous nature of the soil, the uplift or heave is seldom, if ever, uniform.

The secret is to deny the soil the 3 percent change in moisture or alter the properties of the clay constituent to the extent that influences of differential water are neutralized. The former has been discussed in preceding chapters; the latter can be accomplished by treating the problem soil with certain chemical agents. The stabilization procedure depends to some extent upon one's comprehension of the nature of the specific clay constituents.

6.7.1 Clay mineralogy

Basically, the surface clay minerals are composed of various hydrated oxides of silicon, aluminum, iron, and, to a lesser extent, potassium, sodium, calcium, and magnesium. Since clays are produced from the weathering of certain rocks, the particular origin determines the nature and properties of the clay. Chemical elements present in a clay are aligned or combined in a specific geometric pattern referred to as structural or crystalline lattice, generally sheetlike in appearance. This structure, coupled with ionic substitution, accounts principally for both the various clay classifications as well as their specific physical/chemical behavior.

By virtue of a loose crystalline structure, most clays exhibit the properties of moisture absorption (and ion exchange). Among the more common clays, with the tendency to swell in decreasing order, are montmorillonite, illite, attapulgite, chlorite, and kaolinite. Figure 6.1 shows the areas of general and local abundance of high-clay, expan-

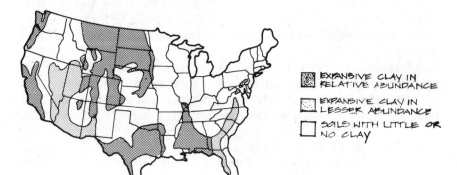

Figure 6.1 Expansive soil areas.

sive soils. The darker areas indicate those states suffering most seriously from expansive soil problems.

These data (provided by K. A. Godfrey, *Civil Engineering*, October, 1978) indicate that 8 states have extensive, highly active soils and 9 others have sufficient distribution and content to be considered serious. An additional 10 to 12 states have problems which are generally viewed as relatively limited. As a rule, the 17 "problem" states have soil containing montmorillonite, which is, of course, the most expansive clay. The 10 to 12 states with so-called limited problems (represented by the lighter shading) generally have soils which contain clays of lesser volatility, such as illite and/or attapulgite, or montmorillonite in lesser abundance.

A specific clay may adsorb and absorb water to varying degrees— from a single layer to six or more layers—depending on its structural lattice, presence of exchange ions, temperature, environment, and so on. The moisture absorbed may be described as one of three basic forms: interstitial or pore water, surface adsorbed water, or crystalline interlayer water. This combined moisture accounts for the differential movement (e.g., shrinking or swelling) problems encountered with soils. In order to control soil movement, each of these forms of moisture must be controlled and stabilized.

The first two forms, interstitial (or pore water) and surface adsorbed water, are generally accepted as capillary moisture. Both occur within the soil mass external to individual soil grains. The interstitial or pore water is held by interfacial tension and the surface adsorbed water by molecular attraction between the clay particle and the dipolar water molecule. Variations in this combined moisture are believed to account for the principal volume change potential of the soil.

On the other hand, soils can take on or lose moisture. Within limits, this moisture exchange involves pore or capillary water, sometimes referred to as free water. (It is recognized that capillary water can be transferred by most clays to interlayer water, and vice versa. However, the interlayer water is normally more strongly held and, accordingly, most stable. This will be discussed at length in the following paragraph.)

In a virgin soil, the moisture capacity is frequently at equilibrium even though the water content may be well below saturation. Any act which disturbs this equilibrium can result in gross changes in the moisture affinity of the clay and result in either swelling or shrinking. Construction, excavation, and/or unusual seasonal conditions are examples of acts which can alter this equilibrium. As a rule, environmental or normal seasonal changes in soil moisture content are confined very close to the ground surface. That being the case, it would appear that, for on-grade construction, it should be sufficient to control the soil moisture only to that depth.

At this point it should be emphasized that, for capillary water to exist, the forces of interfacial tension and/or molecular attraction must be present. Without these forces, the water would coalesce and flow, under the force of gravity, to the phreatic surface (top boundary of water table). The absence of these forces, if permanent, could fix capillary moisture capacity of the soil and aid significantly in the control of soil movement. Control or elimination of soil moisture change is the basis for chemical soil stabilization.

Interlayer moisture is the water situated within the crystalline layers of the clay. The amount of this water that can be accommodated by a particular clay is dependent upon three primary factors: the crystalline spacing, the elements present in the clay crystalline structure, and the presence of exchange ions. As an example, bentonite (sodium montmorillonite) will swell approximately thirteen times its original volume when saturated in fresh water. If the same clay is added to water containing sodium chloride, the expansion is reduced to about threefold. If the bentonite clay is added to a calcium hydroxide solution, the expansion is suppressed even further, to less than twofold. This reduction in swelling is produced principally by ion exchange within the crystalline lattice of the clay. The sorbed sodium ions (Na^+) or calcium ions (Ca^{2+}) limit the space available to the water and cause the clay lattice to collapse and further decrease the water capacity. As a rule (and as indicated by this example), the divalent ions such as Ca^{2+} produce a greater collapse of the lattice than the monovalent ions such as Na^+.

An exception to the preceding rule may be found with the potassium ion (K^+) and the hydrogen ion (H^+). The potassium ion, due to its atomic size, is believed to fit almost exactly within the cavity in the oxygen layer. Consequently, the structural layers of the clay are held more closely and more firmly together. As a result, the K^+ becomes abnormally difficult to replace by other exchange ions. The hydrogen ion, for the most part, behaves like a divalent or trivalent ion probably through its relatively high bonding energy.

It follows that, in most cases, the presence of H^+ interferes with the cation exchange capacity of most clays. This has been verified by several authorities. R. G. Orcutt et al. indicate that sorption of Ca^{2+} by halloysite clay is increased by a factor of 9 as the pH is increased from 2 to 7.[1] Though these data are limited and qualitative, they are sufficient to establish a trend. R. E. Grim indicates that this trend would be expected to continue to a pH range of 10 or higher.[2] (The cation exchange at high pH, particularly with Ca^{2+}, holds significant practical importance, i.e., the stabilization of expansive soils with lime

[Ca(OH)$_2$].) The pH is defined as the available H$^+$ concentration. A low pH (below 7) indicates acidity; 7 is neutral, and above 7 is basic. Cement or lime stabilization of roadbeds represents one condition in which clays are subjected to Ca^{2+} at high pH. It should be recognized that under any conditions the ion-exchange capacity of a clay decreases as the exchanged-ion concentration within the clay increases. Attendant on this, the moisture-sorbtion capacity (swelling) decreases accordingly.

The foregoing discussion has referred to changes in potential volumetric expansion brought about by induced cation exchange. In nature, various degrees of exchange preexist, giving rise to widely variant soil behavior even among soils containing the same type and amount of clay. For example, soils containing Na$^+$-substituted montmorillonite will be more volatile (expansive) than will soils containing montmorillonite with equivalent substitution of Ca^{2+} or Fe^{3+}. This is true because Na$^+$ is more readily replaced by water and the absorption and/or adsorption of the water causes swell.

To this point, the discussion has been limited to inorganic ion exchange. However, available data indicate that organic ion adsorption might have even more practical importance to construction problems.[3] The exchange mechanism for organic ions is basically identical to that discussed above, the primary difference being that, in all probability, more organic sorption occurs on the surface of the clays than in the interlayers and, once attached, is more difficult to exchange. Gieseking[4] reports that montmorillonite clays lost or reduced their tendency to swell in water when treated with several selected organic cations. The surface adsorbed water (or double diffuse layer) which surrounds the clay platelets can be removed or reduced by certain organic chemicals. When this layer shrinks, the clay particles tend to pull closer together (flocculate) and create macropores or shrinkage cracks (intrinsic fractures).

The effect is to increase the permeability of the expansive soil.[5] This action should be helpful to reduce ponding, reduce run-off, and facilitate chemical penetration for stabilization. The extent of these benefits would be dependent upon the performance of the specific chemical product. From a broad view, certain chemical qualities tend to help stabilize expansive clays. Among them are high pH, high OH substitution, high molecular size, polarity, high valence (cationic), low ionic radii, and highly polar vehicles. Examples of organic chemicals which possess a combination of these features are polyacrylamides, polyvinylalcohols, polyglycolethers, polyamines, polyquarternary-amines, pyridine, collidine, and certain salts of each.

Since none of the above organic chemicals possess all the desired qualities, they are often blended with other additives to enhance their performance. For example, the desired pH can be attained by addition of lime [Ca(OH)$_2$)], hydrochloric acid (HCl), or acetic acid (C$_2$H$_3$OOH); the polar vehicle is generally satisfied by dilution with water; high molecular size can be accomplished by polymerization; and surfactants can be utilized to improve penetration of the chemical through the soil.

Generally, the organic chemicals can be formulated to be far superior to lime with respect to clay stabilization. The organic products can be rendered soluble in water for easy introduction into the soil. Chemical characteristics can be more finitely controlled, and the stabilization process is more nearly permanent. About the only advantages lime has over specific organics at present are lower treatment cost, more widespread usage (general knowledge), and greater availability.

The point will be made in later discussions that foundation repair generally is intended to raise lowermost areas of a distressed structure to produce a more nearly level appearance. The repair could be expected to be permanent only if procedures were implemented to control soil moisture variations. This is true because nothing within the usual repair process will alter the existing conditions inherent to an expansive soil. Alternatively, chemical stabilization tends to alter the soil behavior by eliminating or controlling the expansive tendencies of the clay constituents when they are subjected to soil moisture variations. If this reaction is, in fact, achieved, the foundation will remain stable, even under adverse ambient conditions.

Several organic-based products are currently available to the industry. One such product, Soil Sta, is discussed in the following paragraphs. This particular product was selected principally because of the availability of reliable data about it and its apparent effectiveness. All descriptive information was supplied through the courtesy of Brown Foundation Repair & Consulting, Inc., Dr. Cecil Smith, Professor Civil Engineering, Southern Methodist University, and Dr. Tom Petry, Professor Civil Engineering, University of Texas, Arlington, all of Dallas, Texas, and Dr. Malcom Reeves, Soil Survey of England and Wales, London, England.

Soil Sta is basically a mixture of surfactant, buffer, and polyquaternaryamine in a polar vehicle. By virtue of its chemical nature, Soil Sta would be expected to have a lesser influence on kaolinite or illite. Prior research has also indicated that soils exhibiting LL less than 35 or PI less than 23 (montmorillonite content less than about 10 percent by weight) would not swell appreciably.[6] Hence, in the soils utilized in the laboratory and field procedures, montmorillonite as a soil constituent was in relative abundance, at least above 10 percent.

A superior chemical stabilizing agent must be both "economical" and "effective." However, the definitions of these terms can be quite arbitrary. As a start, the economical aspect was assumed to be at a cost somewhat competitive with that for conventional lime. The effective aspect was more elusive. The chemical should be:

1. Effective in reducing swell potential of clay and reasonably competitive with lime, but it should be more readily introduced into the soil. (Lime is sparsely soluble in water and therefore difficult to use where cutting and tilling is inappropriate.)

2. Compatible with other beneficial soil properties.

3. Free from deleterious side effects such as a corrosive nature toward steel or copper, herbicidal tendencies, and smell.

4. Easy to apply with few if any handling problems for the applicators or equipment.

5. Permanent.

At first it might seem that the chemical should actually dehydrate the clay or, in field terms, "shrink the swollen soil." The problem lies in the fact that such dehydration is most often unpredictable and nonuniform. It seems that a simpler approach would be to treat the clay to prevent any material change in the water content within the clay structure. Soil Sta was formulated to hopefully meet all the noted criteria. The mechanism by which this occurs is to both replace readily exchangeable hydrophilic cations (such as Na^+) and adsorb on the exposed cation exchange sites to repel invading water.

6.7.2 Laboratory testing of a soil-stabilizing chemical

For some time, different groups have tested various chemicals as stabilizing agents to prevent the extensive swell of specific clays, montmorillonite in particular. These studies have involved the petroleum as well as the construction industry, and several materials exhibiting varying potential have evolved. As far as the construction industry was concerned, the general emphasis was on new construction. Considering all factors, hydrated lime [$Ca(OH_2)$] has been difficult to displace in types of applications in which a controlled, intimate mix with the clay/soil was feasible.

However, in remedial applications, such as stabilizing the soil beneath an existing structure, lime has its inherent shortcomings: Lime is difficult to introduce into the soil matrix with any degree of uniformity, penetration, or saturation. This stems largely from the facts that (1) lime is sparsely soluble in water and (2) the clay/soil needing stabilization is both impermeable and heterogeneous. A rather comprehensive state-of-the-art report on lime stabilization can be found in Dr.Blacklock's publications, the latest of which is referenced.[7]

As early as 1965, certain surface-active organic chemicals were evaluated and utilized with some degree of success. One very successful chemical utilized in the late 1960s and early 1970s was unquestionably successful in stabilizing the swell potential of montmorillonite clay. The chemical was relatively inexpensive and easily introduced into the soil. However, the product maintained a "nearly permanent" offensive aroma which chemists were never able to mask. Generally this product was a halide salt of the pyridine-collidine-pyrillidene family. In the late 1970s, the quest began to focus more on the potential use of polyamines, polyethanol glycolethers, polyacrylamides, etc., generally blended and containing surface-active agents to enhance soil penetration.[8] It was found that certain combinations of chemicals seemed to be synergistic in behavior (the combined product produced results superior to those noted for any of its constituents).

Starting in 1982, Dr. Cecil Smith, C.E., Professor at Southern Methodist University, Dallas, supervised a series of tests utilizing various potential stabilants. These tests utilized a synthetic soil composed of 15 percent sodium montmorillonite and 85 percent kaolinite. Considering one product (of the several tested), Soil Sta, these preliminary evaluations were quite interersting.

Important Note: The product Soil Sta is proprietary to the author. This presentation is not intended to be commercial. Necessity suggests a focus on this particular product because similar laboratory and field data are not publicly available for any other stabilizer, except perhaps lime. Organic stabilizers function differently from lime, and no standardized testing procedures existed for the evaluation of these types of products. The following discussions and data should prove beneficial to others wishing to evaluate an organic chemical clay stabilizer

First, while Soil Sta applied at the rate of ⅛ gal/ft^2 (0.5ml/cm^2) surface areas reduced the swell pressure of the simulated soil by a factor of 2.6[67.2 to 25.6 lb/in^2 (4.7 to 1.8 kg/cm^2)], no appreciable reduction in the Atterberg parameters was noted. Second, the maximum superior reduction in swell seemed to result at the extreme dilution of 1:50. At this point, it became evident that better test procedures were demanded. This phase of testing at Southern Methodist University was completed in May, 1983.

In late 1983, another test program was initiated at the University of Texas, Arlington, under the direction of Dr. Tom Petry, Professor of Civil Engineering. This procedure involved several phases. From the first segment of phase 4, the data seemed, again, to prove one important fact: Soil Sta at the application rate of $\frac{1}{8}$ gal/ft^2 was effective in reducing the swell of montmorillonite clay. These tests involved a true soil with Atterberg parameters of LL = 59.8, PL = 30.3, PI = 29.5, and LS = 23.5. The initial soil moisture for the control was 13.9 percent. The final moisture content in the control was 34.4 percent, and the average percent swell was 9.13. Soil Sta reduced the percent swell to an average of only 2.61, a reduction by a factor of about 3.5. (Soil engineers generally consider a swell potential of 3 percent to be within the capability of most foundation designs.) Interestingly enough, the Atterberg parameters were again not substantially influenced.

Tests performed in the extended phase 4 (1984) produced the information in Fig. 6.2. Basically these data indicate Soil Sta is completely effective when the soil to be treated meets the basic parameters of expansion and exhibits an initial moisture content of 10.5 percent or higher. (Initial moisture contents less than 10.5 percent tend to be relatively rare under real-world conditions. Nonetheless, Soil Sta reduced the swell in these lower ranges by a factor of at least 4, although the swell potential remained above the arbitrary 3 percent.)

Although the reduction in swell was, at this point, satisfactorily established, it was still evident that additional tests were required to establish the optimum dilution, reduce the standard deviation between repetitive tests, investigate the application procedures more fully, evaluate permanency of stabilization, etc.[9]

In late 1986, Dr. Petry completed a series of wetting and drying tests using Soil Sta and two London clays. These tests were designed to simulate cyclic weather conditions. Over repeated cycles of wetting and drying, the Soil Sta–treated specimens retained the resistance to swell. More surprisingly, Soil Sta reduced shrinkage by some 11 to 50 percent. The data persisted in showing a standard deviation between repetitive tests which was higher than preferred. Obviously, some refinement of test procedures is still in order.

Simultaneously with the latter tests performed by Dr. Petry, Dr. M. J. Reeve, Soil Survey of England and Wales, conducted a series of tests using a Gault clay taken from a depth of 0.7 to 0.9 m (2.3 to 3 ft). The intended application for these tests was 0.5 ml/cm^2 (0.125 gal/ft) Soil Sta. Interestingly, Reeve elected to look into the effects of Soil Sta on the clays' shear strength and permeability, two areas not investigated in prior research. His preliminary results indicated a twofold increase in shear strength and an eightfold increase in permeability. Test results on shrink/swell and Atterberg limits generally agreed with the results reported by Petry. Again, the deviation between repetitive tests involving Soil Sta was greater than that noted for the control.

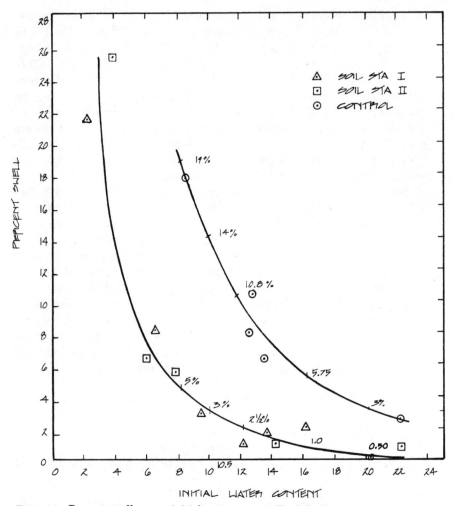

Figure 6.2   Percent swell versus initial water content (Eagleford).

Figure 6.3 shows data similar to those in Fig. 6.2. The tests performed by Dr. Reeve utilized Soil Sta at half strength compared to prior laboratory tests. Hence, the comparative application rate would be reduced to 0.25 ml/cm^2 (0.0625 gal/ft^2).

6.7.3   Field testing of a soil-stabilizing chemical

The following particular application was selected for several reasons. First, the single-story, brick veneer dwelling supported on a conventional slab-on-grade foundation had been virtually condemned for

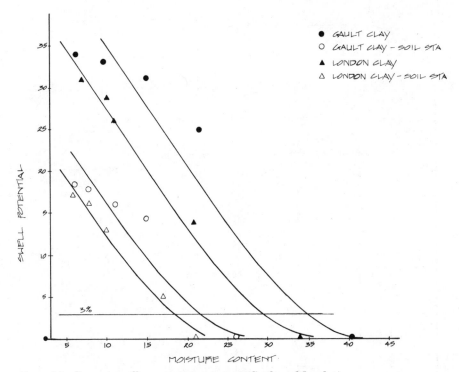

Figure 6.3 Percent swell versus water content (Gault and London).

habitation. The property, which had been vacant for several years, is situated in an area where extensive foundation problems are common. The terrain is hilly (conducive to improper drainage), and the soil exhibits a high montmorillonite content with a PI in or near the 50s. The scenario for restoration commenced in June 1983, as disclosed from company records, was as follows:

1. Over the period June 29 and 30, 1983, the slab was drilled preparatory to mudjacking and Soil Sta was concurrently poured through the drilled holes at the rate of 1 pint/ft^2 (0.125 gal/ft^2 or 0.5 ml/cm^2).

2. Excavations were created at the locations marked with the X in a box, as indicated in Fig. 6.4. These excavations were approximately 3 ft (0.9 m) square and 3 ft (0.9 m) deep. This phase commenced on July 21, 1983, and was completed on July 22, 1983.

3. Soil Sta was poured into the bottom of the excavations at the rate of ½ gal (1.9 l) (0.055 gal/ft^2 or 2.4 l/m^2) each on July 23, 1983.

4. Concrete pads were poured into the excavations on July 25, 1983.

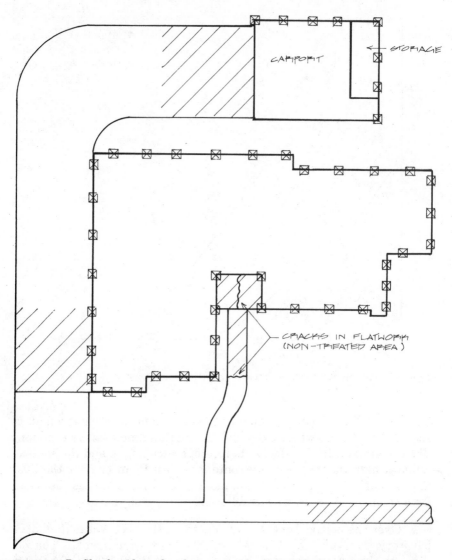

Figure 6.4 Profile of residence foundation treated with Soil Sta showing locations of excavations for spread footings.

Heavy rains inundated the area on August 5 [1.94 in (4.9 cm)] and August 19 [2.89 in (7.3 cm)].

5. On August 10, 1983, the foundation crew returned to the job site for the purpose of bailing the water from the excavation. As a side thought, the job superintendent decided to set jacks on the pads to "see what would happen." The beam was raised without problem with the

exception of one hole where the pad displayed the anticipated tendency to sink into the wet soil. On perhaps 2000 prior jobs, under similar conditions, any raising would have been delayed for a week or more to allow time for the soil underneath the pads to dry. This experience itself was most impressive.

6. On September 12, 1983, the leveling operation was completed.

7. The remodeling contractor was advised to correct all drainage problems, and chemical was sprayed on the soil surface in partial areas where flatwork would be poured. The unshaded areas on Fig. 6.4 indicate approximate limits of the treated areas. The designated areas were omitted because the contractor had not removed old concrete. In all, about 150 gals (568 l) of Soil Sta was injected over 1200 ft^2 (111 m^2), (0.125 gal/ft^2 or 0.5 ml/cm^2). Chemical placement was completed in late September, 1983. All repairs were effectively completed in October 1983.

8. Over the 12 months, from start of repairs until the property was sold, temperature ranged from 5 to 103°F (-15 to 39°C). The accumulative rainfall was in excess of 29 in (74 cm), and it occurred mostly during the months of August, October, February, March, and May. More precisely, the rain was predominantly spread over an accumulative 15 days with the daily average rain being 1.38 in (3.5 cm). Attempts to correct the drainage were not initiated until June 1984, nearly 1 year after the chemical had been placed, and had not been properly completed nearly 4 years later.

Following the repairs and stabilization, the foundation remained stable until May 1985, some 2½ years. The movement noted in May was fairly insignificant; it involved slight settlement principally in the long hall at the south end. The cause of the recurrent problem was total lack of maintenance on the part of the owner. Limited additional work was done in June 1985. The property was reinspected in August 1985 and found to be stable. This is truly amazing, since the property sat unoccupied for over 10 months subsequent to chemical treatment, under the most extreme exposure of temperature and rainfall. Further, the area is noted for frequent and excessive differential foundation movements.

The outstanding result was not completely anticipated, because the laboratory test had suggested some time lag for Soil Sta to adequately disperse into the soil upon gravitational application. As a matter of fact, some slight movement was noted at isolated interior locations a few months after the initial foundation leveling. However, the displacement was not sufficient to require additional foundation repair and occurred prior to interior redecorating. This occurrence was attributed to the time lag. Eighteen months after the flat work had been poured, as shown in Fig. 6.4, at least 90 percent of the stress cracks affected the untreated areas. A saying common in the referenced geographical location is that only three things are certain with concrete: "It will get hard, turn gray, and crack." It appears that proper chemical treatment might alter this statement.

The second field application involved a process identical to the first except for two factors. First, no flat work was treated and, second, the property was occupied and reasonably well maintained. The chemical treatment was completed on June 2, 1984. Although this area also represents one of high incidence of foundation distress, no subsequent movement has been recorded up to the time of this writing.

Subsequent to June 1984, a number of test applications were performed. Of these, one of the most impressive and best documented projects involved treating some 12 multiple-story buildings supported by concrete slab-on-grade foundations of 11,000 ft^2 (1000 m^2) area each. The buildings had suffered severe upheaval to a varying degree that was sufficiently serious to cause the lenders, city engineer, and consulting engineers to consider tearing out the slabs and starting over. Needless to say, the expense associated with that approach would have been astronomical. Instead, Soil Sta was used on an experimental basis in an effort to stop the upheaval and save the buildings. The injection procedure and coverage rate were the same as those previously described. The project was completed in early August 1984. The job cost was $0.50/ft^2 ($5.55/m^2) of treated area, or $5500 per building.

In this instance, grade elevations were taken prior to the injection of Soil Sta, 30 days later, and again 60 days later. Additional readings were planned every 2 weeks for 6 months and then monthly for at least 1 year. The results of the last elevations taken indicated absolutely no measurable upheaval in any of the slabs. The measurements were discontinued in late 1984 or early 1985. Soil tests labeled the soil to be CH with average values of PI 43, LL 68, 1.83 percent swell potential (at natural moisture), and 31 percent in situ moisture. The high initial moisture would tend to imply that minimal additional soil swell (upheaval) would be likely even without the use of Soil Sta; however, the moisture contents were not uniform and tended to vary appreciably from test to test. (This uncertainty caused the decision-making authorities to go with Soil Sta.) It was acknowledged that the high moisture content would cause the soil to be more impermeable and thus resist the penetration of Soil Sta into the matrix. The latter, as it turned out, seemed to present only minimal problems. Figure 6.5 presents swell data similar to those shown in Fig. 6.2 for the Eagleford clay.

More recently, from November 1985 through 1987, an estimated

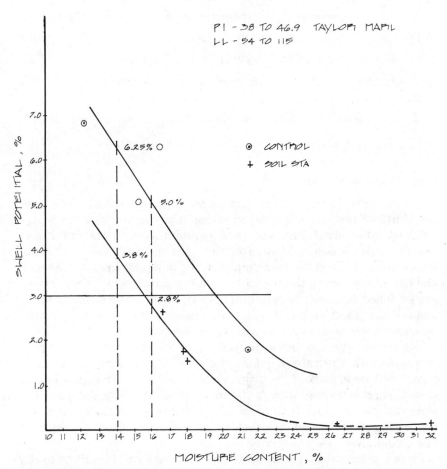

TRINITY PLACE PROJECT
MESQUITE, TEXAS

PI - 38 TO 46.9   TAYLOR MARL
LL - 54 TO 115

6.25% O   ⊙ CONTROL
                 + SOIL STA

O 5.0 %

3.8 %

2.8 %
+

+
+

⊙

Figure 6.5   Swell potential versus moisture content (Taylor Marl).

1900 Soil Sta applications were performed with no known product failures. Most of these field tests involved remedial applications in the Dallas Metroplex, several were in London, England, and a few were pretreatments of construction sites prior to pouring the foundation. Basically, the soils treated were similar to those described in preceding paragraphs. In all instances, the problem clay was montmorillonite, although the amount present might vary considerably from soil to soil. In most field cases described heretofore, the chemical had been introduced to the soil surface and allowed to soak into the matrix.

The concern of the above-mentioned tests, as with the field applications, was to:

1. Confirm the effectiveness of Soil Sta as a chemical stabilant for expansive soil

2. Establish procedures for introducing the chemical into the soil

3. Evaluate various treatment procedures

4. Confirm the longevity of the chemicals' effects

5. Verify the resistance of the chemical to elutriation by water (in particular, rain)

6. Evaluate possible diminishing effects of other ambient conditions

Almost without exception, tests so far have been encouraging.

6.7.4 Pressure Injection

In special cases in the United States and for most applications within the United Kingdom, chemical injection is performed through a specially designed stem (Fig. 6.6). In the system utilized, the Soil Sta is injected under pressure to some depth—usually 4 to 6 ft (1.2 to 1.8 m). Penetration of the stem is accomplished by pumping through the core and literally washing the tool down. Once positioned, the hand valves are switched to close the core and divert flow into the annular space and out the injection ports (Fig. 6.7). The stem can be raised during pumping to cover the desired soil matrix section.

In some instances, a particular soil might tend to resist Soil Sta penetration. Both the rate of penetration and the volume of chemical placed can be enhanced by utilizing hydraulic pulsation (high pressure of short duration) during the injection phase. Alternatively, the stem can be equipped with a packer assembly to isolate zones selectively (Fig. 6.8). This equipment permits higher injection pressures and also allows zone selectivity.

From a practical viewpoint, minimal concern should be given to the exact volume of chemical injected into a specific hole. The primary intent is to distribute the treatment volume reasonably uniformly over the area to be treated. Time (days, weeks, or months—dependent upon the specific site conditions) will produce a nearly equal distribution.

A similar analysis would be true for depth interval injection. Within a short depth (i.e., 6 ft or less) most of the chemical is going to penetrate the same depth interval almost independently of the position of the stinger. This condition could change if two factors coexisted: (1) The depth of penetration is increased substantially, that is, 15 to 20 ft (4.6 to 6 m), and (2) packers or other positive seal methods are used to isolate each zone to be injected. Even in the latter example, true zone penetration may not occur if the placement pressure or specific soil characteristics favor communication between zones.

To illustrate the point, no matter what precautions might be taken,

Figure 6.6 Chemical injection through a specially designed stem.

the normal heterogeneous and fractured nature of the soil would tend to preclude exact placement of a specified volume. Further, at a pressure differential of about 3.5 lb/in^2 (24 kPa), the system illustrated in Fig. 6.7 would theoretically place about 12 gal/min (45 l/min) neglecting line friction. Hence, 10 sec would be required to place 2 gal (7.6 l)

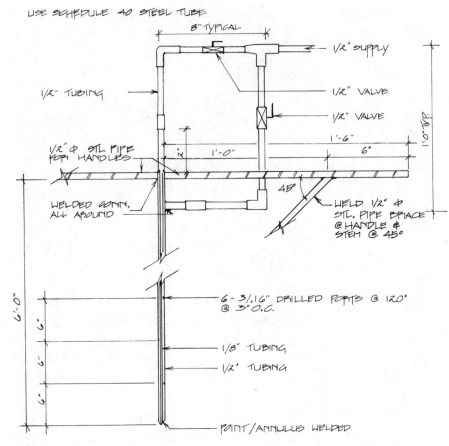

Figure 6.7 Pressure injection stem.

of chemical through the stinger perforations. [This volume equates to ⅛ gal/ft² on a 4-ft (1.2-m) spacing pattern.]

By timing the injection period and maintaining a reasonably constant supply pressure, an acceptably uniform treatment spread would result. Carelessness in either timing or pressure would not be disastrous, so long as it was not blatant. [In field practice, a pressure differential of about 60 lb/in² (414 kPa) delivered 2 gal (7.6 l) of chemical in 30 sec through the stinger and approximately 60 ft (18.3 m) of ½-in (1.27-cm) ID hose.] The following equations are used to calculate velocities and pressure differentials:

Annular velocity: $V_a = \dfrac{Q}{A} = 1.84Q$ ft/sec   (6.1)

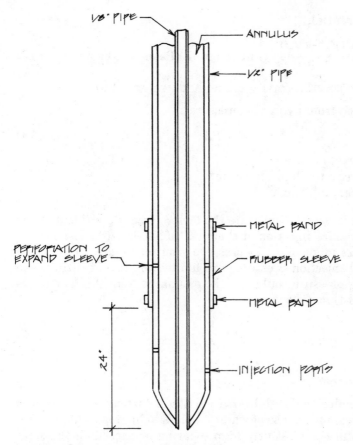

Figure 6.8 Injection stinger with pack-off.

where the annular area is 0.175 in^2 and Q is in gal/min.

Port velocity: $$V_P = \frac{4Q}{D_P^2 \pi n C_D} = 2.4Q \qquad \text{ft/sec} \qquad (6.2)$$

where D_P is 3/16 in, the number of ports n is 6, and Q is in gal/min. This equation is reduced from

$$V_p = \frac{Q}{A_p C_D} \quad \text{and} \quad A_p = \frac{D_P^2 \pi n}{4}$$

The orifice discharge coefficient C_D can be assumed to be 0.80.[10]

Pressure differential:

$$\Delta P = \frac{\rho_f (V_p^2 - V_a^2)}{149} \qquad \text{lb/in}^2 \ (1027 \text{ kPa or } 10.43 \text{ kg/cm}^2) \qquad (6.3)$$

where ρ_f is the specific gravity of the fluid (water = 1.0).

Force developed from hydraulic pressure:

$$F = PA \qquad (6.4)$$

where F = force, lb_f or kg
P = pressure, lb/in^2 or kg/cm^2
A = area, in^2 or cm^2

This equation is used to illustrate the factors creating a lifting force. Generally, pressure injection of chemical soil stabilizers does not involve lifting, as mudjacking or pressure grouting would. In fact, as a rule, chemical injection pressures are limited to prevent lifting. The safe operating pressure could then be estimated from the rearrangement of Eq. (6.4) as follows:

$$P = \frac{F}{A} \qquad (6.5)$$

6.8 Water Barrier

The use of chemical soil stabilizers (Soil Sta in particular) has focused renewed interest on the use of water barriers.[11] In areas where the in situ soil moisture is relatively high (nearing or exceeding the soil's plastic limit), a combined technique utilizing Soil Sta to control soil swell and the moisture barrier to prevent soil moisture loss (shrinkage) appears to have substantial merit. This approach is being considered in the United Kingdom by at least one repair contractor, Robert Wade Brown (U.K.), Ltd. In this instance, the slit trench [approximately 3 in (7.6 cm) wide by 60 in (1.5 m) deep] is dug as near to the foundation perimeter as conditions permit and filled with concrete. Refer to Fig. 9.5. Soil Sta is injected according to the selected procedure as described in preceding paragraphs. The barrier prevents the peripheral loss of soil moisture due to either evaporation or transpiration. (Soil Sta has a minimal effect on soil moisture loss to transpiration. Otherwise, the chemical would be detrimental to vegetation.)

Obviously, the foregoing procedure is designed and intended to stabilize the soil moisture (and foundation) "as is" with negligible, if any, leveling. Where leveling is desirable or necessary, conventional methods are employed. They may or may not include this stabilization technique.

6.9 Irrigation

An irrigation system similar to that shown in Figs. 9.1 and 9.2 could also overcome any peripheral loss of moisture. This system simply replaces any moisture otherwise lost from the soil by either evaporation or transpiration. The key to the effectiveness of this approach lies principally within the metering and monitoring equipment. The moisture returned by the system should be carefully controlled to replace water lost but, at the same time, to maintain a constant soil moisture.

6.10 References

1. R. G. Orcut et al., "The Movement of Radioactive Strontium through Naturally Porous Media," *AEC Report*, November 1, 1955.
2. R. E. Grim, *Clay Mineralogy*, McGraw-Hill, New York, 1953; *Applied Clay Mineralogy*, McGraw-Hill, New York, 1962.
3. H. C. McLaughlin et al., "Aqueous Polymers for Treating Clays," *SPE Paper No. 6008*, Society Petroleum Engineers, Bakersfield, Calif., 1976.
4. J. E. Gieseking, "Mechanics of Cation Exchange in the Montmorillonite-Beidilite-Nontronite Type of Clay Mineral," *Soil Science*, vol. 4, pp. 1–14, 1939.
5. D. E. Foreman et al. "Permeation of Compacted Clay With Organic Chemicals," *Journal of Geotechnical Engineering*, July 1986.
6. M. A. Sherif et al., "Swelling of Wyoming Montmorillonite and Sand Mixtures," *Journal of Geotechnical Engineering*, January 1982, pp. 33–45.
7. J. R. Blacklock and A. D. Pengelly, "Soil Treatment for Foundations on Expansive Soils," *ASCE Paper*, Nashville, Tenn., May 1988.
8. L. H. Williams and D. R. Undercover, "New Polymer Offers Effective, Permanent Clay Stabilization Treatment," *Society of Petroleum Engineers Paper 8797*, January 1980.
9. T. M. Petry and R. W. Brown, "Laboratory and Field Experiences Using Soil Sta Chemical Soil Stabilizer." ASCE paper presented at San Antonio, Tex., October 3, 1986. *Texas Civil Engineer*, February 1987, pp. 15–19.
10. R. W. Brown and B. Gilbert, "Pressure Drop Across Perforations Can Be Computed," *Petroleum Engineer*, September 1957.
11. R. W. Brown, *Residential Foundations: Design, Behavior and Repair*, 2d ed., Von Nostrand Reinhold, New York, 1984, p. 83.

Foundation Failures

7.1 Causes of Foundation Failures

Generally, people tend to associate foundation failures with expansive soils. Basically, the association is correct, especially with residential properties. However, problems are encountered in areas with non-expansive soils as well. The following paragraphs will discuss situations most commonly linked to differential foundation movement. In general, the statements are applicable whether the foundation design is residential or commercial. For simplicity, the presentation is subdivided into nonexpansive soils and expansive soils. In all cases, it is assumed that the foundation will be appropriately designed and of concrete construction.

7.1.1 Nonexpansive soils

Often the nonexpansive soils are also referred to as noncohesive. This is generally true, except that some cohesive soils can be relatively nonexpansive; an example is kaolinite. Typical nonexpansive soils are sands, gravels, coral, and sometimes (though to a lesser extent) certain peats, silts, and clays. Soils with a swell potential of less than 1.0 percent are often considered to be nonexpansive. Foundations situated on these types of soil can suffer distress failure usually as a result of one or more of the following:

1. *Frost heave.* Frost heave occurs as a result of soil water freezing with sufficient expansion to cause the foundation member to heave or, in some cases as with basement walls, to collapse inward. Soils in subfreezing climates which are porous and permeable are the most susceptible to this problem.

2. *Undercompaction.* Bearing soils consisting of fill or disturbed native material often must be compacted to provide a competent, con-

sistent bearing surface to carry the structural load. Well-graded sands and gravels (dry and relatively pure) will consolidate almost immediately upon application of load and, accordingly, would offer few problems. On the other hand, low-density, heterogeneous, expansive, or wet soils could represent a principal concern. Since undercompaction is followed by consolidation, the differential foundation movement, if any, would be settlement.

3. *Overcompaction.* Overcompaction can be a natural consequence when overburden is removed from a soil and not replaced by an equivalent or greater load. In other instances, fill could be mechanically overcompacted. In either event the net result could be an upward thrust of the structure (upheaval).

4. *Removal of water.* Removal of excessive water from the cell structure of these soils often results in consolidation of the soil, sometimes to the extent that structural subsidence follows. This could be the result of pumping water from aquifers (Mexico City) or simply lowering the level of a nearby lake (Florida). This phenomenon is often described as a consolidating soil.

5. *Addition of water.* Under appropriate conditions, specific soils are susceptible to a substantial reduction in void ratio upon addition of water. These soils might exist naturally at low moisture content with apparent high strengths largely attributable to some particle bonding. Water destroys this structural bond and allows local compression. The majority of soils which tend to experience this collapse are aeolian (wind) deposits such as sands, silts, sandy silts, and clayey sands of low plasticity in which there is a loose structure with relatively low densities. As opposed to time-dependent consolidation (reduction of void ratio permitted by removal of pore water), settlement of these collapsing soils occurs somewhat immediately upon the influx of water.[1]

6. *Decay of organic material in fills.* Organic materials decay. In the process, methane gas is produced and a void is created. If the volume of the organic material is sufficient, structural subsidence is likely to follow. The exception is when the foundation bearing surface is below the level of the organic material. As a rule, when the process of decay is on-going, methane gas can be detected.

7. *Construction on a sloping site with downdip soil bedding planes.* In this condition, a downslope stress is transmitted to the foundation. If the sliding stress is sufficient, unless the foundation support is situated below the problem soil–soil interface, downslope movement of the structure could occur. Horizontal, parallel bedding planes would not suggest this problem (Fig. 7.1).

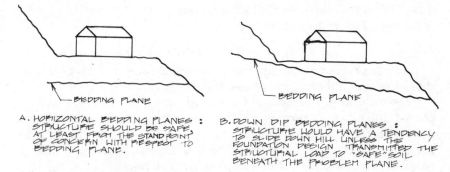

A. HORIZONTAL BEDDING PLANES :
STRUCTURE SHOULD BE SAFE,
AT LEAST FROM THE STANDPOINT
OF CONCERN WITH RESPECT TO
BEDDING PLANE.

B. DOWN DIP BEDDING PLANES :
STRUCTURE WOULD HAVE A TENDENCY
TO SLIDE DOWN HILL UNLESS THE
FOUNDATION DESIGN TRANSMITTED THE
STRUCTURAL LOAD TO "SAFE" SOIL
BENEATH THE PROBLEM PLANE.

Figure 7.1   Construction on a natural slope.

8. *Marginal bearing capacity.* Some soils, such as silts and loess, have a low bearing capacity which tends to make them unsuitable for foundation support. In that case, special foundation design procedures are required as for (7).

9. *Lightning, earthquakes, slides, etc.* These possible occurrences will not be considered.

Note in particular that of the few foregoing potential causes of water-related distress, none are relative to changes in *combined* soil moisture, e.g., surface absorbed or crystalline interlayer water. Further, in no instance was a significant physical change noted for the soil particles.

7.1.2   Expansive soils

The subject of foundation failure relative to differential movement takes on a new significance with the introduction of a new parameter: expansive soils. In addition to the problems described above, the soil itself now becomes a principal contributor to the movement. Expansive soils will shrink upon loss of moisture and, even worse, will swell upon introduction of water. The expansive clay constituent within these soils represents the basic problem. One such clay, montmorillonite can swell up to 20 times its volume.

Soils with montmorillonite present to the extent of 40 percent total solids volume have been known to show swell potentials in excess of 30 percent with expansive pressures in excess of 20,000 lb/ft^2 (97,600 kg/m^2). The swell potential of a soil is dependent upon several things in addition to the percent and type of clay, such as initial and final moisture content. A soil with a natural moisture content 1.0 percent or so above its plastic limit will have already experienced most of its swell. As a rule of thumb, residential foundations are designed to tolerate swell potentials up to about 3 percent. Above that, damage may occur. With the new trouble factor in mind, the frequent causes for foundation failure include:

1. *Abnormal soil moisture at the time the foundation is poured.*   As a rule, this problem is mostly relegated to slab construction, generally that of residential or light commercial design.

If the natural soil moisture is unusually low at the time the slab is poured, the return to normal moisture in surrounding soil could cause the perimeter to heave or cup up. This could be true even though the placement of the slab itself would tend to increase the soil moisture beneath the foundation. However, capillary movement of water in a clay soil is restricted because of the extremely low permeability. On the other hand, ambient conditions can introduce relatively copious quantities of water to the exterior exposed surfaces. This differential in moisture content between perimeter (wetter) and interior (dryer), although sometimes of limited duration, can cause the foundation to shift up and down with attendant distress to the structure's appearance.

If the soil moisture is abnormally high when the foundation is poured, the reverse is true. The high moisture content beneath the foundation is protected (bottled up, if you will) while the exterior is exposed to the drying effects of wind and summer heat. The net result appears as perimeter settlement. Refer to Fig. 7.2 for a simplified illustration of the two conditions.

2. *Undercompaction.*   Basically the same as nonexpansive soils (Sec. 7.1.1).

3. *Overcompaction.*   Somewhat the same as nonexpansive soils except that the new parameter of soil swell is introduced.

4. *Frost heave.*   Frost heave is often not too serious a problem in areas with expansive soils because of the soil's extremely low permeability and normally low porosity. Water must be present within the soil matrix at a depth sufficiently shallow to be affected by freezing temperatures. In some cold-climate, wet areas, the expansive soil has sufficient root channels, intrinsic fractures, or slickensides to provide the necessary permeability and porosity to become the exception. As

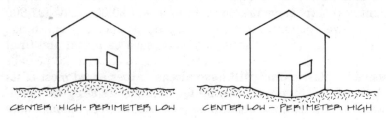

CENTER HIGH- PERIMETER LOW   CENTER LOW – PERIMETER HIGH

Figure 7.2 Foundation distress due to natural soil moisture.

the name implies, since the movement is one of expansion, upheaval is the mode of failure. Refer also to (1).

5. *Decay of organic material.*   See Sec. 7.1.1, numbered paragraph 6.

6. *Plant roots.*   Plants tend to sap more soil moisture through transpiration than wind and heat do through evaporation. As long as this moisture loss is confined to capillary water (sometimes referred to as pore or interstitial water), the soil itself is not particularly affected, as would also be the case with nonexpansive soils. However, at some point, other moisture is pulled from the clay and results in soil shrinkage and potential foundation settlement. Generally, foundation distress relative to transpiration is probably much less than is normally assumed.

Vegetation feeder roots tend to be shallow and to be limited in radial extent from the plant trunk. Most botanists suggest that the feeder roots of many trees and plants exist within the top 1 to 2 ft (0.3 to 0.6 m) below the ground surface. If the perimeter beam is over 2 ft deep, intruding roots are not likely to cause any serious concern with respect to the interior foundation areas. Roots already in place might be another story, as might be trees located quite close to a shallow foundation. The latter conditions could also give rise to mechanical upheaval of the foundation beam as the roots grew in diameter. Under these conditions, similar effects could be ascribed to foundation problems on nonexpansive soils.

On the other hand, tree roots can be beneficial to foundation stability, since they tend to act as a soil reinforcement and increase the soil's shearing resistance.[2] The practical result of this effect could be to impede foundation settlement and reduce soil cracks even though the roots do remove soil moisture.

Refer to Fig. 7.3, which shows the relation between tree roots and foundation. These representations were taken from leading botanists such as Dr. Don Smith, Professor at North Texas State University, and Neil Sperry's book, *Complete Guide to Texas Gardening*, Chap. 1.

7. *Loss of soil moisture.*   Any condition which causes an expansive soil to lose moisture has the potential to cause foundation settlement. As a rule, settlement represents the least worrisome foundation problem, since generally the extent of movement is relatively limited and the condition is often easily reversed by the introduction of proper watering procedures. Deep foundations rarely suffer from this problem because moisture loss is quite limited in depth.

8. *Gain of soil moisture.*   With limited exception, an expansive soil will swell when subjected to excess water. However, some clay soils will lose structure (cohesion) and creep at extremely high moisture

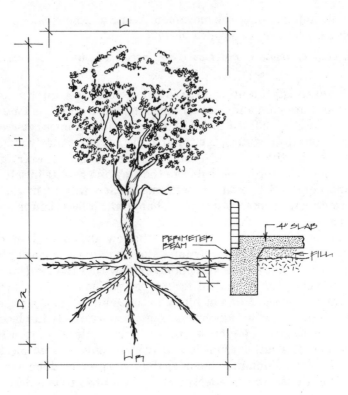

H = HEIGHT OF TREE
W = WIDTH OF CANOPY (UNPRUNED)
D_2= DEPTH OF ROOTS (MOSTLY STRUCTURAL)
D_1= DEPTH OF FEEDER ROOTS
W_R=WIDTH OF FEEDER ROOT SPREAD (OFTEN
    REPORTED AT 1.25 W)
D_B=DEPTH OF PERIMETER BEAM

Figure 7.3 Development of tree root system versus foundation.

contents above or near the liquid limit. In this relatively rare instance, the expansive soil might give the impression of shrinking.

Soil swell and foundation heave represent the most serious problem
to foundation stability in dealing with an expansive soil. The source of
water could be rainfall (improper drainage), utility leaks (principally
slab foundations), wet weather aquifers, subsurface water, etc.

9. *Construction on a sloping site with downdip bedding plane.* The
soil-soil interface at the bedding plane has a lower shear resistance,
because of reduced contact friction, and the soil is therefore more subject to sliding. This is particularly true with expansive soils. In sliding, the mode of failure is not up or down but horizontal.

10. *Cut-and-fill site.* Anytime a foundation is based on cut and fill, the inherent tendency toward instability exists. The cut soil may lose desirable properties, and the fill area represents a soil of different or altered properties. The latter tends to be true even if the fill is native material supposedly compacted to original density and moisture. The disturbed reconstituted soil seldom, if ever, exhibits properties identical with those of the natural undisturbed soil. Refer also to (9).

11. *Marginal bearing capacity.* Same as numbered paragraph 8, Sec. 7.1.1.

The foregoing paragraphs presented the basic factors which threaten the safety and stability of foundations in general. The following discussions will be more specific.

7.1.3 Summary

To date, much attention has been given to avoiding foundation failures resulting from distress (or differential movement) brought about by design deficiencies or environmental extremes. Annual rainfall, temperature ranges, clay content of the supporting soil, soil composition, etc., combine to help produce the design and construction requirements for foundations. In highly plastic clay soils, such conditions as the relative moisture content in the soil immediately prior to construction can affect the future stability or behavior of the foundation.

Each of these factors can have a direct influence on settlement (soil shrinkage) as well as upheaval (soil swelling). The following paragraphs will introduce an argument, supported by filed results, that upheaval, not settlement, is in fact the most serious and prevalent deterrent to slab-on-grade construction in most areas of the United States—perhaps accounting for as high as 70 percent of all failures. This assumes an expansive soil with an ambient moisture no higher than perhaps a percent or so above the plastic limit.

To avoid any problems of semantics, it is advisable to define the terms "settlement" and "upheaval." Generally, this chapter addresses slab foundations. Similar results and problems are encountered with pier-and-beam foundations, but slab construction recently has become numerically dominant over pier and beam.

7.2 Settlement

Settlement is that instance in which some portion of the foundation drops below the original as-built grade. This occurs as a result of loss of bearing—compaction of fill, erosion of supporting soil, dehydration (shrinkage of supporting soil), etc. As an example of settlement brought about by loss of soil moisture, Poor & Tucker reported a change of ½ in (1.27 cm) in vertical displacement of a slab foundation

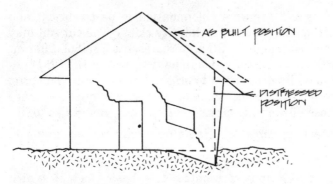

Figure 7.4 Typical foundation settlement.

over a period of about 6 months from the winter of 1971 to the summer of 1972. The conditions of exposure (and loss of soil moisture) were more severe than one would expect for normal residential conditions, since the slab was completely exposed (the house had been removed) and the perimeter had not been watered.[3]

Generally, settlement originates and is more pronounced at the perimeter of the slab, and more particularly at a corner. Settlement progresses relatively slowly and can often be reversed and/or arrested by proper watering. Figure 7.4 shows a typical example of foundation settlement. The dashed lines depict the as-built position and the solid lines the distressed position.

7.3 Upheaval

Upheaval relates to the situation in which the internal and, on rare occasion, external areas of the foundation are raised above the as-built position. Figure 7.5A and B show typical examples of foundation upheaval. In high-plastic soils this phenomenon results, almost without exception, from the introduction of moisture under the foundation. Upheaval can develop rather rapidly depending upon the quantity of available water and the clay constituent within the soil. The author has recorded instances in which 3- to 4-in (7.5- to 10-cm) vertical deflections occurred in a slab foundation over a time interval of less than one month! Admittedly, that was unusual, but it does happen.

The moisture may originate from normal precipitation (improper grade), underground water, or, more frequently, from domestic sources such as leaks in supply or waste systems. Visual observations will usually reveal any grade problems. An understanding of the particular locale will help predict or evaluate the prevalence of underground water. A qualified plumbing check will verify or sometimes eliminate the possibility of any domestic leak.

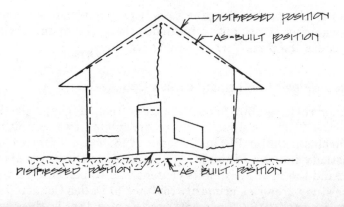

A

B

Figure 7.5 (A) Typical foundation upheaval. (B) Upheaval in interior slab floor. The drainpipe is straight and level. Note the space at either end. The gap at the left end is between 3 and 4 in (7.5 and 10 cm) and at the right end, between 1 and 2 in (2.5 and 5 cm).

Watering around the perimeter can sometimes temporarily retard the noticeable progress of upheaval but will not normally reverse the problem. The latter is true for two reasons: (1) In the case of slab foundations, the weakest area (the interior) is domed and stressed into a deformed contour. Watering may tend to raise the perimeter, but the interior area is likely to merely move upward as well, or, when the availability of water ceases, the exterior soil moisture decreases and the beam settles back. (2) In the case of pier-and-beam foundations, surface watering is not apt to influence the grade of the perimeter beam because the piers tend to act as anchors.

7.4   Occurrence of Settlement versus Upheaval

The author reviewed 502 foundation inspections during a particular study period.[4,5] The basic soils within the subject area exhibit representative plastic limits (PL) in the range of 18, liquid limits (LL) of 60, and plasticity indices (PI) of 42. The natural moisture was about 18 percent, and the montmorillonite content was 40 percent, plus or minus. The study area was primarily confined to Dallas County, Tex. Of the cases reported, 216 (43 percent) were no bids; that is, there was no problem which required attention other than adequate maintenance. (Most structures exhibited the result of some settlement, but often the movement was not considered serious enough to warrant repairs. Identifying upheaval tendencies early enough might have avoided repairs if the source of water could have been identified and eliminated. Virtually all structures within the study area showed some signs of distress.)

The remaining 286 cases were considered to have problems sufficiently serious to warrant foundation repairs; 87 of those foundation failures were obvious, unquestioned conditions of settlement, and 199 cases exhibited some indication of various degrees of upheaval. From these data, it appears settlement versus upheaval would occur on the basis of 87 to 199, or 30 percent as compared to 70 percent. Other studies have developed similar data for comparable soils.

Many individuals have been reluctant to accept the preponderance and seriousness of upheaval. However, the available data give proof that upheaval is indeed a most serious deterrent to slab-on-grade construction. It is also interesting to note that in most cases the movement arrests sometime after the source of water has been eliminated. What does all this mean? Water under a foundation is truly a serious problem and must be avoided. This suggests measures to control subsurface water and surface drainage as well as to prevent deficiencies or leaks in the plumbing systems. Failing to do so will almost certainly invite problems.

Surface grade can be easily handled, and construction in areas subject to problem subsurface water can be avoided or the condition remedied prior to construction. Simple quality control would probably eliminate a majority of the plumbing-induced problems. According to the plumbing contractors, whose findings and data helped to provide the basis of this chapter,[4] the principal or most common plumbing problems stem from:

1. Faulty or omitted shower pans
2. Faulty installation of water closets (collapsed lead sleeves)
3. Faulty or ill-designed drain waste valves
4. Ill-fitted or careless installation of connection joints
5. Substandard sewer line materials

In other words, added attention to the plumbing installations might reduce foundation failures in slab-on-grade construction by as much as 50 to 60 percent within areas of soils similar to those studied. Bear in mind two facts: Water from leaks beneath the slab is accumulative, and any water under the slab, regardless of source, tends to accumulate in the plumbing ditch. Sewer lines are graded for gravity drainage away from the foundation, but the ditches in which they are situated may not be. Anything that could be done to alleviate the accumulation of water in the plumbing ditch would obviously be beneficial to slab-on-grade construction.

Also be advised that seldom does the water accumulate at the source of the leak and very little water is needed to cause serious upheaval. In fact, assuming (1) a 1000-ft^2 (93-m^2) affected slab area, (2) a soil with a PI of 42, (3) an initial 22 percent moisture, (4) a soil porosity of 10 percent, and (5) that 86 percent of principal soil moisture change occurs within the top 3.5 ft (1.1 m), a 3 percent change in moisture would likely cause upheaval in the foundation of approximately 1.25 in (3.2 cm) and would require only 1.5 oz/hr (44 ml/hr) of water over the period of a year. (The foundation area most often affected is the weakest point: the interior slab.) Since water is accumulative, nearly any sort of persistent leak or drainage deficiency would handily account for the stated amount of water. In some drier soils, a 3 percent change in moisture would account for substantially higher swells. Conversely, a soil with a moisture content near to or in excess of the plastic limit would normally exhibit little retentive swell potential.

7.5 Diagnosis of Settlement versus Upheaval

Upheaval, as previously stated, is virtually always the result of some water accumulation beneath the slab. Settlement describes the condition in which some area of the foundation falls below the original grade. The differentiation between the two is most critical and difficult: it requires extensive experience and knowledge. Consider Fig. 7.6. Did the slab foundation heave near the interior partition, or did the perimeter settle? Consider the evidence:

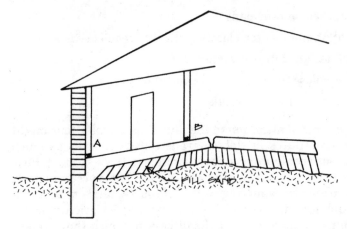

Figure 7.6 Example of foundation deflection.

1. The door frame is off 1 in (2.5 cm) across the 30-in header with the inside jamb being high. The grade change from point B to point A is 4.75 in (12 cm). [The distance from B to A is 12 ft (3.6 m).]
2. The brick mortar joint shows a high area near the midpoint of the wall (A).
3. The cornice trim at both front and rear corners of the side wall is out less than ½ in (1.27 cm).
4. At both corners the mortar joints down adjoining walls are reasonably straight (excepting the single high area previously cited).
5. There is no appreciable separation of brick veneer from window frames in the end walls.

Analysis of the data gives rise to only one conclusion: The center has heaved. Alternatively, had the perimeter settled, the greatest differential movement [4.75 in (12 cm)] would show at the corners and observations 3, 4, and 5 would have been impossible. To further complicate the matter, both settlement and upheaval often exist in the same structure. Before proper repair procedures can be established, the cause of the problem must first be diagnosed.

Failures diagnosed as interior slab settlement can actually be the result of a slab having been installed during a period of prolonged dry weather when the soil moisture might be abnormally low. When rains and/or domestic watering supply the perimeter areas with moisture, natural swelling occurs and raises the perimeter, giving the overall appearance of interior settlement. The opposite situation (i.e., construction of a slab after extended moist weather) can occur and give the impression of central slab upheaval when the perimeter area bearing soil returns to lower, normal moisture content and leaves the central slab area high. (In either event, the vertical displacement is still brought about by variations in moisture content within the expansive soil.)

7.6 Sliding

A third type of movement, sliding, sometimes occurs when a structure is erected on a slope. Here the movement is not limited to up or down (vertical) but possesses a lateral or horizontal component. In expansive soils, cut-and-fill operations can be particularly precarious. The clay constituents in the cut tend to become unusually expansive even though recompacted to or near their original density. This is due in large part to the breakup of cementation within the cut soil, poor compaction of fill, and/or, to some lesser extent, the change in permeability or infiltration of the fill.

Figure 2.2 shows an example of construction on a filled slope, and Fig. 2.3 shows the use of a step beam to conform to the contour of the land. The applied forces are basically the same in either example, and foundation failure generally results in movement down the slope. As a rule, restoration of this problem is handled as settlement. The lower areas can be raised and restored to a vertical position, but rarely is the horizontal component reversed. Fortunately, this type of movement is relatively rare.

7.7 References

1. S. L. Houston, W. N. Houston, and D. J. Spadola, "Prediction of Field Collapse of Soils Due to Wetting," *Journal of Geotechnical Engineering*, Vol. 114, No. 1, January 1988.
2. T. H. Wu et al., "Study of Soil-Root Interaction," *JGE*, vol. 114, Dec. 1988.
3. R. L. Tucker and A. Poor, "Field Study of Moisture Effects on Slab Movements," *Journal of the Geotechnical Engineering Division, ASCE*, April 1978.
4. R. W. Brown, "A Field Evaluation of Current Foundation Design vs. Failure," *Texas Contractor*, July 6, 1976.
5. R. W. Brown and C. H. Smith, Jr., "The Effects of Soil Moisture on the Behavior of Residential Foundations in Active Soils," *Texas Contractor*, May 1, 1980.

8

Foundation Repair Procedures

8.1 Introduction

When foundations do fail for one reason or another, prompt and competent repairs are demanded; otherwise, the problems would increase and jeopardize the value and safety of the structure. The repair procedures discussed in this chapter have been developed over the last 25 years basically through a process of trial and error. When a technique proves successful over several thousand field evaluations, the conscientious contractor is reluctant to attempt unproven changes. In foundation repair, results far outweigh theory. As time goes on, new methods (or variations) will be introduced and, results warranting, perhaps accepted.

Before proceeding, it might be interesting to consider a few facts relative to the forces involved with leveling or raising a structure. An average, single-story, brick wall with roof load exerts a downward force of approximately 10 lb/in^2 (0.7 kg/cm^2 or 6.9 kPa). In order to lift this wall vertically, a force only slightly in excess of 10 lb/in^2 is required. A 4-in- (10-cm-) thick unloaded slab would require a lifting force less than 1.0 lb/in^2 (0.07 kg/cm^2 or 6.9 kPa). (This analogy neglects the aspects of breakaway friction, mechanical binding, etc.) The shear strength of regular five-sack concrete is probably in the neighborhood of 350 lb/in^2 (24.5 kg/cm^2) but might approach 1500 to 2000 lb/in^2 (105 to 140 kg/cm^2). (The true value depends upon the conditions of applied stress and the investigator conducting the test.[1,2])

From these numbers, it is easy to realize how structures can be raised without shearing the slab. It should be acknowledged, however, that in many cases the settlement is not uniform, and, because of the weight and load distribution, requires an increased and variable lifting force at different points. This is a situation requiring caution, experience, and a carefully prepared approach, without which the structure could be sheared and shattered or unevenly raised. This becomes increasingly obvious when the forces available for lifting are recognized.

The hydraulic pumps used in mudjacking are capable of exerting pressures ranging from 100 to 500 lb/in^2 (7 to 35 kg/cm^2), which is clearly in excess of that required to raise the mass of the structure. A 30-ton (27,273-kg) mechanical jack can exert approximately 8500 lb/in^2 (595 kg/cm^2) assuming a 3-in (75-cm) head or load area. It is no wonder, then, that this equipment in the hands of a careless or incompetent operator can cause extensive and severe damage. On the other hand, this lifting force is sometimes required to overcome breakaway friction or mechanical binding, and, as such, must be available.

Note: Opinions have been expressed which tend to minimize the effectiveness of mudjacking. For example, in the *Foundation Engineering Handbook*, edited by Winterkorn and Fang, Edward White states, "This method [mudjacking], is rarely successful unless the entire consolidation of the ground has taken place." Such a statement is, at best, misleading, particularly as far as residential or light commercial foundations are concerned. The mudjacking is more "permanent" than the unconsolidated soil beneath. Recurrent problems would be the result of continued loss of soil-bearing capacity and not the failure of the mudjacking.

If the soil problem is one of poor consolidation, this condition should be corrected if the foundation is to remain stable. Mudjacking, or a variation thereof—pressure grouting—is most often quite successful in cementing and consolidating or compacting loose soils. As an aside, the 7-day compressive strength of typical grout is 230 lb/in^2 [33,120 lb/ft^2 (161,626 kg/m^2)] (from Robert Wade Brown, *Residential Foundations: Design, Behavior and Repair*). Specific mixes can be selected to provide a wide choice of strength. In any event, the grout provides a bearing capacity highly superior to that of even the most favorable soils and could hardly be classified as "inferior."

If the soil problem is one attributable to expansive clay constituents, the volumetric tendencies of the soil must be neutralized to allow foundation stability—regardless of the underpinning or repair method. This done, mudjacking is as permanent as extraneous conditions allow.

Mudjacking is not intended to be a "cure all"; it is intended to provide specific benefits. In truth, the "rap" against mudjacking per se is ill-founded and based on lack of understanding, misapplication, or both. As a rule, mudjacking is essential to the proper repair of residential slab foundations.

Moisture variations within expansive soils cause a preponderance of all foundation failures. The soil swells when wet (upheaval) and shrinks when dry (settlement). This volumetric change in the bearing soil in turn causes differential movement in the supported foundation. According to Earl Jones and Wes Holts in the August 1973 issue of *Civil Engineering*, 60 percent of all residential foundations constructed on expansive soils will experience some distress caused by differential foundation movement and 10 percent will experience problems sufficient to demand repairs. Specific areas suffer an even higher percentage of failures.

Corrective procedures depend upon both the nature of the problem and the type of foundation. Settlement is corrected by raising or restoring the affected area to the approximate original grade. Upheaval is corrected by raising the lowermost areas around the raised crown to a new grade sufficient to "feather" the differential. See Table 8.1 for a concise, abbreviated presentation of repair approaches to various problems. Specific repairs will be discussed in detail in following paragraphs.

All foundation failures are generally manifested in one or more of the following signs: interior or exterior wall cracks, ceiling cracks, sticking doors or windows, pulled roof trusses, and broken windows (Fig. 8.1). A common misconception is that foundation movement occurs "instantaneously." The mistake is promoted by the fact that some of the signs of distress do seemingly appear to be instantaneous. However, the walls, ceilings, and other structural features are somewhat elastic in nature and ultimate failure (cracks, for example) occurs when the applied stress exceeds the elasticity of the particular surface. The behavior is somewhat analogous to that of a stretched rubber band. Stress is not evident until the band parts.

These indications are realized in pier-and-beam as well as slab foundations. In correcting any failure, it is first necessary to isolate and recognize the particular problem. For example, it is often difficult (and always critical) to differentiate between settlement and upheaval. Many of the outward signs of differential foundation movement are similar whether the actual distress is relative to settlement or upheaval; see for example, Figs. 7.4 and 7.5. Both show cracks and both show lateral displacement of the perimeter walls. Many foundation problems have been aggravated rather than solved by errors in analysis of source of distress. However, once the cause of foundation movement has been determined, proper restitution can commence. The gen-

TABLE 8.1 Foundation Repair Options for Residential and Light Commercial Foundations

Problem	Cure	
	Nonexpansive soils	Expansive soils
Frost heave	Problem is best addressed in original foundation design. Foundation base support should be below level of frost line, and subgrade walls should be reinforced to resist inward stress. Taking steps to prevent water accumulation in shallow soils, both as a component of original design and as a remedial approach, will also help.	Not often a serious problem because of inherent lack of soil permeability and porosity. Could be approached as suggested for nonexpansive soils if the need should arise.
Undercompaction	Generally shows as a problem relatively rapidly after construction, if at all.	The settlement is corrected, as a rule, by underpinning the perimeter and either mudjacking and/or pressure grouting beneath the interior slab (slab foundations) or shimming off interior pier caps to level interior floors (pier-and-beam construction). See Figs. 8.2, 8.5, and 8.6.
Overcompaction	Not normally a serious problem to shallow foundations.	Same as nonexpansive soils. When exceptions occur, the procedures described above could be applicable.
Water drain or wetting	Restitution or stabilization would require replacement of lost water or filling the void space by pressure grouting. Often, after the voids are filled, the structure is leveled by underpinning the perimeter and mudjacking the slab or reshimming interior pier caps on pier and beam.	Not often a problem within the definition.
Decay of organics	Collapsing soils are treated the same regardless of classification. The cure is to fill voids and create a cemented volume sufficient to carry the applied structural load. In the case of compressible materials, such as peat, the material is not likely to be cemented, but compression to a pressure above the intended load is adequate. Once the deep-seated problem has been cured, the surface appearance can be remedied by the conventional leveling procedures described above.	
Construction on slope	Slopes with downdip bedding planes create similar problems regardless of the soil type. True, expansive soils experience a greater propensity to this failure, but the cure is almost identical. Remedial choices generally require underpinning the foundation with the added support members extending safely below the problem slip plane into solid bearing. Most often the underpinning technique requires installation of drilled concrete piers or driven pilings. Releveling the stabilized structure would most often require mudjacking (slab foundations) or reshimming interior pier caps (pier and beam). In rare instances, the interface at the slip surface might be pressure-grouted with a cementitious grout to retard the slip.	

Abnormal soil moisture at time of construction	Not normally a point of particular concern.	Natural moisture differentials between the foundation bearing soils and the exterior create shrink/swell tendencies, especially when slab-on-grade foundations are concerned. Dry soil at the perimeter can often be watered to the extent that differential movement is minimal. Dry interior soil might allow the slab to settle to the extent that mudjacking would be required. In extreme cases, any repair approach might include chemical stabilization of the clay to control the affinity to water.
Plant roots	Seldom a problem.	Plant roots steal moisture from the soil, sometimes to the extent that foundation stability is at risk—particularly with respect to slab foundations. Prevention is preferable to cure. However, when a situation develops, the cure is to (1) create a situation which restores the moisture, (2) construct a root barrier at the foundation perimeter to exclude root intrusion, or (3) if the situation demands, raise the perimeter beam by underpinning and mudjack the interior slab.
Loss of soil water (combined)	Seldom a serious concern, but any remedial approach would be consistent with that for expansive soils.	Remedial approach similar to that described above except, with pier-and-beam foundations, the interior floors would be releveled by shimming on existing pier caps.
Gain of soil water	Seldom a serious problem.	Excess water beneath a foundation causes upheaval—especially with slab foundations. The first problem is to eliminate the source of water, which could require plumbing repairs, drainage correction, the installation of French drains, etc., dependent upon the source of the water. Once this is done, the foundation is leveled by conventional means as described above. The principal exception would be the desirability to treat the soil with a chemical stabilizer such as Soil Sta.
Marginal bearing capacity	The solution to this problem would be the same with either expansive or nonexpansive soils. As is always the case, avoiding the problem is more desirable than cure. However, if need be, the bearing capacity of the soil can often be increased by the introduction of chemicals, often of a cementitious nature. Nonexpansive soils show a greater propensity to suffer this problem than expansive soils.	

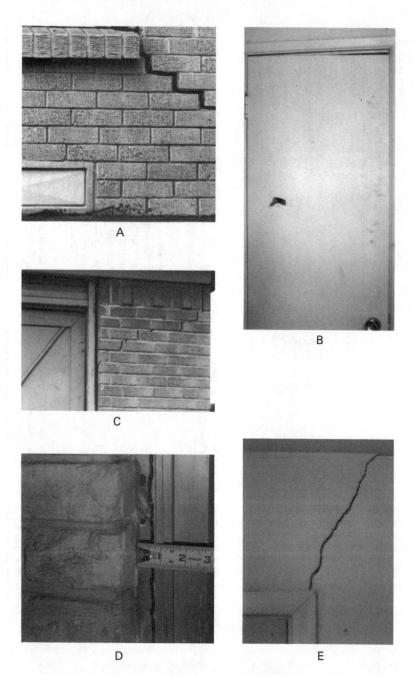

Figure 8.1(A) Separation in brick mortar. (B) Interior door not plumb. Note wide gap at top right corner of door. (C) Separation of brick veneer from garage door jamb. (D) Separation of brick veneer from window frame. (E) Wallboard crack above door.

eral delineation for the following discussions will be based on the type of foundation—either slab or pier and beam.

8.2 Pier-and-Beam Foundations

Pier-and-beam foundation movement is generally confined to settlement, although, in limited cases, upheaval is observed. For practical purposes, the solution for upheaval is again to treat the lowermost sections of the foundation as though settlement had occurred and raise them to the higher grade. Settlement is generally alleviated by mechanically raising the beam and sustaining the beam position by installing new supporting structures. Interior floors are leveled by shimming on pier caps.

8.2.1 Underpinning

Typically, the supports might be spread footings which consist of (1) steel-reinforced footings of sufficient size to adequately distribute the beam load and poured to a depth relatively independent of seasonal soil moisture variations and (2) a steel-reinforced pier tied to the footing with steel and poured to the bottom of the foundation beam (Fig. 8.2). Design and placement of these spread footings is critical if future beam movement is to be averted. The footing design must consider the problems of both possible future settlement and/or upheaval and should be of sufficient area to develop adequate bearing by the soil. The pier should be of sufficient diameter or size to carry the foundation load. It also should be poured to intimate contact with the irregular configuration of the under surface of the beam.

The foregoing paragraphs have described mechanical repairs by the use of spread footings. The principle of the footing design is to distribute the foundation load over an extended area at a stable depth and thus provide increased support capacity on even substandard bearing soil. The typical design represented by Fig. 8.2. provides a bearing area of 9 ft^2 (0.8 m^2). Effectively, a load of 150 lb/ft^2 (732 kg/m^2) applied over 1 ft^2 (0.09 m^2) would require a soil-bearing strength of 150 lb/ft^2 (732 kg/m^2). The same load distributed over 9 ft^2 (0.8 m^2) would require a soil-bearing strength of only 17 lb/ft^2 (83 kg/m^2). Expressed another way, a 9-ft^2 (0.8-m^2) spread footing on a soil with an unconfined compressive strength q_u of 1500 lb/ft^2 (7320 kg/m^2) would provide a load resistance of 13,500 lb (6136 kg) ($Q_r = q_u A$). This capacity would exceed the structural loads imposed by residential construction by a wide margin. The spread footings are predominately used when the overburdened soil is thick and the soil-bearing strengths are low or marginal. Generally, the diameter of the pier cap is greater than or at least equal to the width of the existing beam. Since the pier is essen-

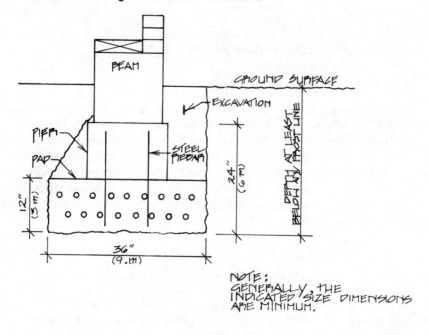

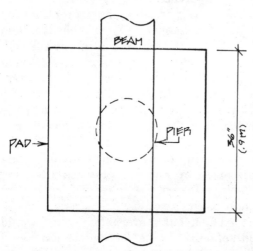

Figure 8.2 Underpinning: typical design of spread footing.

tially in compression, utilizing the principal strength of concrete, its design features are not as critical as those for the footings.

As previously stated the spread footing should be located at a depth sufficient to be relatively independent of soil moisture variations due to climate conditions. In the United States this depth is reportedly in the range of 2 to 3.5 ft (0.6 to 1.1 m) (Ref. 2, Chap. 1 Appendix and Ref. 3, Chap. 9). In Australia the depth is considered to be about 4 ft (1.25 m) (Ref. 3, Chap. 1 Appendix). Proper soil moisture maintenance will help ensure the stability of the footing.

An alternative to the spread footing is the pier or piling. Generally, the piers or pilings depend upon endbearing and skin friction (except in high-clay soils) for their support capacity. Piers or pilings are normally extended through the marginal soils to either rock or other competent bearing strata. This obviously enhances and satisfies the support requirement. The use of piers or pilings, however, is generally restricted to instances in which adequate bearing materials can be found at reasonably shallow depths. When that is possible, the installation of the piers or pilings is sometimes less costly than the spread footing. Generally speaking, for residential repairs, a competent stratum depth below 10 to 15 ft (3 to 4.5 m) resists the use of the pier or piling technique.

On occasion, the piers or pilings are used in conjunction with the spread footing (haunch). Here the theory is to utilize the best support features of each design in the hope of achieving a synergistic effect. In practice, the goal is not normally attained. When soil conditions dictate the spread footing, the pier provides little, if any, added benefit. However, the integration of the deep pier as part of the spread footing has no deleterious features, provided the cross-sectional area of the footing is not diminished and the pier does not penetrate a highly expansive substratum which has some access to water. Along these lines, consider Fig. 8.3. Water in contact with the CH clay at a 5- to 7½-ft (1.5- to 2.3-m) depth could cause the pier to heave, whereas the spread footing would be stable.[3] Certain steps have been taken to avoid or minimize friction (upheaval) in the design of shallow piers. These efforts include (1) the "needle" or "slim" pier (reduced surface area), (2) belling the pier bottoms (usually effective only with conventional-diameter shafts), and (3) placing a friction reducing membrane between the pier and the sidewall of the hole.

Regardless of the type of support, two precautions must be exercised. First, no exposed steel or wood should be utilized below grade either as shim or pier materials. Second, the pier should be poured in place to ensure intimate contact between the pier and the irregular bottom of the perimeter beam. In the first instance, the exposure to the soil and water will corrode the steel and rot the wood within an unusually short period of time. In the latter instance, flat surfaces in contact with the irregular bottom surface of the beam will result in either immediate damage to the concrete beam or subsequent resettlement due to the same effect over a period of time, e.g., crushing of concrete protrusions.

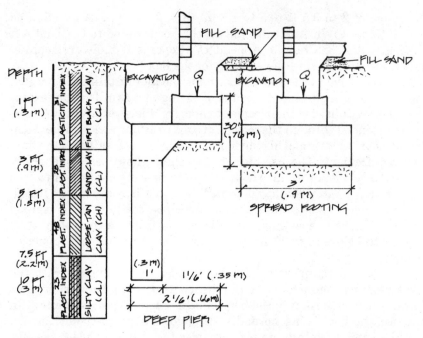

Figure 8.3 The deep pier alternative to the spread footing method of foundation repair.

Also bear in mind that none of the underpinning techniques attempt to "fix" the foundation to prevent upward movement. This is by design to avoid subsequent, uncontrolled damage to the foundation and emphasizes the fact that, if shallow, expansive soils are subjected to sufficient water, the soil expansion will raise the foundation off the supports.

8.2.2 Interior floor shimming—
pier-and-beam foundations

For practical purposes, the residence interior is leveled by shimming on existing pier caps. This shimming will not guarantee against future recurrence of interior settlement, since the true problem has not been addressed. However, reshimming is relatively inexpensive, and the rate of settlement decreases with time because the bearing soil beneath the pier is being continually compacted. True correction of the problem would normally require the installation of new piers and pier caps, at considerable expense, since the flooring and perhaps even the wall partitions would need to be removed to provide clearance for drilling.

In some instances, existing interior pier supports are unacceptable. This could relate either to concrete piers which, for one reason or an-

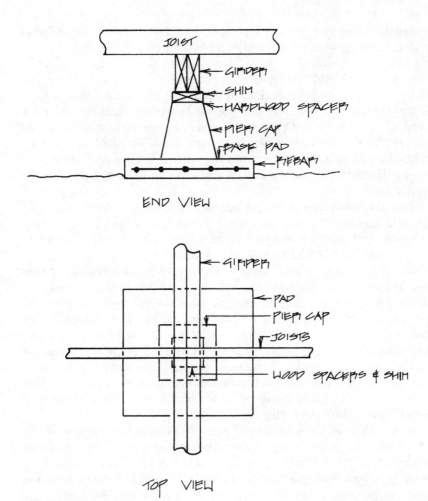

Figure 8.4 Typical interior pier cap.

other, have lost their structural competency, or to deficient wood piers. In either event, a proven method has been to construct new "surface" piers or pier caps. Again, the ideal solution would be the installation of new piers drilled into a competent bearing stratum. As noted earlier, this approach is prohibitively expensive for existing structures. Hence, the usual approach is to provide pier caps supported essentially on the surface soil. The best compromise has been a design represented by Fig. 8.4.

The support depicted in Fig. 8.4 involves a concrete base pad, a concrete pier cap, suitable hardwood spacers, and a tapered shim for final adjustment. The base pad can be either poured in place or precast. The choice and size depend on the anticipated load. For single-story frame construction, the pad can be precast, at least 18 by 18 by 4 in (46 by 46 by 10 cm) thick, with or without steel reinforcing.

In single-story and normal two-story brick construction load conditions, the pad should be steel-reinforced and at least 24 by 24 by 4 in (61 by 61 by 10 cm) thick. For unusually heavy load areas, e.g., a multiple-story stairwell, the pad should be larger, thicker, and reinforced with more steel. In the latter case, the pad is normally poured in place. (The added weight creates severe handling problems.) In any event, the pad is leveled on or into the soil surface to produce a solid bearing. Conditions rarely warrant any attempt to place the pads materially below grade.

When the structure is supported on wood piers and/or wood stiff-legs, it is also rarely justified to replace only a portion of the wood supports with the superior concrete design. Normally, it would represent little, if any, benefit and be a waste of money.

Once the pad is prepared, the pier cap can be poured in place or precast; in most cases, the limited work space demands the precast cap. Figure 8.4 shows one precast design. Alternatives to the precast design include cylinders, hadite blocks, and square blocks. (Ideally, the head of the pier cap should be as wide as the girder to be supported.) Either material is acceptable for selected loads. The hadite blocks, for example, are occasionally inadequate for multiple-story concentrated loads unless the voids within the blocks are filled with concrete. The precast concrete can be designed to support a load comparable with that of a poured-in-place pier cap.

The wood spacers are hardwood and are of suitable size and thickness to fill most of the space or gap between the pier cap and girder to be supported. When the pier cap head is not as wide as the supported girder, the hardwood spacers should be. If the grain of the wood in the spacer is perpendicular to the plane of the girder, the width and length can be the same. If the wood blocking is placed with the grain in line with the beam, the length should be at least twice the width. The final leveling is accomplished by the thin shim or wedge (usually a shingle). The combined thickness of the shims should normally not exceed 7/8 in (2.2 cm).

8.3   Slab Foundation Mudjacking

8.3.1   Upheaval

Upheaval of a slab foundation presents the most serious restoration problem. If the upward movement is pronounced, the only true cure is to break out the slab, excavate the affected base to proper grade, prepare the base, and repour the slab section. If the movement is nomi-

Figure 8.5   Mudjacking equipment.

nal, the lowermost slab areas can be raised to the grade of the heaved section. This operation is extremely touchy, since the grade of the entire structure is being altered. At the same time, particular care must be exercised not to aggravate the heaved area. The leveling is accomplished by what is termed mudjacking, often in conjunction with the supplementary use of spread footings as described above.

Mudjacking is a process whereby a water and soil-cement or soil-lime-cement grout is pumped beneath the slab, under pressure, to produce a lifting force which literally floats the slab to the desired position.[4,5] Figure 8.5 depicts the normal equipment required to mix and pump the grout. The grout is introduced through small holes drilled through the concrete. Figure 8.6 illustrates the mudjacking process through an exterior beam.

Mudjacking has the attendant feature of some chemical stabilization of the soil, which helps preclude future differential movement produced by soil/moisture variations (previously discussed as a preventive treatment).

8.3.2   Settlement

Slab settlement repair is a relatively straightforward problem. Here the lower sections are merely raised to meet the original grade and thus completely and truly restoring the foundation. The raising is accomplished by the mudjack method as described above. In some instances when concentrated loads are located on an outside beam, the mudjacking may again be augmented by mechanical jacking (installation of spread footings or other underpinning). In no instance should

Figure 8.6 Mudjacking a slab. (A) Mudjack hole through a perimeter beam. Pump hose in foreground. (B) Mudjacking through a beam. Top of shovel monitors the raise. (C) Mudjacking an interior slab. (D) Mudjacking an exterior patio.

an attempt be made to level a slab foundation by mechanical means alone.

Rather than provide support (and stabilize the subsoil) mechanical raising creates voids which, if neglected, may ultimately cause more problems than originally existed. As a rule, foundation slabs are not designed as structural bridging members and should not exist unsupported. (Mechanical techniques normally make no contribution toward correcting interior slab settlement.) Raising the slab beam me-

A

B

Figure 8.7   Mudjacking. (A) Before: The floor is separated from the wall partition by about 4 in (10 cm). (B) After: The separation is closed.

chanically and backfilling with grout represents a certain improvement over mechanical methods alone but still leaves much to be desired. This method loses the benefits of pressure injection normally associated with the true mudjack method. In other words, the voids are not adequately filled, which thus prompts resettlement.

C

D

Figure 8.7 (C) Before: Approximately 2-in (5-cm) separation of brick veneer from door frame and 2-in (5-cm) crack in mortar. (D) After: Cracks and separation are closed.

Figure 8.7 illustrates the effect of leveling. In this particular instance, the foundation was of slab design and was leveled by mudjacking. In A, the separation under the wall partition, an indication of foundation distress, is obvious; in B, the separation is closed, illustrating that the movement has been reversed or corrected. In this particular example, the leveling operation produced nearly perfect restoration. This is not always the case, as discussed in various chapters in this book.

8.4 Perma-Jack and Variations

In 1976, a patented process to correct failed foundations was introduced. This technique, labeled Perma-Jack,[6] utilizes a hydraulic ram to drive slip-jointed sections of 3-in- (7.5-cm-) diameter, 3-ft- (0.9-m-) long steel pipe supposedly to rock or suitable bearing. When a solid base or other resistance is reached, continued exertion of the hydraulic ram will raise the foundation. Once at grade, the pipe is pinned through the jack bracket to hold the foundation in place. The jack brackets can be positioned from the interior (Fig. 8.8) or exterior. In the case of slab foundations, the void beneath the slab must then be filled by mudjacking.

The Perma-Jack (or similar) process is more expensive than conventional methods and in most areas has not seemed to provide comparable results. It would appear that the technique might have some use to the foundation repair contractor in areas where the more conventional methods demonstrate inadequacy. Two basic problems with the technique are the uncertainty of alignment and the imminent corrosion of the steel pipe exposed to the wet soil. Refer to Fig. 8.8 and Sec. 8.10.3. Note that none of the underpinning techniques prevent the foundation from raising off the support.

In several alternatives the slip joints are replaced by threaded or welded (usually with epoxy) couplings. One variation is to fill the driven pipe with concrete. This provides little, if any, improvement.[7] Another technique is to drill the pier holes, case them (if necessary), and place steel reinforcing and concrete. This approach would offer the advantages of both a properly aligned pier and elimination of the corrosion concern, but it could introduce the more serious problem of pier uplift. With slim piers, this threat is reduced. Another technique sometimes used to reduce upheaval is to sleeve the uppermost several feet of the hole with a so-called friction reducer, such as cardboard or polyethylene. Belling the pier shaft is most often the best preventive against heave. Refer to Sec. A.5.3 for more detailed information.

The experimental Brown post-tension pier may represent the best alternative as a support pier. Each of the design improvement parameters suggested in the preceding paragraph can be incorporated into the design. The major novel innovation rests in the post-tension ben-

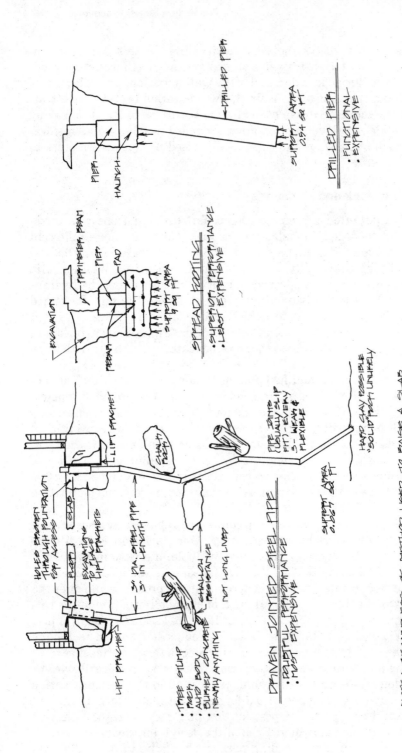

Driven Jointed Steel Pipe

- HOLES BROKEN THROUGH FOUNDATION FOR ACCESS
- LIFT BRACKET
- RAISE SLAB
- TREE STUMP
- ROCK
- AUTO BODY
- BURIED CONCRETE
- NEARLY ANYTHING
- EXCAVATION TO PLACE LIFT BRACKETS
- 2" DIA. STEEL PIPE 3' IN LENGTH
- CHALK PIER
- SHALLOW RESISTANCE
- NOT VERY LONG
- PIPE JOINTS USUALLY SLIP FIT — EVERY 3' — WEAK & FLEXIBLE
- HARD CLAY POSSIBLE "SOLID" PUSH UNLIKELY
- SUPPORT AREA 0.024 SQ FT
- LIFT BRACKETS

DRIVEN JOINTED STEEL PIPE
- DOUBTFUL PERFORMANCE
- MOST EXPENSIVE

Spread Footing

- PERIMETER BEAM
- PIER
- PAD
- BEAM
- PIER
- EXCAVATION
- SUPPORT AREA 4 SQ FT

SPREAD FOOTING
- SUPERIOR PERFORMANCE
- LEAST EXPENSIVE

Drilled Pier

- PIER
- HAUNCH
- DRILLED PIER
- SUPPORT AREA 0.54 SQ FT

DRILLED PIER
- FUNCTIONAL
- EXPENSIVE

NOTE: REGARDLESS OF METHOD USED TO RAISE A SLAB FOUNDATION THE VOIDS CREATED MUST BE FILLED IN ORDER TO RESTORE THE BEARING SUPPORT.

Figure 8.8 Comparison of underpinning techniques. Regardless of the method used to raise a slab foundation, the voids created must be filled to restore the bearing support.

efits (Fig. 8.9). The post-tension pier offers the added benefit of not being subject to franchise, royalty, or related fees, which contribute to
the inordinate cost of the other, similar methods. The pier can be utilized in new construction as well as in remedial procedures. In new
construction, the haunch would be replaced by the perimeter beam or
pier cap. Cost, difficult installations, and alternative possibilities may
preclude wide acceptance and use of this method.

"Pod" piers beneath spread footings represent yet another variation.
Shallow piers, on a bipod or tripod pattern, are installed beneath the
pads used with the conventional spread footings (Fig. 8.2). As a rule,
the piers are of 6- to 8-in (15- to 20-cm) diameter and 3 to 6 ft (0.9 to
1.8 m) deep. This technique was carefully evaluated in the mid- to late
1960s and discarded. Field tests indicated that the inclusion of the
shallow piers added nothing to the stability of the pads (conventional
spread footing).

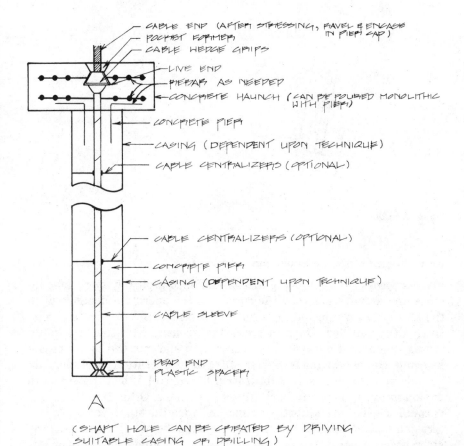

Figure 8.9 Post-tension pier.

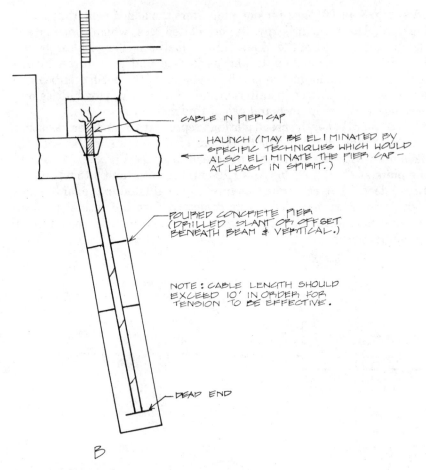

CABLE IN PIER CAP

HAUNCH (MAY BE ELIMINATED BY SPECIFIC TECHNIQUES WHICH WOULD ALSO ELIMINATE THE PIER CAP — AT LEAST IN SPIRIT.)

POURED CONCRETE PIER (DRILLED SLANT OR OFFSET BENEATH BEAM & VERTICAL.)

NOTE: CABLE LENGTH SHOULD EXCEED 10' IN ORDER FOR TENSION TO BE EFFECTIVE.

DEAD END

B

Figure 8.9 *Continued*

8.4.1 Deep grouting: introduction

For purposes of the following discussion, deep-grouting operations include any activity whereby the success of the operation depends upon the ability of an injected material to penetrate and permeate a relatively deep soil bed. Once in place, the grout must either set into a strong, competent mass or intersperse with and into the soil to create a strong, competent mass. Specifically, these operations include: subgrade waterproofing, soil stabilization for control of bearing strength or sloughing, and certain back-filling operations. Often this technique is coupled with mechanical leveling or hydraulic stabilization to correct foundation problems originating deep below the soil surface. Upon occasion, grouting is used to "freeze in" foundation piers or stabilize fill beneath foundations.

For optimum penetration, the consistency (viscosity) of the invading grout should be controlled. For maximum penetration, the consistency should be minimal. In other cases it may be desirable to restrict penetration by increasing the consistency. In the latter case, it is normally sufficient to merely decrease the water-to-solids ratio; in the former, the solution is not so simple. Although grout consistency can be decreased by increasing the water-to-solids ratio, this approach is highly restrictive because increasing the water content will drastically reduce the compressive strength of the set grout and the additional water will create severe handling problems brought about by separation between solids and liquid during transportation (pumping).

It is apparent that, as far as reduced consistency is concerned, another control method might be considered. Several additives suitable for this purpose were discussed in *Residential Foundations: Design, Behavior and Repair*, 2d ed. Grout consistency is approximated in the field by timing a measured volume to flow from a cone or funnel. Refer to U.S. Corp of Engineers CRD-C 611—Flow Cone Method for Grout Consistency.

8.4.2 Mechanics of grouting applications

The specific mechanics required for a grouting operation depend entirely upon the type of operation involved. For certain kinds of grouting it is necessary to form a continuous consolidated boundary or area of sufficient strength, often referred to as a grout curtain, to permit excavation or provide adequate bearing strength. The hole pattern used to introduce the grout will depend upon the particular problem, and each project should be carefully designed and engineered.

In general, however, the fewer the holes and the wider the spacing, the more economical the operation. For the operation to be practical, the grout must flow efficiently, once again pointing out the need for a consistency control. Along these same lines, the diameter of the grout injection pipes is influenced by the grout consistency as well as the rate of grout placement.

8.4.3 Placement of injection pipes

The placement of the grout injection pipes can be either quite simple or quite complicated. The easiest solution is to either drive or push the pipes to depth. Pneumatic paving breakers equipped with a drive head are used to drive the pipes. Front-end loaders, forklifts or the equivalent, can often be used to drive the pipes. In either case, care must be taken to keep the pipes from being plugged during placement.

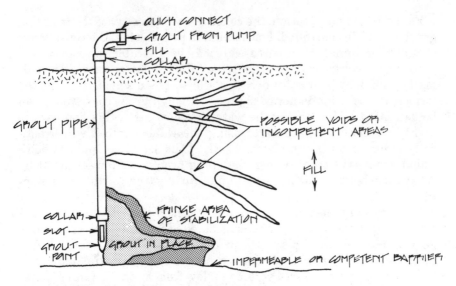

Figure 8.10 Pressure grouting to consolidate fill.

More often than not, the side-slotted design shown in Fig. 8.10 is adequate. Any intruding soil or foreign materials can often be either blown out with air or washed out with water. Another approach would be the use of a pointed drive cap or plug which is loose fitting and is removed by injection pressure or pulling the pipe upward slightly. In either event, the cap or plug is left in the hole.

The more complicated (and expensive) alternative requires drilling the holes, with or without casing. In this technique, the injection pipes normally require some method of packing off or sealing the annular space between the grout injection pipe and the casing or wall of the hole as the case may be. A spin-off to this approach is so-called jet grouting. In this technique grout slurry is pumped through a small-diameter drill pipe and forced laterally through small-diameter orifices or ports. The high-velocity grout impacts the soil matrix. The pipe is rotated and withdrawn slowly to create an enlarged-diameter column of grout and grouted soil. Pump pressures are often in the range of 4000 lb/in^2 (280 kg/cm^2). The withdrawal rate is on the order of 1 ft/min (0.3 m/min), and the grout composition is often a 1:1 mix of cement and water.

Figure 8.11 illustrates pressure grouting in progress. The pipe to the left in the figure is being pumped. The pipe at right has been set and is ready. The air hammer, lower right, is fitted with the pipe driving head used to set pipes.

Figure 8.11   Pressure grouting in progress.

8.5   Subgrade Waterproofing

Since the processes of deep grouting are more common to repair procedures for commercial foundations, the following presentation will be brief and limited to the applications most likely to involve residential foundations. One example of deep grouting would be waterproofing subgrade basements and foundation walls. Another example would be deep grouting to fill voids and increase bearing qualities of deep fills—particularly organic fills.

Waterproofing subgrade walls is a rather routine, straightforward operation. The real difficulty lies in the fact that the stoppage of water intrusion at one point often results in the reappearance of water at unpredictable new locations. Technically, subgrade waterproofing is not materially different from regular mudjacking, the differences being that, in subgrade waterproofing, (1) rather than pumping through a floor slab the grout is injected through the walls, (2) working or injection pressures are higher, and (3) the grout composition is often modified, principally by increasing the cement content. Since each situation is different, the appropriate repair technique must be designed for the specific problem.

The results obtained from this process are generally satisfactory. Upon occasion, as noted above, the intrusion of water may reappear at a new location or the water flow may be reduced to an intolerable seepage. In either instance, the grouting operation is normally repeated. From cases within the author's personal knowledge, the initial procedure was successful in over 80 percent of the cases. Less than 5 percent of the cases required a third application, and none required a fourth. Success varies directly with technique, nature of the water problem, and, on occasion, the particular job or site conditions.

8.6 Soil Consolidation

Consolidation of deep fill by pressure grouting represents a more involved operation. The grout must be placed to fill voids as well as permeate the soil matrix to a sufficient extent to develop the desired bearing strength of the fill segment. The quality and nature of the fill material dictate the grout composition. Often a cement grout, with or without chemical additives, is acceptable. In any event, the selected grout is mixed and pumped into the target soil. Generally the placement commences at the lowermost elevation and proceeds upward to the surface or to some predetermined level. Consistent with this, the grout pipe is placed at the bottom of the zone to be grouted and progressively raised in lifts to accommodate the upper levels.

Pumping normally continues at each level until either some selected resistance pressure is encountered or undesired movement is detected at the surface. Figure 8.11 shows a typical pressure-grouting operation. The represented "void areas" are not meant to imply that either voids or incompetent sections follow any defined pattern. The grout placed alternately may develop into a "bulb" configuration around the grout pipe with little or no penetration into the soil. This might well be satisfactory, provided the placement pressure is sufficiently high to cause either mechanical consolidation of the surrounding fill or the grout permeates and penetrates the matrix soil to the extent that sufficient "cementitious" consolidation occurs.

The so-called fringe area of stabilization (Fig. 8.10) may or may not occur, depending on the particular properties of the specific grout. Generally, the aqueous phase of the grout is responsible for this benefit, which often results in a significant improvement to the competency of the soil matrix.

On occasion, stage grouting is required to provide the desired results. Here the grouting operation is merely repeated until acceptable consolidation is achieved. Generally, no more than two to three stages are required within a given area to produce the desired results.

8.7 Special Problems which Adversely Affect Leveling

This section will touch on the inherent problems which impede the intended foundation leveling or some related operation. In most cases, specific and marked improvement of the condition is experienced although the overall results might be less than desired. Factors to be considered include upheaval, warped wood members, and various construction or "as-built" conditions.

8.7.1 Upheaval

As noted in preceding chapters, upheaval is the condition in which some area of the foundation is forced above the original grade. Upheaval is caused by water accumulation and subsequent swell of the clay soil, which exerts an upward force on the foundation. When this condition occurs, it is rare that the foundation can be completely restored to a level condition. As a rule, the lowermost surrounding areas are raised to approximate or "feather" the heaved crown, and the foundation is then stabilized to prevent future distress. This is normally acceptable as far as utilization is concerned.

8.7.2 Warped substructures

Warped wood members are another antagonist to foundation leveling. This problem normally involves pier-and-beam construction, but it can also include slab construction where the floors are laid on a wood screed system. In either event, a wood member warps into an arc because of the externally applied stress caused by differential movement in the foundation. In the stressed condition, the wood is in tension and thus is often tight against the foundation supports. When the extremities (ends) of the wood are raised in the leveling attempt, the stress may be relieved but the member retains the warped or distorted state; see Fig. 8.12. The floor surfaces at points A and B are level after the raising operation, but the midsection at C is above the desired grade.

From a foundation repair standpoint, nothing further can be done to improve the situation. Often, given time, the wood will "relax" and the crown will depress to approximate normal. In an effort to encourage this event (hopefully) appropriate space is left above the shim at point C. In cases of slab construction with wood screed, the analogy is identical except that the screed rather than the girder is warped.

8.7.3 Construction interferences

Often, specific conditions of construction will restrict or prevent the desired foundation repair results. A few specific examples will be discussed in the following paragraphs.

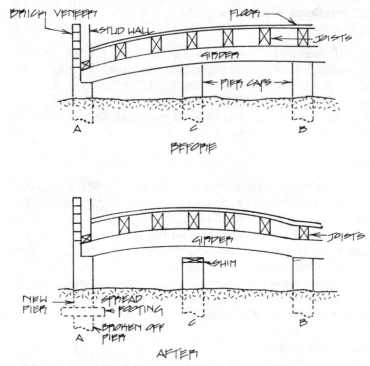

Figure 8.12   Warped substructures before and after foundation repair.

8.7.3.1 Add-on or remodeling without correcting preexisting foundation distress.   In one situation that often exists an add-on is constructed abutting an existing structure which has had previous and has ongoing differential movement. In time, the condition progresses to the extent that foundation leveling is desired. With pier-and-beam construction, the only technique is to underpin (mechanically raise) the affected beam section. To accomplish this, proper access must be provided. Generally, this would require tearing out floor sections in either the add-on or the original structure and doing the work from within. Obviously this would be quite expensive. For slab construction, the problem area might be restored to an intermediate grade by mudjacking inside the original structure. Generally this is not a serious problem, when applicable, and the results are satisfactory.

In either event, slab or pier and beam, the original structure is restored to that grade or to the level existing when the add-on was constructed, though not necessarily to level. To attain a nearly true level would require raising the entire add-on to proper established grade consistent with the original structure. Again this approach would involve considerable expense and generally the results would not justify or warrant the cost.

Remodeling operations can create a similar problem. Suppose a wall partition is added in an area where the floor is not level. If the partition is built rigid, one of two things will occur; either some wall studs will be longer than others or one or both plates will be shimmed. Leveling the floor will then push the "longer" stud area through the ceiling. If this condition is intolerable, the leveling must be curtailed short of the desired results. (The *plates* are wood members placed horizontally at each end of the studs. The ceiling plate forms the top header and the floor or sole plate the bottom. See Fig. 5.1 for an example.)

8.7.3.2 Creation of new distress. Most structures are not initially constructed perfectly level. Any attempt to correct an as-built problem will result in the creation of new distress. For that reason, a foundation is normally raised to a level appearance rather than a true level. Even then, some compromise is often required to equate the degree of levelness with practical job conditions. For example, if a leveling operation intended to close a ¼-in (0.6-cm) crack develops an offsetting ½-in (1.27-cm) crack, nothing is being gained and a decision or compromise must be made. Usually all attempts to raise are stopped.

The same thing is true in the instance of offsetting doors. Assume two doors are opening in opposite directions, either on 180° or 90° planes. If door A is plumb and door B is not, little or nothing constructive can be gained by attempting to level door B. Efforts to improve door B will most often cause an equivalent offsetting movement to door A.

Occasionally an upper floor will develop a sag in an area not directly supported by the lower floor or foundation. Since there is no vertical connection between the problem area and the lower floor, foundation leveling will neither affect nor improve the sag. One solution has been to install wood beams across the lower floor ceiling, properly anchored, to raise and support the area. Alternatively, where practical, columns might be installed to provide the support and/or to provide contact with the foundation. This latter solution is often not acceptable, particularly in residential construction. The columns would be obstructive to movement and generally unsightly.

8.7.3.3 Incompetent foundations. The competency of the foundation materials is sometimes below standard and hence prevents or deters proper foundation repairs. Generally, this condition involves older concrete foundations either poured with faulty concrete or deteriorated by unusual chemical or weather attack. In other instances, the problem might involve rotted or deficient wood. If the foundation will not withstand the stress required for leveling, little can be accomplished.

In some marginal conditions, long steel plates can be placed under the foundation member to distribute the load and facilitate leveling. This process is relatively expensive and does not replace the deficient materials. Faulty wood can generally be replaced economically if proper access or work space is available. Replacing faulty concrete is generally quite expensive and, since older properties are most often involved, not economically feasible.

8.7.3.4 Interior fireplaces. When interior fireplaces settle, expensive problems also develop. Even with slab foundations, the usual repair technique requires the installation of spread footings (typical) and mechanical raising. Access then becomes a serious and costly obstacle. If the movement is not substantial, an acceptable approach is to either cut the surrounding areas loose from the fireplace and level the floors by normal shimming operation (pier-and-beam foundations) or, in the case of slabs, stabilize the foundation to, hopefully, prevent future progressive movement.

8.7.3.5 Crossbeams, interior piers, and intensive loads (slabs). In slab construction, the condition that sometimes develops is a problem area that involves a stiffened slab (crossbeams) or intensified load offset by a normal slab floor section. An attempt to raise the weighted area by mudjacking would risk crowning the weaker slab. In this instance, hydraulic leveling attempts (mudjacking) must be avoided to protect the remaining slab. The alternative would be to break out the adjacent slab for access and mechanically underpin the problem area. As a rule, this is not advisable from both a cost and a structural viewpoint. The identical problem is encountered where interior piers (belled or otherwise) are tied into the slab. Again, the general selection would be to level to a practical extent and stabilize to prevent future, progressive movement.

8.7.3.6 Lateral movement. Under certain conditions, one foundation member may move laterally with respect to another. Specific examples are a patio slab moving away from the perimeter beam and a perimeter beam moving horizontally from an interior floor. In either instance, the problem member can be raised vertically quite easily; however, it is altogether another problem to move that structure laterally to restore the original position. As a rule, that is beyond reasonable expectation. Prevention is therefore the best solution.

There are other conditions which interfere with proper or desired foundation leveling, but those presented in the preceding sections are the most common.

8.8 Review of Repair Longevity

For a comprehensive evaluation of the relative success of foundation repairs, refer to Table 8.2. The data were collected from repair records compiled essentially from Dallas, Texas.[3,8] However, similar results could be anticipated from any area if one assumes competent repair procedures were utilized. These data do include random results from Louisiana, Arkansas, Mississippi, Florida, and virtually all of Texas. No form of soil stabilization was incorporated in the example repairs.

Table 8.2 also emphasizes the relative occurrence of upheaval versus settlement as a reason for redo. Also, it is obvious that the redo rate is quite favorable, with an overall success ratio of better than 90 percent (upheaval and settlement combined). These data do not distinguish between slab and pier-and-beam foundations. However, overall, the ratio of slab repairs to pier-and-beam repairs was about 3:1. In recent times, when the so-called deep piers rather than spread footings have been used, the relative success does not appear to be nearly so impressive.[3]

For our purposes, the term "redo" refers to any rework of the foundation during the initial warranty period, usually 12 months. It might be interesting to note, however, that less than 1 percent of the foundations repaired developed recurrent problems after a year. At this point, a careful analysis of the data presented in Table 8.2 is in order.

At the time the 1964–1969 data were compiled, the slab repairs were performed by mudjacking alone—spread footings (or piers) were not utilized to supplement the raising. Further, the prevalence of upheaval was not fully recognized. The 1977–1979 data cover a span containing an inordinately wet cycle. In fact, the period of December 1977 through about May 1978 represented one of the wettest periods re-

TABLE 8.2 Relative Success of Foundation Repairs

Success of foundation repairs			Cause of failure		
Test period	Number of jobs	Total redos*	Upheaval	Settlement	Indeterminate
1/82–6/82	166	7 (4.2%)	6 (3.6%)	1 (0.4%)	—
1981	336	29 (8.6%)	23 (6.8%)	6 (1.7%)	—
1980	302	36 (11.9%)	22 (7.2%)	14 (4.6%)	—
Totals	804	72 (8.9%)	51 (6.3%)	21 (2.7%)	
12/78–12/79	243	20 (8.2%)	12 (4.0%)	5 (2.0%)	3
12/77–12/78	291	32 (10.9%)	18 (6.2%)	8 (2.7%)	6
Totals	534	52 (9.7%)	30 (5.6%)	13 (2.4%)	9
7/64–1/69	380	18 (4.7%)	4 (1.1%)	4 (1.1%)	10

*Excludes simple reshim of pier-and-beam interior floors.

corded in Texas history. The heavy precipitation gave rise to an unusually high proportion of redos, particularly upheaval. Along these
lines, the overall redo rate expressed for this period is 9.7 as compared
to 4.7 percent for the earlier period, a nearly twofold difference. Further, the relative rates of recurrent settlement vary by about the same
ratio, 2.4 versus 1.1 percent.

The significant variation involves the reported comparative incidence of recurrent upheaval, namely 5.6 versus 1.1 percent. This dis-
proportionate difference is likely due to the following facts: (1) up to
the 1970s, foundation repair contractors were not properly aware of
the tendencies toward upheaval and probably mislabeled some of the
causes and (2) the 1977–1979 data were accumulated during a cycle of
excessive and unusual moisture, which prompted increases in upheaval. The third set of data, previously unpublished, covers the 30-
month period immediately prior to July 1, 1982. Again the influence
of climatic conditions is clearly reflected. The 1980 data show the results of a record July heat wave following the extremely wet years
1978 and 1979.

The year 1981 was again a near-record wet year following the unusually dry 1980. The first 6 months of 1982 represent a "return to
normal" trend. The data in Table 8.2 were developed by two separate
firms, the 1964–1969 data by one and the other two sets by another.
Still, all factors considered, there is amazing consistency. Regrettably,
efforts to get reliable data from other sources were unsuccessful.

The incidence of upheaval, as opposed to settlement, as a cause for
redo is at the ratio of a little over 2:1. At least 50 percent and perhaps
as many as 75 percent of the redo cases were brought about by the
refusal of the owner to properly care for or maintain the property.
Along these lines, refer to Chap. 9. Under normal climatic conditions,
the anticipated chance for any type of redo should be about 4 out of
100 jobs performed (96 percent success). This obviously assumes current U.S. construction practices and excludes the use of competent soil
stabilization which should reduce the incidence of failure even further. Since upheaval is caused by excessive accumulation of water beneath the foundation, any measures that prevent the accumulation
will minimize the chance for redo. For that matter, the same precautions will help avoid the initial problem as well.

8.9 Conclusions

Based on the foregoing, it is apparent that

1. Foundation repairs tend to principally protect against recurrent
   settlement.

2. Recurrent upheaval is a concern with slab foundations unless

proper maintenance procedures are instituted concurrent with or prior to proper foundation repairs.

3. Spread footings are equal or superior to "deep" piers as a safeguard against resettlement.

4. Deep piers may, in some instances, be conducive to upheaval.

5. Upheaval accounts for more foundation failures than settlement.

6. Moisture changes which influence the foundation occur within relatively shallow depths.

7. The effects of upheaval distress occur more rapidly and to a greater potential extent than do those of settlement.

8. The cause of foundation problems must be diagnosed and eliminated if recurrent distress is to be avoided.

9. Weather influences foundation behavior.

8.10   References

1. K. A. Gutschick, "Some Market Development, Success," Presentation at National Lime Association Convention, Dorado Beach, Puerto Rico, April 26, 1967.
2. K. A. Gutschick, "Lime Stabilize Poor Soils," *Concrete Construction*, May 1967.
3. R. W. Brown and C. H. Smith, Jr., "The Effects of Soil Moisture on the Behavior of Residential Foundations in Active Soil." *Texas Contractor*, May 1, 1980.
4. R. W. Brown, "A Series on Stabilization of Soils by Pressure Grouting," *Texas Contractor*, pt. 1A, January 19, 1965; pt. 1B, February 2, 1965; pt. 2B, March 16, 1965.
5. R. W. Brown, "Concrete Foundation Failures," *Concrete Construction*, March 1968.
6. G. F. Langenbach, "Apparatus for a Method of Shoring a Foundation," Patent No. 3,902,326, September 2, 1975.
7. T. Petry, Foundation Seminar, UTA, May 20, 1983.
8. R. W. Brown, "A Field Evaluation of Current Foundation Design vs. Failure," *Texas Contractor*, July 6, 1976.
9. P. Pettit and C. E. Wooden, "Jet Grouting: The Pace Quickens," *Civil Engineering*, August 1988.

8.11   Appendix—Interesting Examples of Repair Techniques

Two examples of interesting and unusual foundation repair exercises are described in the following sections.

8.11.1   Florida

This problem involved extreme subsidence brought about principally when the water level in an adjacent lake was lowered several feet. The bearing soil consisted of a top layer of silty sand, a midlayer of decayed organics (peat), and a base of coral sand.

The two-story, brick veneer dwelling suffered from differential foundation settlement reaching 6 in (15 cm) in magnitude. The objectives were to (1) underpin the perimeter beam to facilitate leveling (as well as provide future stability), (2) consolidate the peat stratum by pressure grouting to provide a solid base for the repaired structure, and (3) mudjack the entire foundation area to create a level or more nearly level structure. Figure 8.11 depicts the repair process.

First, excavations were made at strategic locations to provide the base for the spread footings (underpinning). Next, grout pipes were driven through the base of the excavations into the peat identified for consolidation. Steel-reinforced concrete was then poured into the excavations and allowed to cure. While the footing pads were curing, the entire slab was drilled for mudjacking and interior deep grouting. Deep grouting was then initiated, starting with the permanent grout pipes set through the footings and continuing to the interior.

At each site, grouting was continued either to refusal or start of an unwanted rise. Interior grout pipes were removed during the grout process. The permanent, exterior pipes were cleared of grout and capped. After the grout had set, the top section of the perimeter pipes was removed and capped below grade. Refer to Fig. 8.13. This procedure would permit regrouting at some future date should subsidence recur. Next, the perimeter beam was raised to desired grade and pinned by the installation of the poured concrete pier. The final step was to mudjack the entire foundation for the "fine grading."

Repairs were completely successful and have remained so for over 8 years. Prior to the work, the dwelling could be neither inhabited nor sold.

8.11.2   London, England

The soil in the United Kingdom is not materially different from that found in parts of the United States. The plastic indices classically run in the range of 40 to 50 and the problem clay (montmorillonite) in the vicinity of 20 to 40 percent. The U.K. climate forces repair techniques to be somewhat specialized. The annual rainfall is not particularly high, only about 30 in/year (76 cm/year), but the rain is well distributed over the year (150 days), with seldom more than 2 in (5 cm) during one month. The Dallas Metroplex for example, will have about 30 in of rain per year, but perhaps 75 to 80 percent of the total will fall in less than 15 days. (The latter experiences something like 90 percent run-off.) Further, London's high temperatures are generally in the 70°F (21°C) range, whereas the Metroplex highs exceed 105°F (40.5°C). London's climate produces a high, fairly consistent, moisture content within the soil.

Often the soil moisture tends to persistently approach or exceed the

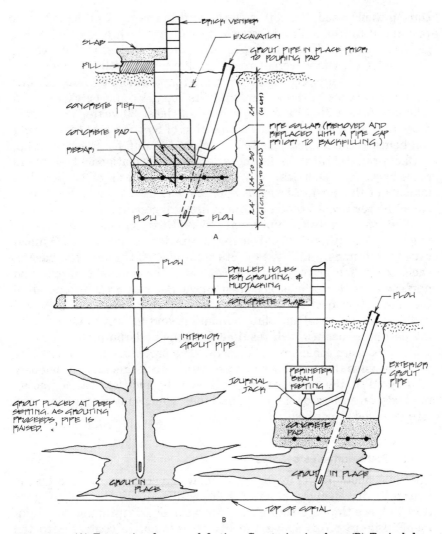

Figure 8.13 (A) Excavation for spread footing. Grout pipe in place. (B) Typical deep grouting procedure.

plastic limit PL, indicating little, if any, normal residual swell potential. [It is interesting to note that moisture contents taken from soil borings in close proximity to trees often show little if any, reduction in percent water between the depth of 1 m (3.3 ft) or so to perhaps 15 m (49 ft). Obviously, this indicates that, over the centuries, the soil has attained a level of unique balance.]

Occasionally a prolonged change in climate does come along which tends to temporarily disturb the balance, such as the drought of 1976.

During that period, the soil moisture within the top 2 m (6.6 ft) or so was significantly reduced, reportedly causing severe and extensive problems of subsidence. Later, upon return of the normal moisture, the problems became even more severe due to soil swell and upheaval.

The London projects involved restoring the foundations of four banks of garages to the extent that the repairs could be expected to alleviate future distress for a period of at least 20 years. The repair procedure included the pressure injection of Soil Sta into the bearing soil beneath the foundations to a depth of 1.8 m (6 ft). Refer to Chap. 6, Chemical Stabilization, for more detailed information on theory and procedures. The chemical was injected on the basis of ¼ gal/ft² (1 ml/cm²) of the surface treated. Soil Sta was used principally to preclude the recurrence of the effects of drought conditions such as those of 1976, specifically the upheaval phase. Next, spread footings were installed beneath the load-bearing perimeter to permit mechanical raising and underpinning. Soil Sta was injected through the base of each excavation prior to pouring concrete. The chemical volume and purpose were the same as specified above. See Fig. 5.11 for a detail of the foundation design. The final stage involved mudjacking to fill voids, raise and level the slab foundation, and fill any voids beneath the perimeter beam which resulted from the underpinning.

The jobs were considered successful. The procedure is substantially less expensive than methods of deep pilings or needle piers previously considered as the conventional approach. In addition, the foregoing methods cause less damage to the landscaping and are quicker and less involved to perform.

8.11.3 Piers—driven steel pipe

The field photographs in Fig. 8.13 show the steel pipe placed by the hydraulic driver and pinned by bolts within the lift bracket. Figure 8.14A shows the pipe slanted inward at over 30° (proving nonalignment). Figure 8.14B shows the lift bracket not in contact with the beam. (The settlement of the pipe could be the result of soil dilatency, clay bearing failure, or ultimate failure in whatever material or object the pier tip embedded.) The "shiny" spots on both pipes represent a prior attempt to adjust the pipes to re-raise the beam. Although Fig. 8.13 represents only one example, this type of performance appears to accompany the current driven steel pipe procedures.

It certainly seems safe to say that this nonperformance represents the rule rather than the exception within certain areas. Another problem, limited to slab foundations, has been the failure of contractors to follow the process with competent mudjacking of the slab. Since the slab is not designed to be a bridging member, the voids, already

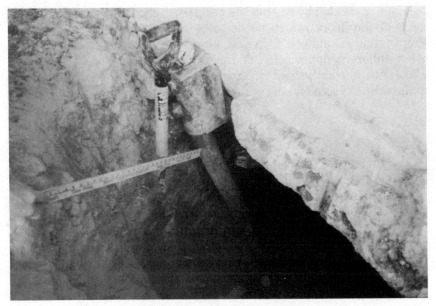

A

Figure 8.14 (A) Pipe slanted inward, proving nonalignment. (B) Lift bracket out of contact with the beam.

existant or created by raising the perimeter, encourage interior settlement of the floors, which needs to be circumvented by mudjacking. Proper mudjacking could, in fact, eliminate or minimize some of the other inherent deficiencies of the driven-pipe process. Mudjacking alone will normally hold a raised slab foundation, provided proper maintenance procedures are instituted and followed (Chap. 9).

9

Preventive Maintenance

9.1 Introduction

Preventing a problem is always more desirable than curing one. Certain maintenance procedures can help prevent or arrest foundation problems if initiated at the proper time and carried out diligently. The following are specific suggestions on how to encourage foundation stability.

9.2 Watering

In dry periods, summer or winter, water the soil adjacent to the foundation to help maintain a constant moisture. Proper watering is the key. Also, be sure drainage is away from the foundation prior to watering.

When cracks appear between the soil and the foundation, the soil moisture is low and watering is in order. On the other hand, water should not be allowed to stand in pools against the foundation. Watering should be uniform and preferably cover long areas at each setting, ideally 50 to 100 ft (15 to 30 m). *Too little moisture causes the soil to shrink* and the foundation to settle. *Too much water—an excessive moisture differential—causes the soil to swell* and heave the foundation.

Along these lines, never attempt to water the foundation with a root feeder or by placing a running garden hose adjacent to the beam. Sprinkler systems often create a sense of false security because the shrub heads, normally in close proximity to the perimeter beam, are set to spray away from the structure. The design can be altered to put water at the perimeter and thereby serve the purpose quite adequately. The use of a soaker hose is normally the best solution. From previous studies of infiltration and run-off, it became evident that watering must be close to the foundation, within 6 to 18 in (15 to 45 cm), and excessive watering can be prevented by proper grading around the foundation.

More sophisticated watering systems which utilize a subsurface weep hose with electrically activated control valves and automatic moisture monitoring and control devices are not available (Figs. 9.1 and 9.2). The multiple control devices are situated to afford adequate soil moisture control automatically and evenly around the foundation perimeter. Reportedly, the control can be set to limit moisture variations to plus or minus 1 percent. Within this tolerance, little if any, differential foundation movement would be expected in even the most volatile or expansive clay soils.

Avoid watering procedures which make outlandish claims; they can often cause more problems than they cure. One example is the so-called water or hydro pier. The claim is that a weep hose placed vertically into the soil beneath the perimeter beam on convenient centers (often 6 to 8 ft) (1.8 to 2.4 m) will develop a "pier" structure by virtue of expansion of the wetted clay soil. This system usually lacks water control in relation to in situ moisture content. This deficiency introduces several problems when dealing with expansive soils. First, moisture distribution within the soil is seldom, if ever, uniform. Second, a soil moisture content approaching the liquid limit (LL) can cause the heaving soil to *lose* strength. (Too much water presents a more serious consequence than does too little.) Third, although consis-

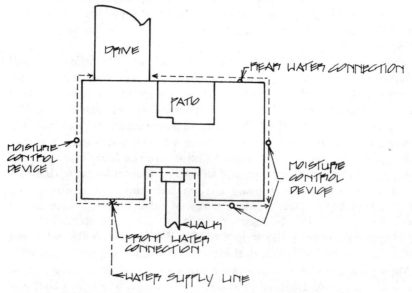

Figure 9.1 Schematic diagram for a system of watering around a perimeter beam.

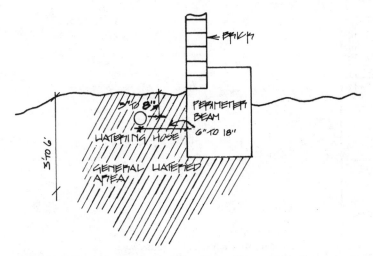

Figure 9.2 Typical watering hose location with respect to the perimeter beam.

tent moisture content in the expansive soil will normally prevent differential deflection of the foundation, the subject process (or processes) will not meet the requirements. And, fourth, water replenishment into an expansive soil will seldom, if ever, singularly accomplish any acceptable degree of "leveling." Minor settlement, limited in scope, might be the exception.

Where large plants or trees are located near the foundation, it could be advisable to water these as well, at least in areas with C_w factors below about 25 (Fig. 5.8). As far as foundation stability is concerned, the trees or plants most likely to require additional water are those which (1) are immature, (2) develop root systems which tend to remove water from shallow soils, and (3) are situated within a few feet of the foundation. See Chap. 1 and Sec. 9.4 for additional information.

9.3 Drainage

For the reasons noted above, it is important that the ground surface water drain away from the foundation. Where grade improvement is required, the fill should be a low-clay or clay-free soil. The slope of the fill need not be exaggerated but merely sufficient to cause the water to flow outward from the structure (Fig. 9.3). The surface of fill must be below the air vent for pier-and-beam foundations and below the brick ledge for slabs. Surface water, whether from rainfall or watering, should never be allowed to collect and stand in areas adjacent to the foundation wall. Consistent with this, guttering and proper discharge of downspouts is quite important. Flower bed curbing and planter

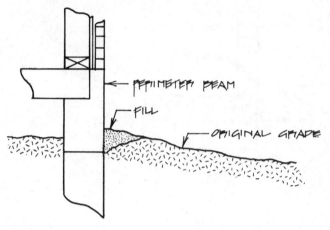

Figure 9.3   Correct drainage: Slope of fill is sufficient to cause water to flow outward.

boxes should drain freely and preclude trapped water at the perimeter. In essence, any procedure which controls and removes excess surface water is beneficial to foundation stability. (See also Chap. 2.)

9.3.1   French drains—subsurface water

French drains are required, upon occasion, when subsurface aquifers permit the migration of water beneath the foundation. When the foundation is supported by a volatile (high-clay) soil, this intrusion of unwanted water must be stopped. The installation of a French drain to intercept and divert the water is a useful approach. As shown in Fig. 2.4, the drain consists of a suitable ditch cut to some depth below the level of the intruding water. The lowermost part of the ditch is filled with gravel surrounding a perforated pipe. The top of the gravel is continued to at least above the water level and often to the surface.

Figure 9.4 illustrates the location of the French drain with respect to the foundation. Provisions are incorporated to remove the water from the drain either by a gravity pipe drain or a suitable pump system. Simply stated, the French drain creates a more permeable route for flow and carries the water to a safe disposal point. If the slope of the terrain is not sufficient to afford adequate drainage, the use of a catch basin/sump pump system is required. The subsurface water normally handled by the French drain is the perched ground water. On occasion, however the lateral flow from wet-weather springs or shallow aquifers is also accommodated.

Where the conditions warrant, the design of the drain can be modified to also drain excessive surface water. This is readily accom-

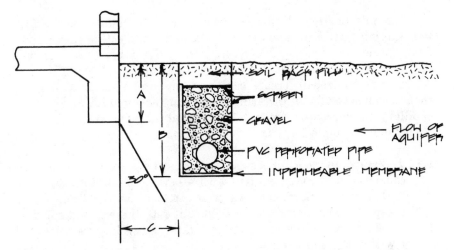

Figure 9.4 Typical French drain. Generally, C is equal to or greater than A and B is greater than A + 2 ft. The drain should be outside the soil-bearing surcharge area.

plished by either adding surface drains (risers) connected to the French drain system or carrying the gravel to the surface level. Water from downspouts should not be tied directly into the French drain; a separate pipe drain system is preferable. The second, solid pipe could, however, be placed in the French drain trench. A French drain is of little or no use in relieving water problems resulting from a spring within the confines of the foundation, since it is almost impossible to locate and tap a spring beneath a foundation. A proper drain intercepts and disposes of the water before it invades the foundation.

When a foundation problem exists before the installation of a French drain, foundation repairs also are often required. In that event, the repairs should be delayed to give ample time for the French drain to develop a condition of moisture equilibrium under the foundation. Otherwise, recurrent distress can be anticipated.

9.3.2 Water or capillary barriers

In an effort to maintain constant soil moisture, measures which impede the transfer of soil moisture can be taken. The barriers may be either horizontal or vertical.

9.3.2.1 Horizontal barriers.
Horizontal, impermeable barriers can be as simple as asphalt or concrete paving or polyethylene film. These materials are used to cover the soil surface adjacent to the foundation and inhibit evaporation. Coincidentally, the covers could also restrict soil moisture loss to transpiration, since vegetation can neither grow nor be cultivated in the protected area.

Permeable horizontal barriers usually consist of little more than landscaping gravel or granular fill placed on the soil surface previously graded for drainage. Moisture within the porous material cannot develop a surface tension and no adhesive forces exist, both of which are required to create capillary (or pore) pressures. Gravity then becomes the factor dictating free water movement. The granular capillary barrier shown beneath the foundation slab shown in Fig. 9.5 is one such example.

9.3.2.2 Vertical barriers. Permeable vertical barriers (VPCB) generally consist of a slit trench filled with a permeable material. Figure 9.5 shows a typical permeable water or capillary barrier.[2] The VPCB will accept surface water and distribute it into the exposed soil matrix. At the same time it tends to block lateral capillary movement of water within the soil itself.

The impermeable vertical capillary or water barrier (VICB) is intended to block the transfer of water laterally within the affected soil matrix. Again refer to Fig. 9.5.[2] Placed adjacent to a foundation, the VICB will hopefully maintain the soil moisture at a constant level within the foundation soil contained by the barrier. Coincidentally, this approach will also prevent transpiration to the soil, since tree, plant, or shrub roots will be prevented from crossing the barrier. In some cases, the soil moisture within the confines of the VICB is increased to a percent or so above the soil's plastic limit prior to construction of the foundation, particularly in the instances of slab foundations. The theory is that the soil is preswelled to a point that increased water is not likely to cause intolerable swell and, at the same time, the barrier will prevent the decrease in soil moisture beneath the foundation. Hence, a stable condition is created.

9.3.2.3 Conclusion. The use of water or capillary barriers offers possible benefit, but field data made public to date leave much to be desired[2,3] (Sec. 5.3.3).

9.4 Vegetation

Certain trees, such as weeping willow, cottonwood, and mesquite, have extensive shallow root systems. These plants can cause foundation (and sewer) problems even if located some distance from the structure. Many other plants and trees can cause problems if planted too close to the foundation. Plants with large, shallow root systems can grow under a shallow foundation and, as roots grow in diameter, produce an upheaval in the foundation beam. Surfaces most susceptible to this include flat work such as sidewalks, driveways, and patios,

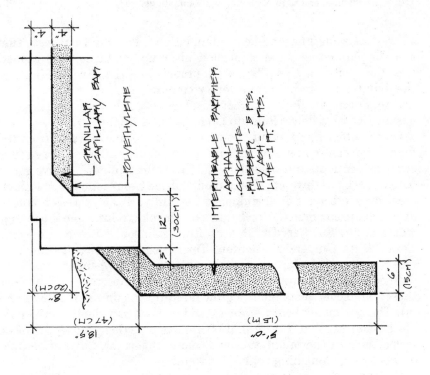

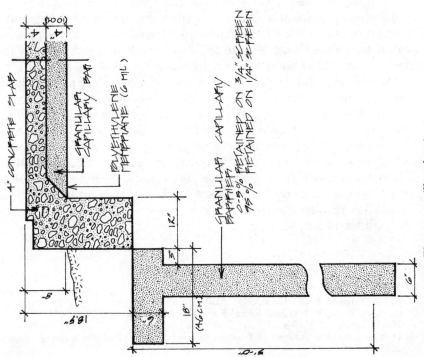

Figure 9.5 Water or capillary barriers.

as well as some pier-and-beam foundations. The FHA suggests that trees be planted no closer than their ultimate height. In older properties this is often not possible. With proper care, the adverse effects to the foundation can be minimized or circumvented. Pruning the trees and plants might limit the root development. Watering as discussed earlier will also help. (Refer to Chap. 1 Appendix.)

On the other hand, plants and trees tend to remove water from the foundation soil (transpiration) and cause a drying effect which in turn can produce foundation settlement. Transpiration can remove moisture to within a few percentage points above the plastic limit without creating excessive soil shrinkage.[1] Certainly, if the process occurred at a moisture content at or below the shrinkage limit, no shrinkage would occur. Further, Dr. Don Smith, Professor of Botany at North Texas State University, Denton, Texas, expresses the opinion that tree roots or other plant roots are not likely to grow beneath the foundation. This is due to several factors, the most important of which are these: (1) Feeder roots tend to grow laterally within the top 24 in (0.6 m). The perimeter beam often extends below that depth and would block root intrusion (Fig. 7.3). (2) Soil moistures (long range) are often lower beneath the foundation and, more important, have no normal access to a replenishing source for water.

For these reasons, it would appear that trees pose no real threat to foundation stability other than that normally associated with plants. Along these same lines, even in a semiarid area with highly expansive soil, it is seldom that a significant earth crack is noted beneath the tree canopy. This suggests an actual conservation of soil moisture.

Any extended differential in soil moisture can produce a corresponding movement in the foundation. If the differential movement is extensive, foundation failure will likely result. Of the two types of failures, settlement and upheaval, the latter is by far the more critical.

Even with proper care, foundation problems can develop. However, consideration and implementation of the foregoing procedures will afford a large measure of protection. It is possible that adherence to proper maintenance could eliminate perhaps 40 percent of all serious foundation problems. Anyone who can grow a flower bed can handle the maintenance requirements!

9.5 References

1. T. H. Petry and J. C. Armstrong, "Geotechnical Engineering Considerations for Design of Slabs on Active Clay Soils," ACI Convention, Dallas, Texas, February 1981.
2. A. Poor, "Experimental Residential Foundations on Expansive Clay Soils," UTA for HUD Contract H-224OR, 1975–1979.
3. D. E. Jones and K. A. Jones, "Treating Expansive Soils," *Civil Engineering*, August 1987.

10

Foundation Inspection and Evaluation for the Residential Buyer

If you are house shopping in a geographical locale with a known propensity for differential foundation movement, it is always wise to engage the assistance of a qualified foundation inspection service. The word "qualified" cannot be overemphasized. It is necessary to both evaluate the existence of foundation-related problems and also determine the cause of the problems when such are found to exist. The latter is particularly important. *Repairs will be futile if the original cause of the distress is not recognized and eliminated.*

Figure 8.1A–E depicts several of the more obvious manifestations of distress relative to differential foundation movement. With only limited experience, one can learn to detect these signs. Often the problems of detection become more difficult when cosmetic attempts have been used to conceal the evidence. These activities commonly involve painting, patching, tuck-pointing, addition of trim, and installation of wall cover, and, as one would guess, they require greater expertise for evaluation.

The important issue in all cases is to decide whether the degree of distress is sufficient to demand foundation repair. This decision requires a great degree of experience, since several factors influence the judgment:

1. The extent of vertical and lateral deflection. Does any structural threat exist or appear imminent?

2. Whether the stress is ongoing or arrested.

3. The age of the property.

4. The likelihood that the initiation of adequate maintenance would arrest continued movement. For example, in cases of upheaval, elimination of the source of water will often arrest the movement.

5. Value of the property as compared to repair costs. Most foundation repair procedures require some degree of compromise. In order to arrive at a reasonable or practical cost, the usual primary concern is to render the foundation "stable" and the appearance "tolerable." In most cases, the cost to truly level a foundation, if it were possible, would be prohibitive.

6. Age, type, and condition of the existing foundation.

7. The possibility that, if the movement appears to be arrested, cosmetic approaches will produce an acceptable appearance.

It is difficult, if not impossible, to properly evaluate the above factors without extensive firsthand experience with actual foundation repairs. One good example of the importance of on-the-job experience is the proper determination of upheaval as opposed to settlement (Chap. 7). If upheaval were evaluated as settlement, the existence of water beneath the foundation would likely be overlooked. In that case, future, more serious, consequences would be nearly certain. However, there are no similar, serious consequences in making the error of labeling settlement as upheaval. Essentially, this is true because all foundation repair techniques are designed to raise a lowermost area to some higher elevation. In cases of settlement, one merely raises the distressed area to "as built"; in those of upheaval, it is necessary to raise the as-built to approach the elevation of the distorted area. The latter is obviously far more difficult. See Chap. 7 for greater detail.

The existence of foundation problems need not be particularly distressing so long as the buyer is aware of potential problems before the purchase. As a rule, the costs of foundation repair are not comparatively excessive, the results are most often satisfactory, and the net results are a stronger, more nearly stable foundation. It is the surprise that a buyer cannot afford. The cost of the residential foundation inspection service is quite nominal; it varies from about $90 to $150 (1988) depending on the time involved and the locale. The following is a simple checklist for evaluating the stability of a foundation. If you have questions, or uncertainty regarding any of the items, consult a qualified authority.

10.1   Checklist for Foundation Inspection

1. Check the exterior foundation and masonry surfaces for cracks, evidence of patching, irregularities in siding lines or brick mortar

joints, separation of brick veneer from window and door frames, trim added along door jam or window frames, separation or gaps in cornice trim, separation of brick from frieze or fascia trim (look for original paint lines on brick), separation of chimney from outside wall, etc..

2. Slight ridge rafter, roof line, and eaves for irregularities.

3. Check interior doors for fit and operation. Check for evidence of prior repairs and adjustment such as shims behind hinges, latches or keepers relocated, and tops of doors shaved.

4. Check the plumb and square of door and window frames.

5. Note grade of floors. A simple method for checking the level of a floor (without carpet), window sill, counter top, etc., is to place a marble or small ball bearing on the surface and observe its behavior. A rolling action indicates a downhill grade. (A hard surface such as a board or book placed on the floor will allow the test to be made on carpet.)

6. Inspect wall and ceiling surfaces for cracks or evidence of patching. *Note*: Any cracking should be evaluated on the basis of both extent and cause. Most hard construction surfaces tend to crack. Often this can be the result of thermal or moisture changes and not foundation movement. However, if the cracks approach or exceed ¼ in (0.6 cm) in width, the problem is likely to be structural. On the other hand, if a crack that is noticed is, say, ⅛ in wide, is it a sign of impending problems? A simple check to determine if a crack is growing is to make a pencil mark at the apex of the existing crack and, using a straightedge, make two marks along the crack, one horizontal and one vertical (Fig. 10.1). If the crack changes even slightly, one or more of the marks will no longer match in a straight line along the crack

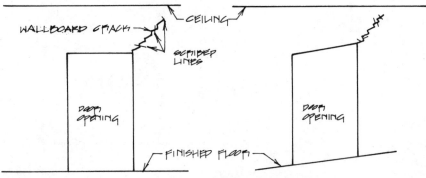

Figure 10.1 Scribe cracks to monitor suspected movement.

Figure 10.2 Movement is confirmed by changes in planes of scribed lines and extension of crack apex.

and/or the crack will extend past the apex mark (Fig. 10.2). A slight variation of this technique is to make a straight-line mark across a door and matching door frame. In a structure older than about 12 months, continued growth of the crack would be a strong indication of foundation movement.

7. On pier-and-beam foundations, check floors for firmness, inspect the crawl space for evidence of deficient framing or support, and ascertain adequate ventilation.

8. Check exterior drainage adjacent to foundation beams. Any surface water should quickly drain away from the foundation and not pond or pool within 8 or 10 ft (2.4 to 3 m). Give attention to planter boxes, flower bed curbing, and downspouts on gutter systems.

9. Look for trees that might be located too close to the foundation. Most authorities feel that the safe planting distance from the foundation is 1 or preferably 1.5 times the anticipated ultimate height of the tree. More correctly, the distance of concern should be 1 to 1.5 times the canopy width. Consideration should be given to the type of tree. Refer also to Chap. 2.

10. Are exposed concrete surfaces cracked? Hairline cracks can be expected in areas with expansive soils. However, larger cracks approaching or exceeding ⅛ in (0.3 cm) in width warrant closer consideration.

A*

Foundation Engineering

A.1 Soil Mechanics and Foundation Engineering

Thus far, the topics have been the applications of soil physics in residential or light commercial foundation investigations. The successful solution to soil problems requires a knowledge and study of a combination of soil mechanics and foundation engineering.

This appendix is limited to a review of the parts of foundation engineering which have the greatest influence on foundation design and repair. They include soil considerations such as sampling, strength, compressibility, compaction, settlement, strength tests, pressure, and bearing capacity. The behavior of the soil controls the behavior of the foundation.

While knowledge of soil mechanics is essential for foundation design, engineering judgment is also helpful in making final decisions. The author believes that, for all practical purposes, it is impossible to predetermine an exact solution to most design problems. As construction proceeds and more information becomes available, soil properties must be reevaluated and engineering judgment utilized to help modify the problem solution.

A.1.1 Site exploration

All residential and commercial building to some extent requires on-site subsurface exploration to obtain information on soil types and properties. Such information can be obtained through boring and sam-

---

*Particular appreciation is extended to Tom Petry, PhD, PE, Associate Professor, Civil Engineering, University of Texas at Arlington, for his editorial assistance with and contributions to this appendix.

pling procedures. Where the soil is not expansive and only the thickness of the soft surficial layer is to be examined, probing with a driven metal tube is an economical method. Where the soil is expansive and it is desired to obtain information at extended depths (i.e., the depth to relatively shallow ground water), hand-operated augers are sometimes used. If the expansive layer is thick, mechanical means of drilling borings such as the auger method or wash boring method can be utilized. These methods can provide enough information from the layers above the bedrock for foundation design of residential and light commercial buildings.

Disturbed samples obtained with auger methods are suitable for determining the soil index and classification in the laboratory. In order to study strength, compressibility, and swell behavior of the soil layer, a hole should be drilled by either the wash boring or auger method and then undisturbed specimens obtained by inserting a soil sampler.

In the housing industry, samples should be taken at 2-ft- (0.6-m-) depth intervals to bedrock or a minimum of 14 ft (4.3 m). For commercial construction such as warehouses or low rise, one sample for each 4-ft (1.2-m) depth section of boring to bedrock, or a minimum of 50 ft (15.2 m), can provide enough information about the soil layer.

In residential foundation projects, soil study should include borings at two corners plus at least one at an interior location with spacing not to exceed 100 ft (30.5 m). For commercial buildings, borings may be located near the boundaries at each corner with intermediate locations such that spacing does not exceed 80 ft (24.4 m).

Boring data are presented in the form of a boring log. Information such as soil indices, classifications, soil consistency, strength or compressibility, and changes in strata rock location and water table is presented on the log. See Fig. 1.5 for an example.

A.1.2   Compressibility of soil:
consolidation and settlement

Stresses in the soil beneath the foundation are relative to the weight of the structure and soil overburden. Terms such as "consolidation" and "compressibility" are used to define this stress. Consolidation occurs when an applied load forces water out of voids and enables the solid particles to become more closely packed. The resultant vertical downward movement is referred to as settlement. The amount of consolidation for a unit increase in applied load (pressure) is called compressibility. The rate at which consolidation can occur is dependent upon the ease with which water can flow through the soil (permeability).

Overconsolidation occurs when the soil has been subjected to loads (pressures) in excess of its current natural overburden. Overconsolidated clays exhibit the inherent tendency to swell. For the foregoing reasons, it is important to foundation stability that past and intended load conditions of the soil be known. As stated above, overconsolidated soils tend to rebound and/or swell and underconsolidated soils tend to settle. Determination of settlement for residential or light commercial buildings can be accomplished by the following approaches:

1. Performing compression tests on soil samples obtained from borings
2. Estimating the compressibility based on information obtained from the index property test

The amount of settlement can be obtained by considering only the vertical stresses, as shown by Eq. (A.1). Short-term settlement depends essentially on compressibility, whereas long-term settlement is a function of consolidation within the soil. The compression or consolidation is rapid in noncohesive soils but time-dependent in cohesive soils. Because of the rapid settlement of the noncohesive soils, there is little concern for foundation problems due to settlement occurring over an extended period.

The compressibility of noncohesive soil is a measure of resistance to movement of the grains into greater-density positions. This resistance depends upon the friction between the grains. It should be noted that the compressibility of a cohesive soil, such as clay, depends upon the double-layer water, particle slickness, and particle elasticity.

One of the conditions that the engineer wants to meet is minimizing the foundation movement related to soil volume change caused, in turn, by change in water content. Shrinkage of soil is directly due to loss of water from the soil by evaporation or transpiration (see Secs. 3.7 and 3.8).

Settlement of a normally consolidated soil can be estimated by the following equation:

$$\Delta H = \frac{H_o}{1 + e_o}\Delta e \quad (\Delta H = H_o - H_t) \tag{A.1}$$

$$\Delta H = \frac{H_o}{1 + e_o} C_c (\log \sigma_s - \log \bar{\sigma}_v)$$

then

$$\Delta e = C_c (\log \sigma_s - \log \bar{\sigma}_v)$$

$$= C_c \log \left(\frac{\sigma_s}{\bar{\sigma}_v}\right)$$

$$\Delta e = (e_o - e_t)$$

where ΔH = amount of settlement

e_o = void ratio before application of load

e_t = void ratio after load application

C_c = compression index

$\bar{\sigma}_s$ = sum of the overburdened soil pressure and the pressure caused by the weight of the structure

σ_v = overburden soil pressure, or effective stress

H_o = initial thickness of stratum

H_t = thickness of stratum after load

In residential foundation design, the compressibility should be established quickly, but the compressibility test requires at least 2 weeks to be completed and is often not economical. To obtain compression index C_c in a short time, the following Skempton relationships are useful:

$$C_c = 0.54(e_o - 0.35) \qquad (a)$$

$$C_c = 0.54(2.6W - 35) \qquad (b)$$

$$C_c = 0.009(LL - 10) \qquad (c)$$

where e_o = in-place void ratio

W = natural water content

LL = liquid limit

Equation (A.1) can be applied only to normally consolidated soil, which is a soil that has never been subjected to pressure or load greater than existing overburden. The settlement of a cohesive soil layer under a spread footing for supporting a bearing wall, chimney, or grade beam can be calculated from Eq. (A.1). The following illustrative example shows the application of Eq. (A.1). Refer also to Fig. A.1.

Example problem A.1   Assume that H_1 is 1 ft, H_2, an expansive clay layer, is 4.5 ft, H_3 is 7 ft, H_o is 9 ft, and γ_o top soil is 95 lb/ft^3, γ_o expansive clay is 115 lb/ft^3, and γ_o compressible clay is 110 lb/ft^3. The void ratio e_o is 0.55 and the compressive index C_c is 0.2. The weight of the structure and footing exerts a stress of 900 lb/ft^2 at midheight of the compressible clay layer ($\Delta\sigma$). Calculate the settlement at the midheight of the compressible clay layer (H_3).

Solution   The settlement is found by

$$\Delta H = \frac{H_3}{1 + e_o} C_c \, (\log \sigma_s - \log \bar{\sigma}_v)$$

where $\bar{\sigma}_v = \Sigma\gamma H$

$$\bar{\sigma}_v + (1 \text{ ft} \times 95 \text{ lb/ft}^3) + (4.5 \text{ ft} \times 115 \text{ lb/ft}^3) + (5.25 \text{ ft} \times 110 \text{ lb/ft}^3) = 1190 \text{ lb/ft}^2$$

$$\sigma_s = \bar{\sigma}_v + \Delta\sigma = 1190 + 900 = 2090 \text{ lb/ft}^2$$

$$\Delta H = \frac{3.5 \text{ ft}}{1 + 0.55}(0.20)(\log 2090 - \log 1190) = 0.11 \text{ in } (0.28 \text{ cm})$$

Note: The value $\bar{\sigma}_v$ can be calculated by either the Boussinesq or Westergaard method, Eq. (A.3). It depends on the site's groundwater, but σ_s (or σ_v) is not affected by the water table.

If the soil layer is overconsolidated, Eq. (A.1) should be modified. In that instance, the engineer should refer to a soil mechanics text.

A.1.3 Volume change in noncohesive soil

The settlement of the foundation in noncohesive soil occurs immediately upon application of a load, and since building loads are developed gradually during the construction, settlement effects can be absorbed by the structure without structural failure. For a sand layer where the modulus of elasticity increases with depth uniformly, the following relationship can be used to calculate the settlement beneath the foundation.

$$\Delta H = \frac{4qB^2}{K_v(B + 1)^2} \qquad (A.2)$$

where B = width of the foundation
q = pressure imposed by the foundation
K_v = modulus of vertical subgrade reaction (Table A.1)

The assumptions for using Eq. (A.1) are that the depth of the foundation below the ground surface is less than the width of the foundation and the foundation width is not greater than 20 ft. Figure A.1 is an

TABLE A.1 Modulus of Vertical Subgrade Reaction K_v^a (Sands)

Condition	Relative density	Value of K_v	
		kips/ft^3	(kN/m^3) $\times$ 10^{-3}
Loose	< 35	100	15
Medium to dense	35–65	150–300	25–50
Dense	65–85	350–550	55–85
Very dense	> 85	600–700	85–110

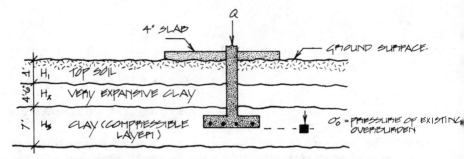

Figure A.1 Illustrative example for calculating settlement under a spread footing.

illustrative example for calculating the settlement under a spread footing. (The value of K_v can be obtained from Table A.1.)

If the water table is at the base of the foundation, use $\frac{1}{2}K_v$.[1]

$$1.0 \text{ kips/ft}^3 = 157 \text{ kN/m}^3 \qquad 1 \text{ kip} = 1000 \text{ lb}$$

Example problem A.2   A total live and dead load of 300,000 lb is supported through a column to a footing. The footing is 4 ft below the surface, and the soil is a thick sand layer with a relative density of 75 percent. If the allowable soil-bearing is 9000 lb/ft², estimate the foundation settlement, ΔH.

Solution

$$\text{Area required} = \frac{300,000 \text{ lb}}{9000 \text{ lb/ft}^2} = 33.33 \text{ ft}^2$$

$$\text{Square footing } B^2 = 33.33$$

$$\text{Then } B = 5.77 \text{ ft} \qquad \text{(use 6 ft)}$$

The K_v value for relative density of 75 percent is equal to 450 kips/ft³ (see Table A.1).

$$\Delta H = \frac{4qB^2}{K_v(B + 1)^2} = \frac{4 \, (9 \text{ kips/ft}^2)(6 \text{ ft} \times 6 \text{ ft})}{(450 \text{ kips/ft}^3)(6 \text{ ft} + 1 \text{ ft})^2} = 0.059 \text{ ft} = 0.71 \text{ in}$$

A.2 Stresses in a Soil Mass due to Foundation Pressures

The stress at a point in a soil mass is the result of the weight of the soil mass above the point plus any structural load. For analysis, the stress in a vertical direction is considered in the magnitude of this stress, which will also be influenced by variations in the groundwater level. The effective stress ($\bar{\sigma}_v$), transmitted grain to grain in the soil, is used for this evaluation.

The stress at a depth H below the ground surface is given by Eq. (A.3).

$$\sigma_v = \gamma H \qquad \text{lb/ft}^2 \tag{A.3}$$

where σ_v = vertical stress, at depth H from the surface
γ = soil unit weight, lb/ft^3
H = depth, ft

When the soil is below groundwater, γ is the submerged unit weight. The resulting stress is then called effective stress, and it is indicated as $\bar{\sigma}_v$ in Eq. (A.4).

$$\bar{\sigma}_v = \gamma_{\text{sub}} H = (\gamma_{\text{sat}} - \gamma_w) H \tag{A.4}$$

where γ_{sat} = soil unit weight above water level
γ_w = unit weight of the water

Figure A.2 illustrates the computation of the stress at a point in a soil mass resulting from various soil and water table conditions. (In field practice, the level of groundwater may or may not coincide with the water table.)

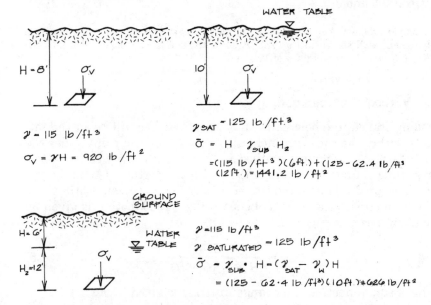

Figure A.2 Vertical stress in subgrade soils.

In some cases, such as basement walls or commercial and residential foundations on a slope, horizontal stress should be calculated at a particular depth from the surface. In such cases, the ratio of lateral stress to vertical stress, or K, the coefficient of lateral pressure should be determined by Eq. (A.5).

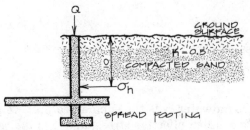

HORIZONAL SOIL PRESSURE = σ_h = K γ H = (0.5)(120 lb/ft³)(10 ft)
= 600 lb/ft²

Figure A.3   Lateral (horizontal) stress.

$$K = \frac{\gamma_h \text{ (horizontal soil pressure)}}{\gamma_v \text{ (vertical soil pressure)}} \qquad (A.5)$$

The value of K for granular loose fill can be taken to be equal to 0.5 to 0.6, for granular compacted fill between 0.2 and 0.5, and for clay between 0.5 and 1.0.

Example problem A.3   Calculate the lateral earth pressure for the concrete basement wall shown in Fig. A.3. Assume the soil to be compacted sand with $K = 0.5$ and a unit weight γ of 120 lb/ft³.

Solution.   See Fig. A.3.

A.3   Vertical Surface Loading

Loading transferred below the foundation member will be spread laterally within the soil with increasing depth from the point under the foundation. The simplest method is to use a 2:1 slope concept or a stress zone defined by an angle (30°) with the vertical. (Actually, the 2:1 slope produces an angle ϕ of 26.7°.) For a spread footing, the change in stress at a depth H beneath the spread footing is given by Eq. (A.6). See also Fig. A.4.

$$\Delta\sigma = \frac{Q}{(B + H)(L + H)} \qquad (A.6)$$

For a square footing the change in stress is given by Eq. (A.7).

$$\Delta\sigma = \frac{Q}{(B + H)^2} \qquad (A.7)$$

where Q = total load applied to foundation
B, L = footing dimensions
H = depth from footing base to the point where stress is desired
$\Delta\sigma$ = change in stress at depth H

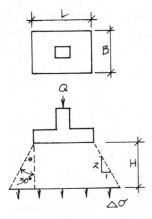

Figure A.4 Vertical surface loading.

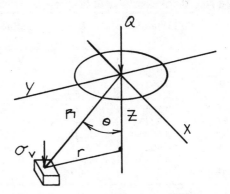

Figure A.5 Graphics of Boussinesq's equation.

A.3.1 Boussinesq method for evaluating soil pressure

The Boussinesq method is based on the assumption that a point load is applied on a surface of an infinitely large, homogeneous, isotropic, elastic half-space to obtain

$$\sigma_v = \frac{3Q}{2\pi Z^2}\left[\frac{1}{1 + (r/Z)^2}\right]^{5/2} \quad \text{lb/ft}^2 \qquad (A.8)$$

The symbols are defined in Fig. A.5. Often, Eq. (A.8) is simplified and used in terms of an influence factor Ip, where

$$Ip = \frac{3}{2\pi}\left[\frac{1}{1 + (r/Z)^2}\right]^{5/2} \qquad (A.9)$$

then, since

$$q = \frac{Q}{Z^2} = \frac{Q}{A} \qquad (A.10)$$

$$\sigma_v = \frac{Q}{Z^2}Ip = qIp \qquad (A.11)$$

Values for Ip are given in Table A.2.[2]

In Boussinesq's method, the foundation is considered to be point load and the modulus of elasticity and Poisson's ratio are not considered, assuming that stress is independent of these properties. This, of

TABLE A.2   Influence Factors for Vertical Pressure (s_v) under Center of Uniformly Loaded Flexible Circular Area of Diameter *D*

$\dfrac{D}{z}$	Influence factor *Ip*	$\dfrac{D}{z}$	Influence factor *Ip*	$\dfrac{D}{z}$	Influence factor *Ip*
0.00	0.0000	2.00	0.6465	4.00	0.9106
0.20	0.0148	2.20	0.6956	6.00	0.9684
0.40	0.0571	2.40	0.7376	8.00	0.9857
0.60	0.1213	2.60	0.7733	10.00	0.9925
0.80	0.1966	2.80	0.8036	12.00	0.9956
1.00	0.2845	3.00	0.8293	14.00	0.9972
1.20	0.3695	3.20	0.8511	16.00	0.9981
1.40	0.4502	3.40	0.8697	20.00	0.9990
1.60	0.5239	3.60	0.8855	40.00	0.9999
1.80	0.5893	3.80	0.8990	200.00	1.0000

*σ_v = influence factor × contact pressure *q*

course, is not strictly true, but the assumptions are justifiable for practical design purposes. Figure A.6 illustrates the variation of vertical stress versus depth below load.

Modifications of Boussinesq's method, taking contact area into account, were presented by Newmark (1942) in chart form. The reader can refer to several soil mechanics textbooks for the Newmark's influence chart. Here the mean vertical stress σ_v at depth *H* beneath a rectangular area, *L* × *B* at load *q*, can be estimated[2] (Fig. A.7).

For residential and commercial buildings, the conditions of a homogeneous and isotropic material are often assumed for clay deposit and human-made fills where the selected fill has been compacted in several layers. This is particularly true when only σ_v approximations are desired for general design purposes. In that event, the foregoing method often proves to be adequate.

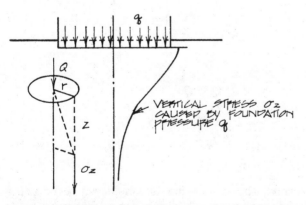

Figure A.6   Variation of vertical stress under a foundation (Boussinesq analysis).

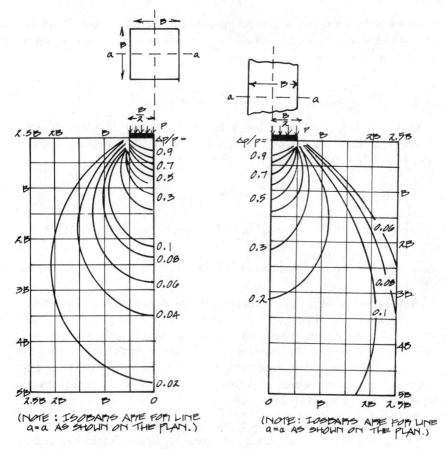

Figure A.7 Vertical pressure isobars under (left) uniformly loaded square footing and (right) uniformly loaded continuous footing. (Based on Newmark's integration of Boussinesq's notation.)

A.3.2 Westergaard's method

For soil deposits consisting of layered strata of coarse and fine materials such as laminated clay and silt or sandy soils, the Westergaard method is sometimes preferred. Westergaard's method is based on the assumption that the thin layers of a homogeneous and isotropic material were sandwiched between closely spaced, thin sheets of rigid materials that would permit compression, but no lateral deformation. Westergaard (1938) presented Eq. (A.12), which is best applied to pavement systems.

$$\sigma_v = \frac{Q}{2\pi Z^2}\left\{\frac{\sqrt{(1 - 2v)/(2 - 2v)}}{[(1 + 2v)/(2 - 2v) + (r/Z)^2]^{3/2}}\right\} \qquad (A.12)$$

where ν is Poisson's ratio $(\Delta\sigma/\Delta L)$ and the other terms are as defined for Boussinesq's equation. When Poisson's ratio is zero, the equation can be simplified to

$$\sigma_v = \frac{Q}{\pi Z^2}\left\{\frac{1}{[1 + 2(r/Z)^2]^{3/2}}\right\} \qquad (A.13)$$

This is a form of Boussinesq's equation. Taylor[3] relates the two forms (Fig. 11.2, page 253) through the use of the constants N_B and N_W. Here N_B is identical with Ip [Eq. (A.9)]

$$N_W = \frac{1}{\pi[1 + 2(r/Z)^2]^{3/2}}$$

When $r/Z \geq 1.25$, for all intents and purposes, numerically $N_B = N_W$.

A.3.3 Application to residential foundation design

In foundation design, the condition of point load is not always practical. The load is applied on an area beneath the footing, thereby creating concern regarding relative stress at different locations. The result of the integration of Boussinesq's and Westergaard's equations for a summation of point loads under the footings has been presented by charts, graphs, and tables. The following examples will illustrate the application of graphs in Figs. A.6 and A.7.

Example problem A.4   A 110-kip load is applied on a spread footing 4 ft square which is located on a homogeneous soil. Calculate the stress at the edge and the center of the footing at a depth of 4 ft. Neglect the stress caused by overburden. Refer to Fig. A.8.

Solution: At the center

$$q = \frac{Q}{A} = \frac{110 \text{ kips}}{4 \text{ ft} \times 4 \text{ ft}} = 6.87 \text{ kips/ft}^2 = 6870 \text{ lb/ft}^2 \qquad (1 \text{ kip} = 1000 \text{ lb})$$

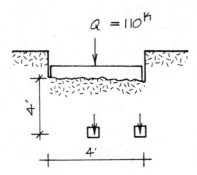

Figure A.8 Load applied to shallow footing.

From Fig. A.7, for a square at center, $\Delta\sigma_v$ in terms of q is 34 percent for depth/width = 4/4 = 1. Then

$$\Delta\sigma_v = (0.34)(6870 \text{ lb/ft}^2) = 2336 \text{ lb/ft}^2$$

For a square at an edge, the factor is 0.27. Then

$$\Delta\sigma_v = (0.27)(6870 \text{ lb/ft}^2) = 1855 \text{ lb/ft}^2$$

Example problem A.5 A top expansive clay soil has been excavated up to 6 ft to fill with a nonplastic soil compacted to 95 percent. The bearing wall of a commercial building is to be constructed on a spread footing that is located 3 ft from the surface. What subsurface stress increase occurs beneath the center of the spread footing at a depth of 15 ft in the middle of a silty clay layer? (Neglect the weight of the concrete slab.) Refer to Fig. A.9.

Solution

$$q_{\text{footing}} = \frac{70 \text{ kips}}{4 \text{ ft} \times 4 \text{ ft}} = 4.4 \text{ kips/ft}^2$$

$$\text{Ratio of depth to width} = \frac{Z}{B} = \frac{12 \text{ ft}}{4.0 \text{ ft}} = 3.0$$

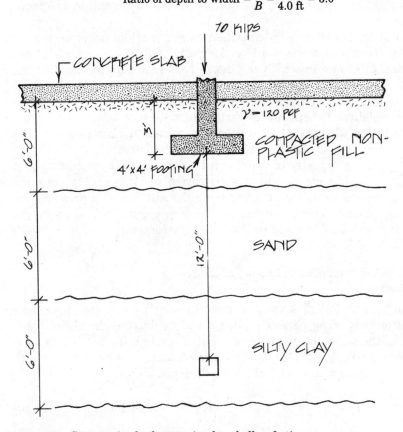

Figure A.9 Construction load transmitted to shallow footing.

Estimate the stress increase by Boussinesq's equation (Fig. A.7).

$$\Delta\sigma_v = 5\% \times q = 0.05(4400 \text{ lb/ft}^2) = 220 \text{ lb/ft}^2 \qquad \text{from foundation}$$

From fill:

$$\Delta\sigma_v = (\gamma_{fill} \text{ lb/ft}^3)(H_{fill} \text{ ft}) = 120 \text{ lb/ft}^3 \times 6 \text{ ft} = 720 \text{ lb/ft}^2$$

Total stress increase = 720 + 220 = 940 lb/ft^2

A.4 Bearing Capacity of Shallow Foundations

Foundations are designed to transfer the loads from structures to the soil without failure or excessive settlement. The maximum pressure that can be applied to the soil mass without causing shear failure is called the soil bearing capacity. This pressure or stress is created by the weight of the structure and is transmitted to the soil by the foundation.

Foundations are broadly classified as shallow and deep; most residential foundations are shallow. Terzaghi[4] (1943) defined a shallow foundation as one in which the depth D is less than or equal to the width B of the footing. More commonly, "shallow foundation" is the term used to describe the structural design wherein loads are carried by the soil directly beneath the structure and "deep foundation" refers to the design wherein structural load is carried to a competent soil at some depth, usually through piers, piles, or caissons.

The bearing capacity of a soil can be determined by application of equations or the utilization of penetration resistance data obtained during the soil sampling or by relating the soil type to a presumptive bearing capacity recommended by building codes. Each of these parameters will be discussed in the following sections.

A.4.1 Shallow foundation bearing capacity equation

Terzaghi and Peck[5] developed general bearing capacity equations based on soil being perfectly plastic and neglecting the shear resistance of the soil above the horizontal plan through the base of the footing (Fig. A.10). In fact, the soil is replaced with a surcharge ($q_o = \gamma D$), where γ = unit weight of soil, lb/ft^3, at depth D feet.

$$q_f = N_c C + N_q D_f \gamma + \tfrac{1}{2} N_\gamma B \gamma \qquad \text{strip footing} \qquad (A.14)$$

$$q_f = 1.3 N_c C + N_q D_f \gamma + 0.4 N_\gamma B \gamma \qquad \text{square footing} \qquad (A.15)$$

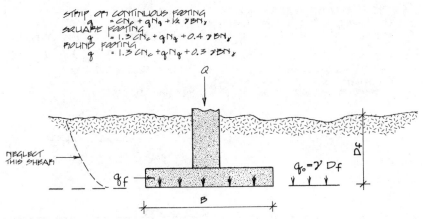

Figure A.10 Shallow foundation bearing.

$$q_f = 1.3CN_c + N_qD_f\gamma + 0.3\gamma BN_\gamma \qquad \text{round footing} \qquad (A.16)$$

where
q_f = ultimate soil bearing capacity; includes weight of soil over the footing and the footing

C = cohesion

B = least lateral dimension of footing (for round footing B = diameter)

γ = unit weight of soil

q_o = pressure of soil above base level of foundation

N_c, N_q, N_γ = bearing capacity factors

D_f = depth of foundation. (A shallow footing is one with the width B equal to or greater than depth D_f.)

Values of N_c, N_q, and N_γ are tabulated for selected angles of internal friction. (N_γ approaches zero for most clays, so the last term becomes negligible.) See Fig. A.11 for the values of capacity factors versus the angle ϕ over which the resultant earth pressure acts. (For shallow foundations where D is less than or equal to B, assuming $\phi = 0$, the bearing capacity terms become $N_c = 5.7$, $N_q = 1.0$, and $N_\gamma = 0$.)

Figure A.12 is an illustration of a local and general shear failure. In local shear failure, a considerable vertical soil movement occurs before soil bulging takes place (punching shear). Terzaghi suggested the following modifications for C and ϕ, using local shear failure mode. For soft clays, ϕ approaches zero. Hence, for deep foundations the reduced cohesion and internal friction become

$$C' = \tfrac{2}{3}C \qquad (A.17)$$

LOADED STRIP, WIDTH B
TOTAL LOAD PER UNIT LENGTH OF FOOTING
GENERAL SHEAR FAILURE: $Q_d = B(cN_c + \gamma D_f N_q + \frac{1}{2}\gamma B N_y)$
LOCAL SHEAR FAILURE: $Q_d' = B(\frac{2}{3} cN_c' + \gamma D_f N_q' + \frac{1}{2}\gamma B N_y')$
SQUARE FOOTING, WIDTH B
TOTAL CRITICAL LOAD: $Q_{ds} = B^2(1.3cN_c + \gamma D_f N_q + 0.4\gamma B N_y)$
UNIT WEIGHT OF EARTH = γ
UNIT SHEAR RESISTANCE: $S = c + \sigma \tan \phi$

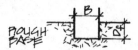

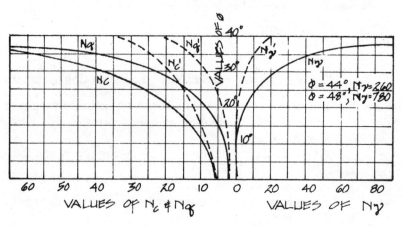

$\phi = 44°, N_y = 260$
$\phi = 48°, N_y = 780$

VALUES OF N_c & N_q VALUES OF N_y

Figure A.11 Relation between [Gfl] and the bearing capacity factors. (*After Terzaghi and Peck*, Soil Mechanics in Engineering Practice.)

and $\tan \phi' = \frac{2}{3} \tan \phi$ (A.18)

Joseph E. Bowles suggests that foundations not be designed for a local shear failure condition because the practice often results in such a large reduction in bearing value that the soil would be compacted to a general shear condition.

In recent years there have been numerous proposals with various assumptions for computation of the ultimate bearing capacity. Among them, Hansen (1970) extended his theory, which is similar to the Terzaghi method and gives better results than Terzaghi equations. For more information, the reader can refer to recent publications and journals. The Terzaghi method has been widely used in the past, but it is not currently so favored. The reasons are that (1) the equations are based on an incorrect failure pattern (angle β, Fig. A.13), which is in

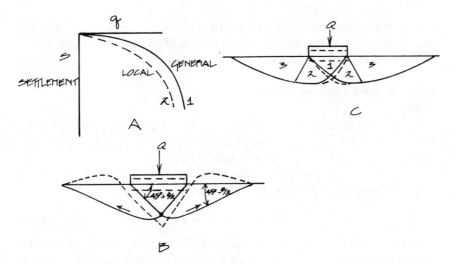

Figure A.12 (A) General and local shear failure; curve 1 depicts a soil resistance against loading with small settlement until sudden failure. (B) General shear failure. (C) Local shear failure. (*After Terzaghi*, 1943.)

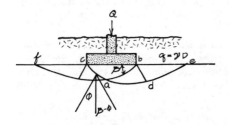

ASSUMPTIONS : REPLACE SOIL BY A SURCHARGE $q = \gamma D$ &
SHEAR ALONG cb IS NEGLECTED
$B = 45 - \phi/2$ FOR SMOOTH BASE
$B = 45 + \phi/2$ FOR ROUGH BASE

Figure A.13 Condition for a shallow foundation assumption for the development of the Terzaghi bearing capacity equation.

reality closer to $45° + \phi/2$ than to ϕ, and (2) the depth effect is not taken into account.

A.4.2 Hansen equations

Hansen equations are based on plane strain values and have been shown to be in agreement with measured values for both noncohesive and cohesive soils. The author suggests using Hansen equations for residential and commercial foundation design and analysis. They afford a reasonable means of estimating bearing capacity and include such factors as shape, depth, inclination, and geometry. The inclusion of these formulas is not considered necessary to the scope of this book.

A.4.3 Bearing capacity of footings on slopes

Footings can be located on or adjacent to a slope. It is obvious that, because of lack of soil overburden on the slope, the bearing capacity of the footings should be reduced (Figs. A.14 and A.15).

G. G. Meyerhof (1957) suggests the following equation for ultimate bearing capacity of a soil under strip footings.

$$q = CN_{cq} + \tfrac{1}{2}\gamma BN_{\gamma q} \qquad (A.19)$$

where N_{cq} and $N_{\gamma q}$ are bearing capacity factors for footings on slopes; the values are shown in Figs. A.14 and A.15. N_s is the stability factor, and other terms are defined by the appropriate figure.

The author believes that, to design a spread footing on, or adjacent to, a slope, the bearing capacity should be known and the slope stability should be investigated. The stability of the slope can be a controlling factor in such a design.

Example problem A.6   A bearing wall for a basement of a commercial building is designed to be adjacent to a slope. For the given conditions, design the size of continuous (strip) footing. Neglect the pressure imposed by slab and the other loads. Assume a safety factor (F) equal to 3. Refer to Fig. A.16, where Q is 5000 lb, and C is 1200 lb/ft^3.

Solution   By trial and error, it is assumed that $D/B = 0.5$ and $b/B = 1$ ($b = 4$ ft). Since $B < H$, from Fig. A.15, $N_s = 0$, $b/B = 1$, and $\beta = 60°$, obtain $N_{cq} = 4.8$. For shallow strip footings on cohesive soil,

$$q_{ult} = CN_{cq} = 4.8C = 4.8 \,(1200 \text{ lb/ft}^2) = 5800 \text{ lb/ft}^2$$

$$q_{design} = \frac{5800 \text{ lb/ft}^2}{fs} = \frac{5800 \text{ lb/ft}^2}{3.0} = 1933.3 \text{ lb/ft}^2$$

The required footing width is

$$B = \frac{Q}{(q_{des} \text{ lb/ft}^2)(1 \text{ ft length})} = \frac{5000 \text{ lb}}{(1933.3 \text{ lb/ft}^2)(1 \text{ ft})} = 2.58 \text{ ft}$$

Use $B = 3$ ft.

A.4.4 Bearing capacity based on building codes

In many cities, there are local building codes for evaluation of allowable soil pressure required for acceptable foundation design. Most of

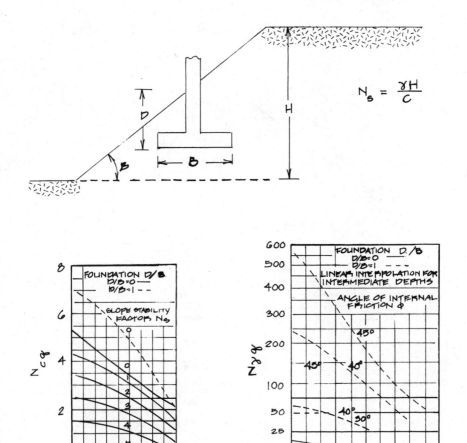

$$N_s = \frac{\gamma H}{C}$$

(a) PURELY COHESIVE SOIL   (b) COHESIONLESS SOIL

Figure A.14 Bearing capacity factors for strip foundation on face slope. (*From Das,*[6] p. 247.)

these codes are based on local experience and visual soil classification justified by laboratory testing.

The author believes these codes are useful only in preliminary stages, since they do not reflect the depth or size of footing, location of water table, or potential bearing soil compaction. Among these codes, the Uniform Building (1964) and the Chicago (1975) are most commonly recommended for residential and light commercial buildings.

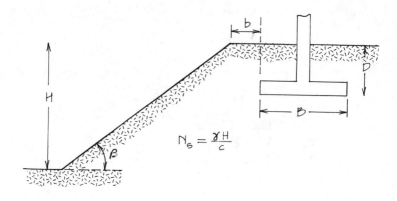

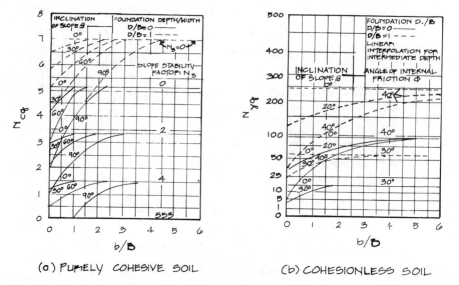

(a) PURELY COHESIVE SOIL   (b) COHESIONLESS SOIL

Figure A.15   Bearing capacity factors for strip foundation at top of slope. (*From Das,*[6] p. 248.)

A.4.5 Safety factors in foundation design

In the design of foundations, complexity of soil behavior and incomplete knowledge of the subsoil conditions always create uncertainty. This can be minimized by obtaining reliable soil data, relative change in probability of failure by changing safety factors, and, finally, changes in soil properties due to soil stabilization. A safety factor (F) between 2 to 3 for spread footings and 1.7 to 2.5 for mat foundations under shear failure mode is recommended.

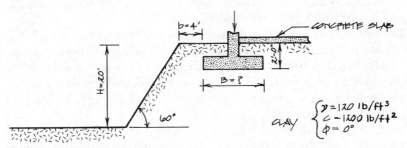

Figure A.16   Basement bearing wall adjacent to a slope.

TABLE A.3   Bearing Capacities from Indicated Building Codes, lb/ft²

Soil description	Chicago 1975	Uniform Building Code 1964
Clay, very soft	500	
Clay, soft	1500	1500
Clay, ordinary	2500	
Clay, medium stiff	3500	2500
Clay, stiff	4500	
Clay, hard	6000	8000
Sand, compact and hard	5000	
Sand, compact and silty	3000	
Inorganic silt, compact	2500	
Sand, loose and fine		1500
Sand, loose and coarse, or sand-gravel mixture		2500
Gravel, loose and compact		8000
Sand-gravel, compact		8000

A.5   Bearing Capacity of Drilled Piers

Over the years, high-capacity drilled piers have been designed for high-rise buildings and heavy loads from industrial facilities where settlement requires that the structure be supported on hard soil or bedrock. Drilled piers have also found application as a means of providing positive support through high-plastic soils and fills for residential and commercial buildings. Particular care should be taken with piers in expansive soils to ensure vertical alignment with the imposed load. Otherwise, the nonuniform soil pressures against the downward loaded pier could result in increased deviation of the pier from vertical. Ultimately this could cause the pier to fail.

Piers are installed by excavating or drilling a shaft (cased or uncased) and then filling it with concrete. When the base is enlarged, the foundation is known as a belled pier. Other terms such as "bored pile," "drilled shaft," and "drilled caisson" are used by foundation engineers to designate the drilled piers.

The bearing capacity of a drilled pier in a homogeneous soil is a combination of the end-bearing resistance and frictional resistance on the shaft. Friction developed along the shaft in a soft soil (fills) or highly plastic soil is at least partially neglected, and the shallow pier should be designed as a compression member with the applied load resisted by the bottom (tip).

The concrete shaft, depending on the design approach, can be reinforced with steel bars either near the top or throughout the pier length. Generally, the latter is most common. Figure A.17 shows a classification of drilled piers.[7] Often the pier shaft is belled as shown in Fig. A.17A,B. This procedure is utilized to increase end-bearing capacity and/or impede the effects of negative skin friction (settlement). When bells are used, the diameter of the bell is normally between 2 and 3 times the diameter of the shaft.

A.5.1 General considerations in analysis

In general, the design of drilled piers is empirical, and local experience and engineering judgment based on presumptive bearing stress can provide the conditions for a satisfactory design. Nevertheless, presumptive bearing stress should be modified by bearing capacity analysis based on soil tests. Soil information, rock location, and groundwater level are the important factors in selecting the depth and determining the size and type of a pier. The load applied to the top of a pier is transferred to the soil or rock by:

1. The skin friction forces or adhesion between the face of the pier and surrounding materials
2. The bearing resistance of the material under the pier base

The total capacity Q_{total} is:

$$Q_{total} = Q_{friction} + Q_{tip} - W \qquad (A.20)$$

$$Q_{total} = fA_{surface} + q_{tip}A_{tip} - W \qquad (A.21)$$

where f = average unit friction or adhesion (undrained) between soil and pier surface (sidewall area, πDH)

$A_{surface}$ = total surface area of pier in contact with soil along the embedded shaft length, πDH

q_{tip} = bearing capacity of soil at pier tips

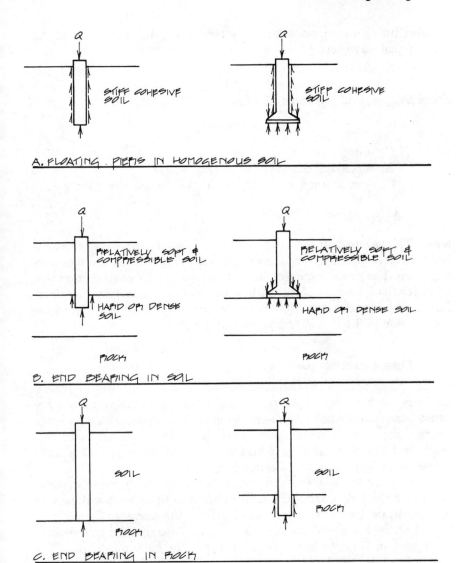

A. FLOATING PIERS IN HOMOGENOUS SOIL

B. END BEARING IN SOIL

C. END BEARING IN ROCK

Figure A.17 Principal classifications of drilled piers. (*From Fang and Winterkorn.*[7])

A_{tip} = pier tip bearing area, $\pi D^2/4$
W = weight of the pier (can be ignored)
D = diameter of pier
H = depth of pier

Note: fA_{surface} is assumed to be zero for shallow piers in soft or highly expansive soils.

Substituting expressions for the ultimate bearing capacities of the pier tip (cohesive soil) gives

$$Q_{tip} = q_{tip}A_{tip} \qquad (A.22)$$

Since $fA_{surface}$ and W can be ignored,

$$Q_{tip} = C_u N_c A_{tip} \qquad (A.23)$$

where $N_c C_u = q_{tip}$
N_c = bearing capacity factor [Eq. (A.31)]
C_u = undrained strength of the soil below the base of the pier
$A_{tip} = \pi D^2/4 = 0.785D^2$

Note: The bearing capacities of drilled piers can be increased substantially by pressure-grouting the effective bearing soils at the pier surface area. The grout increases lateral stresses at the contact interface (skin friction), reconsolidates soils loosened by the shaft drilling operation, and increases the soil bearing capacity at the tip. See Secs. 8.4.1, 8.6, and 8.10.1 for additional discussion.

A.5.2 Piers in granular soils

Drilled piers are seldom installed as end-bearing members in granular soils, such as sand and gravel, below the groundwater level because excavation allows the sand to expand and decreases its load-bearing capacity. However, piers extending through a soft soil layer (such as fill) and located on dense sand above the water table have proved to be economical in a number of cases.

If the water table is encountered, a bentonite slurry may be circulated into the hole during the drilling process to prevent soil cave-in and facilitate lifting the excavated soil to the surface. Concrete is placed at the bottom of the excavation and filled upward in a continuous pour in order to force displacement of the bentonite slurry. If a casing has been used, it is withdrawn as the concrete is poured. Close attention should be paid to prevent the soil walls from collapsing into the hole and contaminating the concrete. A principal disadvantage of bentonite slurry is the fill on the soil surrounding the hole, which tends to reduce the skin friction between the soil and cured concrete. Also, unless extreme care is taken in placing the concrete, the bentonite can reduce the strength of the set concrete.

The friction capacity can be determined by calculating the friction of the sand:

$$f_{sand} = \sigma_H \tan S \qquad (A.24)$$

where σ_H = horizontal soil pressure acting at depth H in the soil mass

tan S = coefficient of friction between sand and the pier surface (see Table A.4 for different values of friction coefficient)

$$\sigma_H = K\bar{\sigma}_v \qquad (A.25)$$

where $\bar{\sigma}_v$ = effective overburden pressure acting laterally at depth H
K = lateral earth pressure coefficient

Therefore,

$$f_{sand} = K\bar{\sigma}_v \tan S \qquad (A.26)$$

$$\bar{\sigma}_v = \gamma_{soil}D$$

$$Q_{friction} = f_{sand}A_{surface} \qquad (A.27)$$

$$= (K\bar{\sigma}_v \tan S)A_{surface}$$

Field tests indicate that constant values of tan S should be considered up to the critical depth, which is 10 pier diameters for loose sand and about 20 pier diameters for dense, compact sand. The lateral earth coefficient K, depending on the excavation technique and the soil condition, can be taken as 0.4 to 0.75 for compacted sand and 0.75 to 3.0 for loose sand. Often K at rest (K_0) is taken as 1 - sin ϕ.

The end bearing capacity q_{tip} can be computed from the bearing capacity equation for deep foundations in noncohesive soils.

$$q_{tip} = \tfrac{1}{2}\gamma BN_\gamma + \bar{\sigma}_w N_q \qquad (A.28)$$

and

$$Q_{tip} = q_{tip}A_{tip}$$

where N_q, $N\gamma$ = bearing capacity factors for deep foundations, which vary with ϕ, the friction angle
B = pier tip diameter or width
γ = unit weight of soil in zone of pier tip

TABLE A.4   Coefficient of Friction

Material	tan S
Wood	0.4
Steel	0.3
Steel, corrugated	tan ϕ of sand
Concrete	0.4 to 0.5

Substituting Eq. (A.28) into Eq. (A.21), the general equation of load bearing of a pier in a noncohesive soil can be obtained:

$$Q_{total} = fA_{surface} + Q_{tip}A_{tip} \qquad (A.21)$$

or
$$Q_{total} = fA_{surface} + \tfrac{1}{2}\gamma BN_{\gamma A_{tip}} + \bar{\sigma}_v N_q A_{tip} \qquad (A.29)$$

The term $(\tfrac{1}{2}\gamma BN_\gamma A_{tip})$ is small compared to $\bar{\sigma}N_q A_{tip}$ and is usually disregarded.

Example problem A.7

$$Q_{total} = fA_{surface} + \bar{\sigma}_v N_q A_{tip}$$

Assume a 12-in-diameter concrete pier 30 ft deep in wet sand,

$$\gamma = 120 \text{ lb/ft}^3 \quad \text{and} \quad \phi = 30°$$

What working load can the pier support assuming a safety factor of 2.5?

Solution

$$A_{tip} = \frac{\pi}{4}D^2 = 0.785 \text{ ft}^2$$

$$\bar{\sigma}_v = (120 \text{ lb/ft}^3 - 62.4 \text{ lb/ft}^3)(30 \text{ ft}) = 1728 \text{ lb/ft}^2$$

$$N_q = 25 \quad \text{(Fig. 3.15)}$$

$$Q_{tip} = (0.785)(1728)(25) = 33{,}912 \text{ lb} = 16.9 \text{ tons}$$

$$Q_{friction} = K\bar{\sigma}_v A_s \tan S \quad \text{where } A_s = \pi DH$$

$$= K\bar{\sigma}_v H\pi D \tan S$$

$$\bar{\sigma}_v = \frac{1728}{2} = 864 \text{ lb/ft}^2 \quad \text{average lateral pressure}$$

$$K = 2, \tan S = 0.45 \text{ (from Table A.4)}$$

$$Q_{friction} = (2)(864)(30)(3.14)(1.0)(0.45) = 73{,}250 \text{ lb} = 36.6 \text{ tons}$$

$$Q_{total} = 16.9 + 36.6 = 53.5 \text{ tons}$$

$$Safe\ load = 53.5/2.5 = 21.4 \text{ tons}$$

Example problem A.8
What working load could a slim pier (4-in-diameter drilled shaft cased with corrugated steel and filled with 3000-lb/in^2 steel-reinforced concrete) safely support under the soil conditions set forth in Example Problem A.7? Again assume a 30-ft pier.

Solution

$$A_{tip} = (0.785)(4/12)^2 = 0.085 \text{ ft}^2$$

$$Q_{tip} = (0.085)(1728)(25) = 3670 \text{ lb} = 1.8 \text{ tons}$$

$$\tan S = \tan 30° = 0.577$$

$Q_{\text{friction}} = (2)(864)(30)(\pi)(0.33)(0.577) = 31,000 \text{ lb} = 15.5 \text{ tons}$

$Q_{\text{total}} = 1.8 + 15.5 = 17.3 \text{ tons}$

Safe load = 17.3/2.5 = 6.9 tons = 6.1 metric tons

A 15-ft slim pier, such as that illustrated above, would safely carry only 3.8 tons, which would suggest marginal application to normal residential construction.

A.5.3 Piers in cohesive soils

For piers in a cohesive soil, the ultimate bearing capacity is the combination of end bearing and skin friction. In the skin friction calculation, the upper 5-ft section and the belled section (if designed) are neglected because of soil disturbance and loss of strength caused by construction, with W considered as negligible. Equation (A.20) becomes:

$$Q_{\text{total}} = Q_{\text{tip}} + Q_{\text{friction}}$$

Substituting Eqs. (A.23) and (A.21):

$$Q_{\text{total}} = C_u N_c A_{\text{tip}} + f A_{\text{pier}} \qquad (A.30)$$

where C_u = undisturbed shear strength of soil at tip
   A_{pier} = surface area of pier that is effective in developing skin friction
   $f = \alpha S C_w$, friction factor

and α = adhesion factor, 0.3, S = shape factor, 1.0 for straight shafts and 1.2 for tapered shafts, and C_w = undisturbed shear strength (fissured) at wall (Ref. 2 page 393).

Generally the soil adjacent to the shallow pier does not experience the shear strain necessary for a significant skin friction to develop, thus:

$$Q_{\text{total}} = Q_{\text{tip}} = C N_c A_{\text{tip}} \qquad (A.31)$$

The value of 9.0 is generally taken for N_c for a homogeneous cohesive soil when skin friction is neglected. Investigation using the finite element method (Ellison, et al., 1971) has indicated that the classical theory is not appropriate because of "tension cracks" that develop in the soil adjacent to the tip of the pier. Consequently, the value of 9.0 for N_c has been modified by others to include a reduction factor (0.75 has been suggested for London clay). A safety factor of 2.5 is most often recommended.

Example problem A.9

$$Q_{\text{total}} = Q_{\text{tip}} + Q_{\text{friction}} = C_u N_c A_{\text{tip}} + f A_{\text{pier}}$$

where $f = \alpha S C_w$

A clay soil affected by seasonal moisture variations to a depth of 5 ft is intended to support a house foundation. The working load per pier will not exceed 6 tons. Below the 5-ft interval, the undisturbed shear strength of the soil varies from 1000 lb/ft^2 at 5 ft to 3500 lb/ft^2 (fissured shear strength) at 25 ft. Design the required pier diameter and depth. A minimum safety factor of 2.5 is required. In order to use light equipment, consider pier depth less than 20 ft. Neglect any adhesion in the top 5 ft.

Solution   Assume 16-in diameter by 12 ft. Average strength increases with depth [1000 lb/ft^2 plus 125 lb/ft^2 per ft].

Shear strength C_w at 12 ft = 1000 lb/ft^2 + 7(125 lb/ft^2) = 1875 lb/ft^2

Average shear strength $C_w = \dfrac{1000 + 1875}{2} = 1437.5$ lb/ft^2

$$Q_{friction} = (0.3)(1440)(7 \text{ ft})(\pi)(1.33 \text{ ft}) = 12,630 \text{ lb} = 6.3 \text{ tons}$$

$$Q_{tip} = \frac{(9)(1875)(\pi)(1.33^2)}{4} = 23,450 \text{ lb} = 11.7 \text{ tons}$$

$$Q_{total} = 6.3 + 11.7 = 18 \text{ tons}$$

Safety factor = 18/6 = 3.0, which exceeds the minimum design. If the pier diameter were reduced to 12 in, what would be the safety factor?

$$Q_f = (6.3 \text{ tons})(1 \text{ ft}/1.33 \text{ ft}) = 4.7 \text{ tons}$$

$$Q_{tip} = (11.7 \text{ tons})(1 \text{ ft}^2/1.33 \text{ ft}^2) = 6.6 \text{ tons}$$

Safety factor = 11.3/6.0 = 1.88, which is unacceptable.
    If the pier diameter is reduced to 14 in, what would be the safety factor?

$$Q_f = (6.3 \text{ tons})(1.17/1.33) = 5.5 \text{ tons}$$

$$Q_{tip} = (11.7 \text{ tons})(1.17^2/1.33^2) = 9.0 \text{ tons}$$

Safety factor = 14.5/6.0 = 2.4, which is not acceptable. However, the 14-in diameter could be used if the pier depth were increased to 15 ft (4.6 m).

Example problem A.10   Assume the conditions established in Example Problem A.9 except that the pier is a 4-in drilled shaft lined with thin-wall steel casing and filled with 3000 lb/in^2 steel-reinforced concrete. Would this pier safely carry the suggested load? Would the concrete pier crush under the imposed load assuming ideal conditions?

Solution

$$A_{tip} = (0.785)(4^2) = 12.6 \text{ in}^2$$

$$A_{tip} \times q_c = (12.6 \text{ in}^2)(3000 \text{ lb/in}^2)$$

$$= 37,600 \text{ lb} = 18.8 \text{ tons}$$

The concrete would safely support the load of 6 tons, assuming a concrete compression safety factor of 3.

Shear strength C_w at 20 ft = 2875 lb/ft^2

Average shear strength C_w = 1000 + 2875/2 = 1940 lb/ft^2

$$Q_{\text{friction}} = (0.3)(1940)(15)(\pi)(0.33) = 9050 \text{ lb} = 4.5 \text{ tons}$$

$$Q_{\text{tip}} = (9)(2875)(0.33^2)(0.785) = 2210 \text{ lb} = 1.1 \text{ ton}$$

$$Q_{\text{total}} = 4.5 + 1.1 = 5.6 \text{ tons}$$

The slim pier would fail, since the safe load would be 5.6/2.5 or 2.24 tons.

Note: The depth of disturbed soil moisture content in semiarid climates, under true field conditions, is greater than routine water content tests would indicate, particularly concerning piers at the perimeter. The fact that the concrete conducts heat causes the soil to lose moisture at depths significantly greater than are suggested by undisturbed considerations. This is particularly true when the soil contains a highly expansive clay in relative abundance.

A.5.4 Negative skin friction

Negative skin friction occurs when the pier or pile shaft traverses loose soil or uncompacted fill followed by soil compaction upon application of surface load. This tends to cause the pier or pile to settle.

Shallow piers drilled into or through expansive clay soils sometimes present the problem of uplift from skin friction (heave) (Fig. 8.3). Reducing the diameter of the pier will reduce skin friction and, ultimately, heave. Also, lining (or sleeving) the top few feet of the drilled hole with a friction-reducing material, such as cardboard or polyethylene, is often thought to be useful for this purpose. However, belling the pier shaft is most often the best preventive against heave.

The design of piers in granular-cohesive soil is based on presumptive bearing values (Table 3.11).

Example problem A.11   If the tensile strength of a 4-in concrete pier 20 ft in length is 350 lb/in^2, what expansive force would be required to separate the pier? Again assume a structural load of 6 tons on the pier.

Cross-sectional area (CSA) = $0.785D^2$ = (0.785)(16) = 12.56 in^2

$$Q_{\text{tensile resistance}} = (350 \text{ lb/in}^2)(12.56 \text{ in}^2) = 4396 \text{ lb} = 2.2 \text{ ton}$$

If this pier were situated in an expansive soil with a PI of 42, initial moisture content W of 20 percent and if the soil would exert an expansive force of 9000 lb/ft^2 upon an increase of 3 percent soil moisture, would the pier be likely to fail? Assume that the pier does not slip (heave).

$$Q_{\text{tensile force}} = (0.45)(1)(9000 \text{ lb/ft}^2)(15 \text{ ft})(\pi)(\tfrac{1}{3} \text{ ft}) = 62{,}949 \text{ lb} = 31 \text{ tons}$$

The concrete pier would fail in tension.

Similarly, if the pier consisted of slip joint pipe filled with concrete, would the pier be likely to fail in tension?

$$Q_{\text{tensile force}} = (0.3)(1)(9000)(15)\pi(\tfrac{1}{3}) = 21 \text{ tons}$$

The pier would fail in tension. (Certain license has been taken to simplify this example, but it is obvious that the conclusion drawn is accurate.)

These examples focus on the inherent weakness of slim concrete piers or piles. The addition of steel reinforcing will increase the tensile capacity. Belling, when mechanically possible, will increase the vertical load capacity at the tip or base. Belling will not influence the tensile capacity and, in most cases, the steel would not eliminate some degree of failure in compression.

Most of the cities in the northern United States are located on a thick layer of glacial till or hardpan overlying the bedrock. Glacial tills consist of clay, silt, gravel, and boulders. Low compressibility of this material provides high bearing capacity and is ideal for load-carrying drilled piers.

TABLE A.5   Presumptive Bearing Values for Glacial Till or Hardpan

Code	Allowable bearing stress, tons/ft^2
Boston	10
Chicago	6
Cleveland	10
Detroit	10
Indiana	4
New York City	8–12
Pittsburgh	8

A.5.5   Bearing capacity of rock

For commercial and industrial buildings and (in some limited cases) for residential buildings, drilled piers are designed to be located on or socketed into bedrock. At the present time, there is no established basis for design of piers on rock. Design is based on presumptive bearing stress on rock allowed by building codes.

If rock cores are tested in a laboratory under an unconfined compressive strength test, usually one-sixth to one-eighth of the test value can be taken as the allowable bearing stress. Depending on the rock quality, a reduction factor should be considered. The reduction factor is related to structural characteristics of the rock such as fissured, closely fissured, thinly bedded, and inclined.

The finite element method for stress analysis of different rocks with different stiffness matrixes, such as transversely isotropic, orthotropic, or anisotropic, can provide good results and will include the fracture effects and any other microscopic geologic defects that alter the behavior of rock under the load.[8]

A.6   References

1. McCarthy, David, *Essentials of Soil Mechanics and Foundations*, Reston Publishing, Reston, Va., 1977.
2. M. J. Tomlinson, *Foundation Design and Construction*, Wiley Interscience, New York, 1969.
3. Donald W. Taylor, *Soil Mechanics*, Wiley, New York, 1948.
4. K. Terzaghi, *Theoretical Soil Mechanics*, Wiley, New York, 1943.
5. K. Terzaghi, and R. B. Peck, *Soil Mechanics in Engineering Practice*, Wiley, New York, 1948, 1949.
6. Braja M. Das, *Soil Mechanics*, Iowa University Press, Iowa, 1979.
7. Hsia-Yang Fang and Hans F. Winterkorn, eds., *Foundation Engineering Handbook*, VNR, New York, 1975.
8. C. R. Scott, *Developments in Soil Mechanics*, *Vol. 1*, Applied Science Publishers, London, 1978.
9. Marcus M. Truitt, *Soil Mechanics Technology*, Prentice-Hall, Englewood Cliffs, N.J., 1983.

Appendix

B

Conversion Factors

To convert	to	Multiply by
acre-feet (acre-ft)	cubic meters (m³)	1.23×10^3
acres (acres)	hectares (ha)	0.405
pounds-mass (lbm)	kilograms (kg)	0.454
miles (mi)	kilometers (km)	1.61
U.S. gallons (gal)	liters (l)	3.79
inches (in)	millimeters (mm)	25.4
kilograms-force (kgf)	newtons (N)	9.81
pounds-force (lbf)	newtons (N)	4.45
kips (k)	pounds (lb)	1000
kips per cubic foot (k/ft³)	kilonewtons per cubic meter (kN/m³)	157
tons (short)	kips (k)	2.0
tons (short)	tons (metric)	0.91
inches (in)	angstroms (Å)	2.54×10^8
inches	micrometers (microns)	2.54×10^4
inches	centimeters (cm)	2.54
feet (ft)	meters (m)	0.30
square inches (in²)	square centimeters (cm²)	6.45
cubic inches (in³)	cubic centimeters (cm³)	16.39
cubic feet (ft³)	cubic meters (m³)	2.83×10^{-2}
cubic yards (yd³)	cubic meters	0.76
pounds per square inch (lb/in²)	kilograms per square centimeter (kg/cm²)	7.0×10^{-2}
pounds per square foot (lb/ft²)	kilograms per square meter	4.88
pounds per cubic foot (lb/ft³)	kilograms per cubic meter (kg/m³)	16.02
pounds-force per square inch (lbf/in²)	newtons per square meter (N/m²)	6.89×10^3
pounds-force per square inch (lbf/in²)	kilopascals (kPa)	6.89
atmospheres (atm)	pounds per square inch (lb/in²)	14.7
kilonewtons per square meter (kN/m²)	kilopascals (kPa)	1.0

Abbreviations of Units of Measure

acre-in/hr	acre-inch or acre-inches per hour
cm	centimeter(s)
cm^2	square centimeter(s)
cm^3	cubic centimeter(s)
cm/year	centimeter(s) per year
°F	degree(s) Fahrenheit
°C	degree(s) Celsius
ft	foot or feet
ft^3	cubic foot or feet
ft/ft	foot or feet per foot
ft/min	foot or feet per minute
ft/sec	foot or feet per second
ft/sec^2	foot or feet per second per second
g	gram(s)
gal/ft^2	gallon(s) per square foot
gal/min	gallon(s) per minute
gal/sack	gallon(s) per sack
in	inch or inches
in/ft	inch or inches per foot
in/hr	inch or inches per hour
in/year	inch or inches per year
kg/cm^2	kilogram(s) per cubic centimeter
kg/m^2	kilogram(s) per square meter
kg/m^3	kilogram(s) per cubic meter

km^2	square kilometers
l	liter(s)
l/min	liter(s) per minute
lb	pound(s)
lb/(ft · sec)	pound(s) per foot per second
lb/ft^2	pound(s) per square foot
lb/ft^3	pound(s) per cubic foot
lb/in^2	pound(s) per square inch
lb/yd^3	pound(s) per cubic yard
m	meter(s)
m/min	meter(s) per minute
mi	mile(s)
mi^2	square mile(s)
μm	micrometer(s) (μ is the Greek letter mu)
min	minute(s)
ml/cm^2	milliliter(s) per square centimeter
ml/hr	milliliter(s) per hour
mm	millimeter(s)
oz/hr	ounce(s) per hour
pints/ft^2	pints per square foot
sec	second(s)
t	metric ton(s) (1000 kg)
t/cm^2	metric ton(s) per square centimeter
yd^3	cubic yard(s)

Glossary*

activity Ratio of plasticity index PI to percent of clay particles, by weight, passing 2 μm.

adequate watering Watering sufficient to stop or arrest settlement brought about by soil shrinkage resulting from loss of moisture.

aeolian soil Soil that has been deposited by wind.

aeration zone The capillary fringe, an intermediate belt (which may include one or more perched water zones) and, at the surface, the soil water belt, often referred to as the root zone.

allowable load The load which may be safely transmitted to a foundation member.

allowable pier or pile load The load permitted on any vertical pier or pile applied concentrically in the direction of the axis. It is the least value determined from the capacity of the pile or pier as a structural member, the allowable bearing pressure on soil strata underlying the tips, the resistance to penetration, the capacity demonstrated by load test, or the basic maximum load prescribed by the building code. The latter may be exceeded when a higher value can be substantiated on the basis of test analysis.

alluvial soil Soil deposited by running waters.

anchor pier or pile A pile or pier connected to a structure by one or more ties to furnish lateral support or to resist uplift. Also, a reaction pile or pier for load testing.

arenaceous soil Sandy soil.

argillaceous soil Clayey soil.

augered or drilled pier or pile A concrete pier or pile cast in place in an

---

*Certain of the entries concerning pile technology were taken from H. W. Hunt, *Design and Installation of Driven Pile Foundations*.

augered hole, which may be belled at the bottom, and suitable for use where the soil is dry and the hole will stand open.

banding   Strapping timber piles with high-tensile steel to prevent their splitting while being driven.

basal spacing   The distance between individual or molecular layers of the clay particles.

batter pier or pile   A pile driven or a pier cast at an inclination from the vertical.

bearing capacity   The allowable pier or pile load as limited by the provision that the pressures in materials along the pier or pile and below the tips, produced by the loads on individual pier or piles and by the aggregate of all piers or piles in a group, shall not exceed the allowable soil-bearing values.

bearing capacity of soil   Maximum pressure which can be applied to a soil mass without causing shear failure. The pressure or stress is created by applied loads and transmitted to the soil by the foundation.

bell (underream)   Enlargement of the bottom end of an augered pier to increase bearing load capacity.

bentonite (montmorillonite)   A colloidal clay used as a heavy slurry to prevent earth sluffing into a drilled hole; also used for waterproofing.

brace pier or pile   A batter pile or pier connected to a structure in a way to resist lateral forces.

brooming   The separation of fibers at the butt or tip of a wood pile generally caused by excessive or improper driving. It can be controlled through the use of a pile ring, driving cap with cushion blocks, on a metal shoe for the pile tip.

butt of a pile   The larger or head end of a tapered pile; usually the upper end of a pile as driven. Also, a general term for the upper portion of a pile.

caisson or caisson pile   A large-diameter shaft hand- or machine-excavated to the bearing stratum inside a protective casing. The shaft may require a cutting shoe to penetrate obstructions.

caliche   Argillaceous limestone or calcareous clay.

canopy (width)   The diameter of tree foliage. Also referred to as *drip line.*

capillary fringe   An area that contains capillary water originating from the water table or perched water zone.

capillary rise (h_c)   A measure of height of water rise above the level of free-water boundary. Capillarity is impeded by the swell of clay particles (loss of permeability) upon invasion of water. Finer soils will create a greater height of capillary rise, but the rate of rise is slower.

cast-in-place pier or pile   A concrete pier or pile poured (either with or without a metal casing) in its permanent location in the ground.

Chicago caisson   A 3- to 12-ft-diameter or square shaft with vertical timber sheathing sunk in about 4-ft increments as bracing and additional sheathing are installed.

clay   A soil that has the finest possible particles, usually smaller than

1/10,000 in in diameter, and often possesses the capacity for extreme volume changes with differential access to water.

clay bearing failure The result of expansive soils exerting nonuniform pressure against a constant downward loading. Such a loading causes the pier to deviate further from the vertical until the pier can no longer support a structural load.

cohesion A cementing or gluing force between particles; requires a clay content.

compacted concrete pier or pile A cast-in-place pier or pile formed with an enlarged base. Concrete in the base is placed in small batches, which are compacted by heavy blows prior to attaining an initial set.

composite pile A pile made up of two types of piles joined together. The connection between the two components should prevent their separation during and after construction.

compressive stress Stress resulting from compressive loading, considered positive in soil mechanics.

consolidation The action that occurs when an applied load forces water out of voids and enables solid particles to become more closely packed. The resultant downward movement is termed "settlement."

creosoted pile A timber pile impregnated with a specified minimum amount of coal tar creosote by an approved process to prevent deterioration.

cushion block Material inserted between the hammer and the pile-driving cap or pile to minimize local damage. Asbestos, micarta, steel, aluminum, coiled cable, wood, and other materials are used.

cut and fill Removal of excess existing soil (cut) to low or deficient areas (fill) for contouring purposes.

cutoff The prescribed elevation at which the top of a driven pile is cut or left; also the portion removed from the upper end of the pile after driving.

cutting shoe Additional metal as an inside or outside cast-steel ring or welded plate at the bottom of an open-end pile or caisson to strengthen the tip.

dead load W_D The weight of the empty structure.

deep foundation A design whereby the structural load is transmitted to a soil at some depth, usually through piers, piles, or caissons.

displacement pile A solid timber or precast concrete pile, or hollow pile driven with the lower end closed, which displaces soil volume by compaction or by lateral or vertical displacement of soil. H and open-end pipe are examples of nondisplacement piles.

doodle or dummy hole An empty tubular section driven into the ground within operating radius of a pile rig. Shell or thin-wall pipe requiring a full-length mandrel for driving is lowered into the hole, and then the mandrel is inserted in the pile. Pile and mandrel are raised together into the leads and moved to the required location.

downdrag   Negative friction or weight of earth gripping a pile in settling soils and thus adding load on the piles installed.

drilled-in caisson   An open-ended pipe driven to rock. It is cleaned out and a socket is drilled into rock to receive a steel core (H, WF, or bars). Then the socket and pipe are filled with concrete.

driving cap or helmet   A steel cap placed over a pile to prevent damage in driving.

effective size D_{10}   Sand particle size such that 10 percent passes that sieve.

elastic modulus E   A factor determined by dividing stress by strain and expressed in pounds per square inch or kilograms per square centimeter.

elevations   Measurements taken by instrument (usually optical) to establish grades.

embedment   The length of the pile from the surface of the ground or from the cutoff below the ground to the tip of the pile. Also, the depth of penetration of the top of pile into the pile cap.

failure of pier or pile foundation   The movement of the pier or pile foundation, or any part thereof, either as settlement upheaval or laterally, to such an extent that objectionable damage results to the structure supported by the foundation. Also, failure of a pier or pile or piers or piles to pass a load test.

field capacity   The residual amount of water held in the soil after excess gravitational water has drained and after the overall rate of downward water movement has decreased (zero capillarity).

fill   Soil added to provide a level construction surface or desired grade.

flexural strength   The maximum stress (tensile or compressive) at rupture. (A fictitious, though sometimes convenient, value because mathematical assumptions for soil behavior at stresses approaching failure are inadequate.) Also referred to as the *modulus of rupture*.

follower   A member interposed between the hammer and the pile to transmit blows when the top of the pile is below the reach of the hammer.

foot, pile   The lower end of a driven pile.

footing   A member, usually concrete, that distributes the foundation load over an extended area and thus provides increased support capacity on any bearing soil.

force   Pressure times area or mass times acceleration.

foundation   The part of a structure in direct contact with the ground which transmits the load of the structure to the ground.

Franki pile   A pile formed by ramming very dry concrete into the ground with a heavy weight, a pressure-injected footing.

free water   Water which can be taken on or lost by the soil without corresponding soil volume change.

French drain   A perforated pipe installed in a cut to intercept and divert the underground water. The cut is below the level of the intruding water, and it is graded to drain the accumulated water away from the site. Sometimes a catch basin and discharge pump are also required if a natural grade does not exist.

friction pile   A pile or pier that supports its load by the friction developed between its surface and the soil through which it is driven.

frost heaving   Expansion that results when a mixture of soil and water freezes. Upon freezing, the total volume may be increased by as much as 25 percent dependent upon the formation of ice lenses at the boundary between the frozen and unfrozen soil.

g_T Unit weight of liquid at temperature T. Expressed in grams per cubic centimeter.

gap-graded soil   A coarse-grained soil containing both large and small sizes but a relatively low proportion of intermediate sizes.

grade   The level of ground surface. Also, the rise or fall per given distance (often 100 ft).

grillage   A framework of structural horizontal members crossed in layers and placed on the tops of piles or pile caps to support a structural load.

grout curtain   A continuous, consolidated boundary or area with strength sufficient to permit excavation without sloughing or provide adequate bearing strength from soils of basic substandard capacity.

grouting   An operation whereby a material is injected to penetrate and permeate a relatively deep soil bed. The purpose is to decrease voids or permeability, increase quality of the penetrated soil, or, on occasion, impede organic decay.

guard pile   A fender pile.

guide pile   A pile used as a guide for driving other piles.

guides   The part of the pile leads that forms a pathway for the hammer. It consists of parallel members which mate with grooves on the hammer.

gumbo   Highly plastic clay from the southern and/or western United States.

gypsum   Anhydrous calcium sulfate ($CaSO_4$).

hammer energy   The capacity of a pile-driving hammer to do work at impact, measured in foot-pounds per blow.

heave of pier or pile   The uplift of earth between or near piers or piles caused by the displacement of soil by pile driving; the uplift of an in-place pile caused by the driving of an adjacent pile; the uplift of an in-place pile or pier caused by cohesive skin friction (expansive soils).

hygroscopic soil Soil that readily takes up and retains water on the surface of its particles.

interception The process whereby precipitation is caught and held by foliage and evaporated from the exposed surfaces.

interior floors Floors that are supported by the girder-and-joist system of a wood substructure wherein the system is, in turn, supported on piers and pier caps.

interlayer moisture Water that is situated within the crystalline layers of the clay and provides the bulk of the residual moisture contained within the intermediate belt.

intermediate belt Soil that contains moisture that is essentially in dead storage and is held by molecular forces. It may include one or more perched water zones.

jacking A means of imposing a static driving force on a pile by jacks. Used extensively to install piles in underpinning existing structures and in static load testing.

jetting The use of a water jet to facilitate the placing or driving of a pile through the hydraulic displacement of parts of the soil. In some cases, a high-pressure air jet may be used either alone or with water.

lateral support Batter piles or reinforcement to resist lateral forces on piles or footings.

leads or leaders A frame, upright or inclined, which supports sheaves at the top for hoisting the pile and hammer and which is equipped with parallel members for guiding the pile and hammer. Leads are known as swinging, hanging, or pendulum when suspended at the top so as to permit vertical or lateral movement or swinging through an arc and as fixed or stationary when constructed or held in a fixed position on a pile driver. Fixed leads may be adjustable for driving batter piles. Also known as *pile guides*.

liquid limit The water content of a soil in which 25 blows from a drop of 1 cm closes a ⅜-in V groove for a length of ½ in in a standard liquid limit LL device.

live load W_L The weight of building contents plus wind, snow, and earthquake forces where applicable.

loess An aeolian deposit of uniform gradation with some calcareous cementation.

mandrel A core that is inserted into a closed-end thin-shell tubular pile. A *solid mandrel* is a heavy tubular section that will transmit the hammer energy to the point; a *collapsible mandrel* is a core, the outer diameter of which can be changed by mechanical or other means, that is capable of transmitting the hammer energy to the bottom of the pile and supporting the wall of thin-shelled casing. It is inserted into the pile in a collapsed condition and expanded to grip the inner surface of the pile with sufficient force to prevent slipping. After the pile is in place, the mandrel is collapsed and withdrawn.

marl A calcareous clay.

mats Heavy timbers bolted together for use as a support and roadway for a pile driver crane.

maximum density The density attained by the addition of sufficient water to fill the voids and help the particles move closer together. Water added beyond that point displaces the heavier solids and thus reduces the density.

moisture barrier A means of maintaining moisture content beneath a foundation (generally slab) consisting of an impermeable barrier extending to some depth and in close proximity to the perimeter beam.

mudjacking A process whereby a water and soil cement or soil-lime-cement grout is pumped beneath the slab, under pressure, to produce a lifting force which literally floats the slab to the desired position.

negative friction The effect on a pile of settling soil that may grip the pile and add its weight to the load to be carried by the bearing strata.

newton A unit of force. 1 N = 1 kg-mass $\times$ 1 m/sec^2 (acceleration).

newtonian fluid A fluid (e.g., water, antifreeze, or salt water) that produces a straight line through the origin when a shear rate–shear stress diagram is plotted.

noncohesive soil A soil in which there is no attraction or adhesion between individual particles.

nonnewtonian fluid A fluid (e.g., cement, soil, or a soil-cement slurry) that does not exhibit a linear shear rate–shear stress diagram.

overdriving Driving in a way that damages material in a pile, most often by continuing to pound after penetration of the pile stops.

pedestal pile A cast-in-place concrete end-bearing pile so constructed that concrete is forced out into a bulb or pedestal at the foot of the pile.

penetration, gross The downward axial movement of a pile per hammer blow as measured at an established point on the pile. *Net penetration* is the gross penetration less the rebound, or the net downward movement of the established point. *Total penetration* is the distance from the point of the pile to the surface of the ground. *Minimum pile penetration* is the depth or length specified to develop the required load-bearing capacity of the soil or required for lateral strength.

perched water zone The region of perched groundwater which develops essentially from water accumulation either above a relatively impermeable stratum or within an unusually permeable lens. It generally occurs after a good rain and is relatively temporary.

Perma-Jack A proprietary device that utilizes a hydraulic ram to drive slip-jointed sections of 3-in steel pipe to rock or suitable bearing soil.

pH A measure of hydrogen ion concentration by which 7 is neutral. Values less than 7 indicate acidity, and values above 7 indicate basicity.

phreatic boundary The surface of the water table which will not normally deflect or deform except under certain conditions in the proximity of a producing well.

pier and beam   A design wherein the perimeter loads are carried on a continuous beam supported in turn on piers drilled into the ground, supposedly to a competent bearing soil or stratum. Interior loads are carried by isolated piers in a grid pattern.

pier and beam, low-profile   A design wherein the crawl space is substantially lower than the exterior grade.

pier and beam, normal design   A design wherein the crawl space is at a grade equivalent to the exterior landscape.

piers   In general, concrete poured into circular holes that, as opposed to piles, are normally of larger cross-sectional area relative to length. A single pier is normally expected to support the entire applied load.

piers or pilings   Members normally extended through the marginal soils to either rock or other competent bearing material.

pile   Long, slender wood, steel, or concrete members usually driven in groups or clusters. They may also be poured concrete, which gives rise to a gray area of differentiation between piles and slim piers.

pile bent   Two or more piles driven in a row transverse to the long dimension of a structure, such as a bridge foundation, and fastened together by capping and bracing.

pile bulkhead   A pile structure generally consisting of vertical piles with brace or anchor piles, wales, and a sheet pile wall framed together and capable of resisting earth or water pressure.

pile butt   The larger end of a tapered pile. Also, a section of pile cut off at top.

pile drive shoe   A metal protection for the foot of a pile to prevent damage, obtain better penetration, and improve the contact area of an end-bearing pile. Designed to take mandrel impact if a mandrel is used.

pile-driving cap   Generally a forged steel or steel casting designed to fit over and around the top or butt end of the pile to prevent damage to the head of the pile while driving. Also known as a *hood* or *bonnet*.

pile encasement   A protective cover for a steel or timber pile. Usually it is concrete added at the water or ground line, where piles of all types are most vulnerable.

pile extractor   A device for pulling a pile out of the ground. It may be an inverted steam or air hammer with a yoke so equipped as to transmit upward blows to the pile body or a specially built extractor utilizing the same principle. Vibratory hammers may be especially effective. All extractor operations require a strong upward force.

pile hammer   One of several devices for driving a pile: (1) *drop hammer* A heavy weight, usually a metal casting with grooves in the sides to mate with leads. It is raised in the leads by ropes or cable and allowed to drop on the pile.

Sometimes called a gravity hammer. (2) *steam or air hammer* A movable ram attached to a piston operating in a cylinder which in turn is mounted in a metal frame with grooves that engage the pile driver leads; it has a hood or bonnet on the lower end with a cushion block that fits the pile head. In the single-acting hammer, steam or air pressure is used only to raise the moving parts, which then fall by gravity and strike the cushion block. In the double-acting and differential-acting hammer, steam or air pressure is also used to accelerate the downward movement of the ram. (3) *diesel hammer* An integrally powered pile hammer operated with the use of diesel fuel oil. A movable ram is raised initially by outside means. When released, the ram falls onto an impact block or anvil which itself rests on the pile. The falling ram actuates ports for admission of fuel and air, compresses the air, and raising the air to a higher temperature; the oil vaporizes and ignites from heat and pressure. The instantaneous expansion of gases supplies additional drive and raises the ram for the next stroke. (4) *vibratory driving machine* A unit with eccentric weights mounted on shafts rotated in different directions for the purpose of applying periodic unbalanced forces to a pile shaft. An electric motor or hydraulic fluid rotates the shaft at about 700 to 2000 vibrations/min. (5) *sonic driver* A machine designed for variation from 3600 to 9000 cycles/min to match the sonic response of soil for very rapid driving. (Vibratory and sonic drivers work very well under some conditions but not efficiently in others. They generally produce little disturbance in surrounding soils.)

pile or pier cap   A structural member placed upon the tops of piers or piles. It is used to transmit and distribute the load of the structure above to the head of a pile, a row of piles, or a pile group.

pile point   A cast-steel or steel drive shoe which may be pointed and is fixed to the pile shaft at the tip for easier driving, improved penetration, protection against damage in dense material or boulders, and improved bearing at the tip.

pile ring   A metal hoop used to bind the head of a timber pile during driving to prevent splitting and brooming.

pile splicer   A metal fitting for quickly joining two similar or dissimilar parts of a pile in or out of the leads.

pile tip   The lower and usually the smaller end of a pile.

pipe flow apparatus   The simplest capillary viscometer. It is, as might be expected, commonly used.

pipe pile   A steel or concrete cylindrical shell of specified strength and thickness. It is driven either open- or closed-ended and is usually filled with concrete.

plastic limit PL   The water content at which a $\frac{1}{8}$-in-diameter thread of soil begins to crumble.

plasticity index PI   A dimensionless constant which bears a direct ratio to the affinity of the bearing soil for volumetric changes with respect to moisture variations. The PI is determined as the difference between the liquid limit LL and plastic limit PL.

plates   Wood members placed horizontally at each end of wall studs. The ceiling plate, or *header*, forms the top, and the floor or sole plate forms the bottom.

poorly graded soil   A coarse-grained soil in which a majority of particles are of one size. Often described as *uniform* or *gap-graded*.

pore water   Water that occurs within the soil mass external to individual soil grains and is held by interfacial tension.

porosity *n*   The ratio of combined volume of liquid and air to total volume of soil.

precast pier or pile   A reinforced concrete pier or pile which is manufactured in a construction yard or at the site and, having been properly cured, is driven like a timber pile.

preexcavation   Removal of soil that may heave. The removal is effected by augering or by driving and cleaning out an open-ended pipe. The objective is to keep the soil volume constant.

prestressed pier or pile   A precast concrete pier or pile which is either pre- or posttensioned to reduce or eliminate tensile stresses to which piers or piles are subjected during transportation and driving and while in service. Pretensioning is used for piling up to about 24 in in sizes for which the wires are stressed prior to casting concrete around them. Posttensioning is used for large open cylindrical piles; wires are pulled through holes left in the walls and stressed against concrete previously cast in the walls.

q_u   The unconfined compressive strength which measures a soil's capacity to carry load.

r   The radius, in centimeters, of a capillary pore.

refusal   The condition reached when a pile being driven by a hammer has zero penetration per blow (as when the point of the pile reaches an impenetrable bottom such as rock) or when the effective energy of the hammer blow is no longer sufficient to cause penetration. When so stipulated, the term "refusal" or "substantial refusal" may be used to indicate the specified minimum penetration per blow. Overdriving of piles after essential refusal can damage them seriously.

rock   In the construction field, a layer of stony material. Contrary to popular opinion, it is not always a superior foundation bed because of such possible factors as bedding planes, faults, joints, weathering, and cementation (or lack thereof) of constituents.

root zone   The upper layer of soil from which plant roots take their moisture.

run-off   Excess water not retained by the soil.

sand pile   A column of sand installed by driving a pipe with an openable end into soil (usually swamp) and then forcing the sand out as a permanent column as pipe is withdrawn. The sand serves as a drain or wick to speed consolidation and improve bearing value of the soil.

sands and gravels Coarse particles which range in size from 3-in diameter down to grains so small they can be barely distinguished by the unaided eye.

sanitary land fill A euphemism for garbage dump.

saturation zone The deepest soil water source. More commonly termed the "water table" or "groundwater."

screw pile A spiral blade fixed on a shaft and screwed into the ground by a rotating force. Quite large piles of this type have been used, but they are little known in the United States.

sensitivity The ratio of unconfined compressive strength of undisturbed clay to that of remolded clay.

set Net penetration per pile-driving blow.

settlement The drop of some portion of a foundation below the original, as-built grade.

settling velocity V_s The rate at which particles settle in a liquid, referred to as Stokes law.

shale A sedimentary rock: indurated clay and/or silt muds.

shallow foundation A foundation in which the depth D is less than or equal to the width B. Refers principally to footings.

shear strength of soil (coulomb) $\tau_f = C + \sigma \tan \psi$, (cohesion plus friction), lb/in^2, kg/cm^2, where C = apparent cohesion, σ = total normal stress on shear plane, and ψ = angle of shearing stress.

shearing strength of clay soil (vane shear test)

$$C = \frac{T}{\pi}\left(\frac{d^2 h}{2} + \frac{d^3}{6}\right) \quad = \quad \text{lb/in}^2 \ (\text{kg/cm}^2)$$

where d = vane width, h = vane height, T = torque required to rotate vane.

sheet pile A pile that may form one of a continuous line or row of timber, pre-cast concrete, or steel piles driven in close contact to provide a tight wall to resist or exclude the lateral pressure of water, adjacent earth, or other material.

shrinkage limit SL Water content immediately above the quantity necessary to fill all the voids of a dry soil.

silt Soil that is intermediate in particle size between sand and clay. It represents particles of ground rocks which have not yet changed in character to minerals.

slab One or another variety of concrete foundation that is supported entirely by surface soils. It probably constitutes the majority of new construction in areas with high-clay soils.

sliding The consequence of erecting a structure on a slope such that movement is not limited to the vertical but has a lateral or horizontal component.

soil All the loose material constituting the earth's crust in varying proportions and including air, water, and solid particles. The solid particles have been formed by the disintegration of rocks.

soil belt   The vertical section that can contain capillary water available from rains or watering. Unless this moisture is continually restored, the soil will eventually desiccate through the effects of gravity, transpiration, and/or evaporation.

soil stabilization   A procedure for improving the natural soil properties to make them a more adequate base for construction.

soil water belt   The vertical section that provides moisture for the vegetable and plant kingdom.

spread footings   Footings that consist of two structural components: (1) steel-reinforced pads that are of sufficient size to adequately distribute the foundation load over the supporting soil and are poured at a depth to be relatively independent of seasonal soil moisture variation and (2) a steel-reinforced pier tied into the footing with steel and poured to the bottom of the foundation beam.

spud   A short, strong member driven and then removed (1) to make a hole for inserting a pile which is too long for placing directly in the pile driver leads or (2) to break through a crust of hard material.

steel pipe pile   Pipe with any wall thickness or diameter. It may be driven open- or closed-end depending on conditions. Closed-end piles preferably have cast-steel points but sometimes have flat plates. Open-end piles may require bottom reinforcement.

step-tapered pier or pile   A cast-in-place pier or pile that has a diameter stepped up in increments, usually in 8- to 12-ft sections of corrugated thin-metal shell, and is driven with a mandrel. It may be pipe reduced in steps and installed with or without a mandrel.

strapping   Banding of timber piles with high-tensile steel to prevent splitting while driving.

strength   The ability to resist force, often measured by the force (stress) required to cause rupture or failure. The basic resistance to failure is due to both cohesion and internal friction. The angle of rupture is a function of the intended angle of friction v. The angle which the plane of failure makes with the axis of loading is considered to be 45°, $\theta/2$. Rupture or failure can result from applied tensile stress (failure in cohesion), shearing stress (sliding), compression stress (crushing), or some combination of the three.

stress   The force at a point in a soil mass that is due to the weight of the soil above the point plus any applied (structural) load.

stringer   A member at right angles to and resting on or clamped to pile caps that forms a support for the superstructure.

strut   A compression member that extends horizontally from bent to bent, or pile to pile in a bent, and serves as a stiffening member.

surface-absorbed water   Water that occurs within the soil mass externally to individual soil grains and is held by molecular attraction between the clay particle and the dipolar water molecule.

swelling pressure   Pressure needed to prevent swell as soil takes on moisture above the stable moisture level.

tensile stress   Stress resulting from tensile forces, considered negative in soil mechanics.

timber pile   A tree trunk, usually driven small end down, probably the earliest form of pile. Frequently it is treated with creosote as a preservative. A fabricated or pressed-steel tip—and frequently a steel ring around the top—insure against damage in driving.

transpiration   The removal of soil moisture by vegetation.

tremie   A procedure and equipment for placing concrete under water.

triaxial shear (compression) strength test   A procedure in which a cylindrical soil sample, generally with a length/diameter ratio of 2 is stressed under conditions of axial symmetry. The sample is subjected to peripheral hydraulic pressure and then the axial stress is applied in gradually increasing increments by applications of compressive load until failure of the sample occurs.

triaxial shear tests   Tests that are basically useful for clays, silts, peats, and soft rocks: (1) *unconsolidated-undrained* Soil water is retained within the sample during the test. Consolidation of sample by peripheral fluid pressure is not allowed. (2) *consolidated-undrained* Drainage of soil water from the specimen is permitted under a specified peripheral fluid pressure until consolidation is complete. Drainage is blocked and the axial stress is applied. Pore water pressures can be measured during the undrained portion of test. (3) *drained* Drainage of the specimen is permitted through the duration of test. The principal stress (axial load) is applied at a rate sufficiently low to ensure that the water pore pressure remains zero. Under conditions in which the test procedures are reflective of field conditions, the undrained strength can be expressed in terms of total stress (C and O) and the drained strength in terms of effective stress (C' and O').

trip   A block in the leads of a pile driver of the drop hammer type that has a device for releasing the hammer and thereby regulating the height of the fall and is also used to drop the ram to start a diesel hammer.

T_{ST} Surface tension of liquid at temperature T^0.

uniform soil   Soil that contains a high proportion of particles within narrow size limits.

uniformity coeffecient C_u   The ratio D_{60}/D_{10}, where each term represents grain size, respectively that which passes 60% (D_{60}) and 10% (D_{10}) by weight.

upheaval   The situation in which areas of the foundation (usually internal) are raised above the as-built position.

viscosity   A single constant which describes the newtonian relationship of shear stress and shear rate.

void ratio e   The ratio of combined volume of water and air to the total volume of the soil sample.

W_t The sum of live loads W_L and dead loads W_D.

water leaks   Water from any domestic source which is accumulated under the foundation. Any water under the foundation, regardless of source, tends to accumulate in the plumbing ditch. Usually of greater concern to slab foundation.

water table   The upper surface of water saturation in permeable soil or rock.

well-graded soil   A soil with a fairly even distribution of grain sizes—no excess of one size and no intermediate sizes lacking.

Index

A line, 48–49
Abbreviations of units of measure, 217–218
Abrasion resistance, 61
Absorption, 101
Activity, defined, 49
Add-on construction, 160
Adelaide soil, 86
ADS pipe, 29, 31
Adsorption, 101
Aeolian deposits, 122
Aeration zone, 5, 7
Aggregate, 64–66
Air-entrained concrete, 59, 61, 67–68
American Standard sieves, 46
Annular velocity, 116–117
Apparent cohesion, 55
Aquifers, deep subsoil, 6
Attapulgite, 2
Atterberg limits, 16, 42–43, 89
Auger method, 184
Australian "pier and beam" foundations, 79, 80

Back filling, 86, 127, 154
Base exchange, 100, 102–103, 105
Basements, 92
  flooded, 32–33
Batter, 23, 24
Beams, 78–88, 126, 141–151
Bearing area, 41, 92–94
Bearing capacity:
  based on building codes, 200–201, 203
  of drilled piers, 203–213
  equations, 196–202
  factors, 196–202
  of footings on slopes, 200–203
  marginal, 123
    repair options for, 139

Bearing capacity (*Cont.*):
  of rock, 212–213
  of shallow foundations, 196–203
Bearing soils, 2–3
  foundation loads on, 92–94
Bearing strength, 38, 40, 41, 54, 154
Bedding planes, 123, 126
Belled piers, 78, 204
Bentonite clay (*see* Clays)
Bentonite slurry, 206
Blowers, forced-air, 79
Borehole log, 15
Boring log, 184
Boussinesq's methods, 191–193
Bowles, J. E., 198
BRAB publication, 81, 83, 84
Bridging members, 81
British Standard sieves, 46
Building codes, bearing capacity based on, 200–201, 203
Building Near Trees, 20
Bulk densities, 54
Bureau of Soils Classification, 46

Cables, reinforcing, 85, 153
Calcium aluminates, 58—59
Calcium carbonate, 57
Calcium chloride, 58
Calcium hydroxide, 102–105
Calcium lignosulfonate (CLS), 58
Calcium sulfate, 57
Canopy width, 16—21, 126
Capillarity, zero, 6
Capillary barriers, 175–177
Capillary fringe, 6
Capillary pore, radius of, 7
Capillary rise, height of, 7
Capillary water, 101, 102
Casagrande's plasticity chart, 49

Catch basins, 28
Cation exchange, 100, 102–103, 105
Ceiling plate, 161
Cement, Portland (see Portland cement
    concrete)
Chemical stabilization:
    of impermeable soils, 99–118
    of permeable soils, 98–99
Chlorite, 100
Classification:
    size, 45–46
    soil, 44–56
Clay content, 89
Clay mineralogy, 100–105
Clay soils, 2, 13–14
    (See also Clays)
Clays, 38–39, 49
    attapulgite, 2, 49, 100
    bentonite, 102
    chlorite, 49, 100
    compressible, shrinkage of, 40–42
    expansive, compaction of, 98
    fat, 14
    illite, 2, 49, 100
    kaolinite, 2, 49
    London, 14
    montmorillonite, 2, 49, 100, 102
        106–107, 140
    relative activity of, 49
    specific gravities of, 53–54s
Climatic ratings, 13
    for continental United States, 84
    soil types and, 83
Coarse-grained soils, 37, 45
Coefficient of lateral pressure, 189
Cohesion, apparent, 55
Cohesive soils, 38, 44–45, 54–55, 99,
        186–187, 209–211
    drilled piers in, 209–211
Collapsing soils, 122
Compaction, 95–98, 136, 158
Compressibility test, 185–186
Compressible clays, shrinkage of, 40–42
Compression index, 185–186
Compressive strength:
    concrete, 71
    unconfined, 54
Concrete:
    air-entrained, 59, 61, 67–68
    bond strength, 58, 61
    compressive strength, 71
    curing, 70–71
    drying shrinkage, 63

Concrete (Cont.):
    freeze-thaw durability, 60–61
    fundamentals, 58–63
    general properties of, 57–76
    hardened, characteristics of, 60–63
    impermeability, 62
    lightweight, 63
    mechanical properties, 71–72
    metal reinforcement, 72–74
    modulus of elasticity, 71
    ordinary, 57
    paste content, 60
    placing, 70
    plastic, characteristics of, 59–60
    Portland cement (see Portland cement
        concrete)
    proportioning, 63–69
    rate of hardening, 60
    ready-mix, 57
    reinforcing, 72–76
    resistance to abrasion and impact,
        61
    shear strength, 71
    shrinkage, 71–72
    strain, 71
    strength, 61
    synthetic fiber reinforcement, 74–75
    tensile strength, 71
    unit weight, 62–63
    "waterproof," 62
    workability, 59–60
Consistency of soil, 54–55
Consolidating soils, 122
Consolidation, soil, 136, 158, 184
    (See also Compaction)
Construction:
    add-on, 160
    interferences with, 159–162
    sequence of, 35
    on slope, repair options for, 138
    on sloping site with soil bedding planes
        down dip, 122, 123, 126
Contour interval, 25
Conversion factors, 215
Coulomb's equation, 55
Cracking, 181–182
Crawl space, 77–79
Cross slope, 23, 24
Crossbeams, 162
Crown, 23, 24
Crystalline structure, 100–104
Cut and fill, 24
Cut-and-fill site, 127, 133

Dead loads, 77
Deep-grouting operations, 154–157, 166–167
Deep pier alternative, 144
Dehydration, 49
Densities:
  bulk, 54
  maximum, 39–40
  optimum, 39–40
  relative, 53–54
Differential foundation movement, 121
Differential movement, 90
Distress, causes of, 121–127, 179
Distress failure, 2
Diversion terraces, 34
Doming, 6
Doors, offsetting, 161
Drainage, 173–176
  correct, 174
  natural, 27
  positive, 23
  proper, 3
  site, 26–29
  subsurface, 29–31
Drains, French, 30, 31, 174–175
Draw-down, 6
Drilled piers:
  bearing capacity of, 203–213
  in cohesive soils, 209–211
  driven jointed pipe, 151–153
  in granular soils, 206–209
Drop inlet trickle tube, 34
Drop inlets, 28
Dry unit height versus water content, 40
Dry unit weight, 39
Drying cycle, 9
Drying shrinkage, concrete, 63
Ductility, 61

Eagle Ford soil, 99
Effective stress, 189–208
Elasticity, modulus of, concrete, 71
Electric-welded wire fabric (WWF), 72
Elevation, spot, 25–26
End bearing, 143–144, 151–152
Energy dissipators, 34–35
Erosion control plans, 26
Evaporation, 8–9
  transpiration and, 17
Expansive clays, compaction of, 98
Expansive soils, 2, 88–89, 123–127
Experimental foundation designs, 88
Exterior grade (*see* Drainage)

Failure(s):
  defined, 2
  foundation (*see* Foundation failures)
Fat clays, 14
Feeder roots, 20–21
  vegetation, 125
  (*See also* Root *entries*)
FHA designs, 81–83
Field capacity, 6, 8
Fill(s), 39
  cut and (*see* Cut and fill *entries*)
  organic decay in, 122
Filled slopes, foundations on, 26–27
Fine-grained soils, 37
Finished grading, 26
Fireplaces, interior, 162
Flocculation, 103
Flooded basements, 32–33
Floor plate, 161
Floors, checking grade of, 181
Florida, foundation repair in, 165–166
Flow cone method, grout consistency, 155
Flowerbed curbing, 173
Flower boxes, 173
Fluid flow potential, 10
Fly ash, 67
  (*See also* Pozzolans and Silica fume)
Footings on slopes, bearing capacity of, 200–203
Force, lifting (*see* Lifting force)
Foundation deflection, 132
Foundation design(s), 77–94
  experimental, 88
  safety factors in, 202
Foundation drain collector, 33–34
Foundation drain connections, 32
Foundation drain systems, 32–34
Foundation engineering, 183–213
  soil mechanics and, 183–188
Foundation failures, 121–133
  causes of, 121–127
  diagnosis of settlement versus upheaval, 131–132
  recurrent, 163–164
  settlement as, 127–128
  signs of, 137, 140
  sliding as, 133
  upheaval as, 128–131
Foundation inspection, 179–182
  checklist for, 180–182
Foundation leveling, problems with, 159–162
Foundation loads on bearing soils, 92–94

Foundation pressures, soil mass stresses due to, 188–190
Foundation repair, 104
  longevity of, 163–164
  procedures for, 135–170
  techniques of, examples of, 165–170
Foundations, 1, 77
  on filled slopes, 26–27
  incompetent, 161–162
  on loess, 97
  pier-and-beam (see Pier-and-beam foundations)
  pouring, with abnormal soil moisture, 124
  on sand deposits, 96–97
  on sanitary landfill sites, 97–98
  shallow (see Shallow foundation entries)
  slab (see Slab foundations)
  on soils, 40, 41
  types of, 1
  water under, 3
Free water, 101
Freeze-thaw durability, 60–61
French drains, 30, 31, 174–175
Friction capacity, 206–207
Fringe area of stabilization, 156, 158
Frost heave, 43, 121, 124–125
  repair options for, 138

Gap-graded soil, 45
Girders, 78
Glossary, 219–232
Godfrey, K. A., 101
Grade, 23, 24
  of floors, checking, 181
Gradients, 25
Grading:
  different terms used in, 23, 24
  finished, 26
  rough, 26
Grading concept, 23
Grain size plot, 45
Granular soils, 96–97
  drilled piers in, 206–209
Gravels, 38
  compaction of, 39
  internal fraction in, 38
Gravity, 8
Gridiron system, 29, 30
Grim, R. E., 102
Ground water, 5
Grout consistency, 155

Grout injection pipes, placement of, 155–157
Grouting:
  deep, 154–157, 166–167
  jet, 156
  mechanics of applications, 155
  pressure (see Pressure grouting)
Gutters and downspouts, 33

Hadite blocks, 146
Haller, J., 20–21
Hansen's equation, 199–200
Hardened concrete, characteristics of, 60–63
Heat of hydration, 58–59
Heavy soils, 7
Herringbone system, 30, 31
Horizontal barriers, 175–176
Hunt, H. W., 219
Hydration, 49
Hydraulic force, 118
Hydraulic gradient, 10, 117
Hydraulic pulsation, 114
Hydraulic ram/driver (see Perma-Jack)
Hydro pier, 172
Hydrochloric acid, 104
Hydrogen ion, 102
Hydrostatic head, 10

Illite, 2
Impact resistance, 61
Impermeable soils, stabilizing, 99–118
Impermeable vertical capillary barriers (VICB), 176
Incompetent foundations, 161–162
Infiltration feature of soils, 9–11
Influence factor, 191–192
Injection stinger with pack-off, 117
Intensive loads, 162
Interception process, 8
Interceptor channels, 34
Interceptor system, 29–30
Interfacial tension, 101, 102
Interior fireplaces, 162
Interior floor shimming, 144–146
Interior pier caps, 145–146
Interior piers, 162
Interlayer moisture, 102
Intermediate belt, 5
Interstitial water, 101
Ion exchange, 100, 102–103, 105
Irrigation system, 118–119
Israeli soil, 20

Jet grouting, 156
Joists (see Beams)

Kaolinite, 2, 49, 106
Kormonik, A., 20, 42

Land planning, 31–32
Landscaping, 31
Lateral earth coefficient (see Coefficient
  of lateral pressure)
Lateral movement, 162
LI (liquidity index), 47
Lifting force, 135–136
Lightweight aggregate, 63
Lightweight concrete, 63
Lime (see Calcium hydroxide)
Lime-silica reaction, 67
Liquid limit (LL), 42, 47, 50
Liquid state, 43
Liquidity index (LI), 47
Live loads, 77
LL (liquid limit), 42, 47, 50
Loads, 77
  dead, 77
  distribution of, 93, 192–194, 199
  intensive, 162
  live, 77
  point, 194
Loess soils, 97
  foundations on, 97
London clay, 14
Low-profile pier-and-beam design, 78, 79

Maintenance, preventive, 171–178
Manholes, 29
Marginal bearing capacity, 123
  repair options for, 139
Measure, units of, abbreviations of,
  217–218
Meniscus angle at wall, 7
Mesophytes, 8
Metal reinforcement, concrete, 72–74
Mildew, 79
Mineralogy, clay, 100–105
M.I.T. Classification, 46
Modulus of elasticity, 71
Modulus of vertical subgrade reaction,
  187–188
Moisture absorption, 100
Moisture imbalance, 3
Moisture regimes, 5–6
Montmorillonite, 2, 49, 100, 102, 104,
  106–107, 140

Mudjacking, 136–137, 168, 170
  slab foundations, 146–151
Mudjacking equipment, 147

Natural drainage, 27
Natural system, 30, 31
Negative skin friction, 211–212
Newark, N. M., 192
Noncohesive soils, 7, 45, 206–209
  volume change in, 187–188
Nonexpansive soils, 121–123

Offsetting doors, 161
Orcutt, R. G., 102
Ordinary concrete, 57
Organic decay:
  of base soil, 165–167
  in fills, 122
  repair options for, 138
Organic ions, 103
Organic polymers, 103–104
Overcompaction, 122, 124
  repair options for, 138
Overconsolidation, soil, 184–185

Packer (packing off), 114, 117, 156
Paste content, concrete, 60
Peck, R. B., 196, 198
Perched water, 6
Perimeter beam, 94
Perma-Jack, 151–153
Permeability, coefficient of, 10
Permeable soils, stabilizing, 98–99
Permeable vertical barriers (VPCB), 176
Petry, T., 17, 37, 106–107, 183
pH, 102–104
Phreatic boundary, 6
Phreatic surface, 102
Phreatophytes, 8
PI (plasticity index), 42, 47, 50
Pier-and-beam foundations, 1, 77–79, 94
  Australian, 79, 80
  movement of, 141–146
Pier caps, interior, 145–146
Piers, 143
  alignment of, 151–152
  belled, 78, 204
  drilled (see Drilled piers)
  driven steel, 151–153
  interior, 162
  "pod," 153
  post-tension, 151, 153, 154
  slim, 143, 151

Piers (*Cont.*):
  steel-reinforced, 141, 142
Pilings (*see* Piers)
Pipe slope, 29
Pipes, 29
Pitch, 23, 24
PL (plastic limit), 42, 47
Plant roots, 125
  repair options for, 139
  (*See also* Root *entries*)
Planting distance, 13–21, 125–126,
    176–178
Plants, 14–22, 176–178, 182
Plastic concrete, characteristics of, 59–60
Plastic limit (PL), 42, 47
Plastic state, 43
Plasticity chart, Casagrande's, 49
Plasticity index (PI), 42, 47, 50
Plates, 161
Plumbing installations, 126, 128–131
Pocket penetrometer, 54
"Pod" piers, 153
Point loads, 194
Poisson's ratio, 194
Polyethylene sheets, 79
Ponds, 34
Poor, A., 17, 20, 21
"Poorly graded," term, 38
Pore water, 101
Porosity, 37, 51
Portland cement concrete, 57–58
  admixtures to, 66–68
  aggregates for, 65–66
  high early strength, 59
  low-heat, 59
  modified, 58
  normal, 58
  sulfate-resistant, 59
Positive drainage, 23
Post-tension piers, 151, 153, 154
Post-tension slab foundations, 85
Potassium ion, 102
Potential soil volume change, 50
Pozzolans, 66, 67
Pressure differential, 117–118
Pressure gradient, 10
Pressure grouting, 99, 156, 157
  soil consolidation by, 158
Pressure injection of soil-stabilizing
    chemicals, 114–118
Pressure injection stem, 115, 116
Preventive maintenance, 171–178
PVC pipe, 29, 31

Rainfall, 11–12
  average intensity of, 28
  frequency of, 28
Rate of sedimentation, 47
Ready-mix concrete, 57
Redo's (*see* Success ratio, foundation repair)
Reeve, M. J., 107–109
Reinforcing concrete, 72–76
Reinforcing steel (*see* Steel reinforce-
    ment)
Relative densities, 53–54
Remodeling operations, 161
Retaining walls, 27
Rock, 39
  bearing capacity of, 212–213
Root growth, 8
Root systems, 13–22
Root zone, 5
Roots:
  feeder (*see* Feeder roots)
  plant (*see* Plant roots)
  tree (*see* Tree root *entries*)
Rough grading, 26
Round bars, dimensions of, 73
Run-off (*see* Water run-off)

Safety factors in foundation design, 202
Sand deposits, foundations on, 96–97
Sands, 38
  compaction of, 39
  internal friction in, 38
  specific gravities of, 54
Sanitary landfill sites, foundations on,
    97–98
Sanitary sewers, 32
Saturation, percent, 51
Saturation zone, 5
Seasonal moisture variation, 83–84,
    89–91
Sediment basins, 34
Sediment traps, 28
Sedimentation, size versus, 46–47
Sedimentation:
  control plans, 26
  rate of, 47
  tests, 45
Semisolid state, 43
Sensitivity, 55
Settlement, 3, 127–128
  incidence of, 164
  of slab foundations, 147–151
  of solids, 47
  vs. upheaval ratio, 47

Sewers:
  sanitary, 32
  storm, 27
Shallow foundation bearing capacity
    equation, 196–199
Shallow foundations, bearing capacity of,
    196–203
Shear strength, 38, 54, 55
  concrete, 71
  undrained, 96
  (*See also* Cohesion)
Shear tests, triaxial, 55
Shimming, interior floor, 144–146
Shrinkage coefficient, 72
Shrinkage:
  of compressible clays, 40–42
  concrete, 71–72
Shrinkage limit (SL), 41–43, 50
Side-slotted design, 156
Sieve analysis, 45–46
Sieves, British and American Standard, 46
Silica fume, 67
Silts, 7, 38–39
Site drainage, 27–29
Site exploration, 183–184
Size, sedimentation versus, 46–47
Size classification, 45–46
Skin friction, 209
  negative, 211–212
SL (shrinkage limit), 41–43, 50
Slab foundations, 1, 79, 81–91
  mudjacking, 146–151
  post-tension, 85
  settlement of, 147–151
Slab-on-grade foundations, 1
Sliding, 133
Slope stability charts, 27
Slopes, 24
  bearing capacity of footings on,
      200–203
  filled, foundations on, 26–27
  steep, 34
Slump, concrete, 59–60
  total mixing water versus, 64, 65
Slump cone, 68–69
Slump test, 68–69
Smectite, 2
  (*See also* Montmorillonite)
Smith, C., 106
Smith, D., 17, 18, 125, 178
Soil(s), 37
  Adelaide, 86
  bearing (*see* Bearing soils)

Soil(s) (*Cont.*):
  chemical stabilization of, 98–99
  classification of, 47
  clay, 2, 13–14
    (*See also* Clays)
  coarse-grained, 37, 45
  cohesive (*see* Cohesive soils)
  collapsing, 122
  compressibility of, 184–187
  consistency of, 54–55
  consolidation of, 122, 136, 158, 184
  creep of, 125
  dry, 43
  expansive, 2, 88–89, 123–127
  fine-grained, 37
  foundations on, 40, 41
  freezing, 43
  gap-graded, 45
  granular (*see* Granular soils)
  heavy, 7
  impermeable, stabilizing, 99–118
  infiltration feature of, 9–11
  Israeli, 20
  loess, 97
  maximum density of, 39–40
  noncohesive (*see* Noncohesive soils)
  nonexpansive, 121–123
  particle size of, 45
  permeable, stabilizing, 98–99
  properties of, 44
  size classification of, 45–47, 64
  specific gravities of, 53–54
  stability of, 2
  strength of, 55–56
  subgrade, vertical stress in, 189
  three-phase, 50–52
  uncovered, 8
  uniform, 45
  virgin, 39
  water behavior in, 5–22
  well-graded, 45
Soil belt, 5
Soil classification, 44–56
Soil classification system, unified, 37, 47
Soil consolidation, 184
  by pressure grouting, 168
Soil engineering, 44
Soil expansion, 81
Soil mass, describing, 50
Soil mass stresses due to foundation
    pressure, 188–190
Soil mechanics, 37–56
  foundation engineering and, 183–188

Soil moisture, 3
  abnormal, at foundation pouring, 124
    repair options for, 139
  gain of, 125–126
    repair options for, 139
  loss of, 9, 125
    repair options for, 139
Soil sampler, 184
Soil Sta, 104–118, 168
Soil stabilization, 95–119
  defined, 95
Soil-stabilizing chemicals:
  field-testing of, 108–114
  laboratory testing of, 105–108
  pressure injection of, 114–118
Soil swelling, 42, 126
Soil types, 37–39
  climatic ratings and, 83
Soil volume change, potential, 50
Soil water, 7
Soil water belt, 5–6
Sole plate, 161
"Solid" rock, 39
Solid state, 43
Sorption, ion, 102
Sperry, N., 20, 125
Spot elevation, 25–26
Spread footings:
  conventional, 92–93
  use of, 141–144
Stability of soils, 2
Stabilization, fringe area of, 156, 158
Stabilizers, chemical:
  inorganic, 102, 105–106
  organic, 103, 106–114
Standard sieves, British and American,
  46
Steel-reinforced piers, 141, 142
Steel reinforcement, 72–74, 77, 78, 85,
  92, 142
Steep slopes, 34
Stem, 114–118
Step beam, 27
Stinger (see Stem)
Stoke's law, 47
Storm drainage system, 34
Storm sewers, 27
Storm water run-off, 27
Strain, concrete, 71
Stress (sse Effective stress)
Strength, compressive (see Compressive
  strength)
Structural lattice, 100

Subgrade soils, vertical stress in, 189
Subgrade waterproofing, 157–158
Subsoil aquifers, deep, 6
Substructures, warped, 159, 160
Subsurface drainage, 29–31
Subsurface water, 174–175
Sucess ratio, foundation repair, 163–164
Sulfonated naphthalene, 58
Sump pumps, 32
Support factor, 81–82
Surface drain, 27–29
Surface grade, 130
Surface tension of liquid, 7
Surface water, 28, 173
Surfactant, 106
Swales, 27, 28
Swelling, soil, 42, 126
Swelling potential, 42, 43, 89, 100–105
Swelling pressure, 42, 89
Synthetic fiber reinforcement, concrete,
  74–76

Taylor, D. W., 46
Tensile strength, concrete, 71
Terzaghi method, 197–199
Three-phase soils, 50–52
Topsoil, 26
Transpiration, 7–8, 178
  evaporation and, 17
Transpiration loss versus distance from
  tree trunks, 18–22
Tree root depths:
  in London, England, 18
  in United States, 17
Tree roots, 125, 126
  (See also Root entries)
Tree trunks, transpiration loss versus
  distance from, 18–22
Tremies, 70
Triaxial shear tests, 55
Tricalcium aluminate, 59
Tricalcium silicate, 59

Unconfined compressive strength, 54
Uncovered soils, 8
Undercompaction, 121–122, 124
  repair options for, 138
Underconsolidation, soil, 185
Underpinning, 141–144
  comparison of techniques, 152
Unified Classification, 47–49
Uniform soil, 45
Uniformity coefficient, 45

Units of measure, abbreviations of, 217–218
Upheaval, 3, 128–131, 159
  incidence of, 164
  of slab foundations, 146–147
Upward deflection, 6

Vane test, 55
Vapor barriers, 79, 175, 176
Vegetation, 176, 178
Vegetation feeder roots, 25
Ventilation, proper, 79
Vertical barriers, 176
Vertical stress in subgrade soils, 189
Vertical surface loading, 190–196
VICB (impermeable vertical capillary barriers), 88, 90, 176
Virgin soils, 39
Void boxes, 78
Void ratio, 37, 51
  water content versus, 52
Volume change:
  in noncohesive soils, 187–188
  soil, potential, 50
VPCB (permeable vertical barriers), 176

Walls, retaining, 27
Warped substructures, 159, 160
Wash, 23, 24
Wash boring method, 184
Water:
  addition of, 122
  behavior in soils, 5–22
  capillary, 6, 101, 102
  crystalline interlayer, 101–103
  under foundations, 3
  free, 101
  freezing, 43
  ground, 5
  infiltration, 11–12
  interstitial, 101
  loss of, 3
  optimum, 39, 40
  percent, 51
  perched, 6

Water (Cont.):
  pore, 101
  removal of, 122
  soil, 7
  subsurface, 174–175
  surface, 28, 173
  total mixing, versus slump, 64, 65
Water barriers, 118, 175–177
Water/cement ratios, 64, 65
Water content:
  dry unit height versus, 40
  void ratio versus, 52
Water drain, repair options for, 138
Water glass, 99
Water infiltration, 9–11
Water pier, 172
Water run-off, 11–12, 28
  coefficient of, 28
  storm, 27
Water table, 5
  surface of, 6
Watering, 171–174
  adequate, 13
"Waterproof" concrete, 62
Waterproofing, subgrade, 157–158
Weather analysis, 91
Weather conditions, 89
Weight, dry unit, 39
"Well-graded," term, 38
Well-graded soil, 45
Westergaard's method, 193–194
White, E., 136
Wind deposits, 122
Wood spacers, 146
WWF (electric-welded wire fabric), 72

Xerophytes, 8

Yield strength:
  concrete, 71
  steel, 73, 74

Zero capillarity, 6

About the Author

Robert Wade Brown is President and Chairman of the
Board of Brown Foundation Repair and Consulting, Inc., a
firm based in Dallas and Garland, Texas, that specializes
in the design and repair of building foundations. Mr.
Brown is a member of the American Society of Civil
Engineers and the Society of Petroleum Engineers. The
author of numerous articles and holder of important
patents, Mr. Brown has written *Residential Foundations:
Design, Behavior and Repair.*